THE POET'S VOICE AND CRAFT

Also by C.B. McCully from Carcanet

Fly-fishing: a book of words
Time Signatures (poems)

The POET'S VOICE *and* CRAFT

EDITED BY C. B. McCully

CARCANET

First published in 1994 by
Carcanet Press Limited
208-212 Corn Exchange Buildings
Manchester M4 3BQ

A CIP catalogue record for this book
is available from the British Library.
ISBN 1 85754 020 4

The publisher acknowledges financial assistance
from the Arts Council of Great Britain

Set in 10pt Bembo by Bryan Williamson, Frome
Printed and bound in England by SRP Ltd, Exeter

Contents

Notes, supplied by the Editor, are given at the end of each essay.

Acknowledgements

Many people helped to promote *The Poet's Voice and Craft* programme. Among those to whom I owe special thanks are the staff at Carcanet Press, Manchester, the staff at the John Rylands University Library, and Janet Allan, then of the Portico Library. However they may try to deny it, Nick Rhodes and Rob Stuart have also been implicated in this project, and I owe them my warm gratitude. NorthWest Arts helped to advertise the programme at home; the British Council advertised our schedule abroad. I also owe a debt to my colleagues in the Department of English; while it is invidious to particularise this, I ought to say that Bill Hutchings, Helen MacLean and the late David Palmer offered the best kind of support – lucid and practical. I was also very fortunate to have had the patient endorsement of Brian Cox and the Poetry Centre Committee.

Two outstanding acknowledgements remain. First, I would like to thank our audiences, who not only turned out in all kinds of Manchester weather (including train- and traffic-stopping snow) but who also – not altogether surprisingly – proved to be informed and cultured listeners. They added a great deal to the momentum of the project. Second, I would like to extend my sincere thanks to Maxine Powell, whose secretarial acumen and skill extended through copious photo-copying, advertising and liaison to co-ordination and final completion of the typescript.

A longer version of the Introduction is to appear in C.C. Barfoot (ed.), *Contiguous Traditions in Post-War British and Irish Poetry* (Amsterdam: Rodopi, 1994).

Introduction
C.B. McCully

In 1988 the Manchester Poetry Centre initiated what the *Daily Tele-graph* (21 October 1988) called 'an ambitious series' of readings and lectures. The series ran under the title *The Poet's Voice and Craft.*[1] The programme subsequently continued until 1991, and involved seventeen poets. The schedule was as follows:

1988-89	Donald Davie
	Patricia Beer
	John Heath-Stubbs
	Anne Stevenson
	Edwin Morgan
	Fleur Adcock
1989-90	Peter Scupham
	Iain Crichton Smith
	Douglas Dunn
	C.H. Sisson
	Grevel Lindop
	Sorley Maclean
1990-91	Brendan Kennelly
	Robert Wells
	Jeffrey Wainwright
	Alison Brackenbury
	Charles Tomlinson

The ambition of the series lay less, perhaps, in the readings than in the following lectures, each of which focused on some aspect of a poet's craft. The term 'craft' is of course relatively meaningless without further definition – metrical craft? the craft of re-writing? – and so to enable the focus, each visiting poet was sent an initial set of guidelines which took the form of specific questions. These are reproduced here:

In each lecture, we would ask you to engage with the structural questions which your work in either contemporary English verse or in verse translation necessarily involves. The questions we would like to explore fall into three main areas of interest; merely as a set of guidelines, you may like to think about the following topics (section 1 owes acknowledgement to a survey that was done some years ago in *Agenda*)[2]:

1. Sound-structure and metrics

How conscious are you of metrical considerations in your work? Are any of your poems triggered off by purely rhythmic suggestions? Do you find that writing metrical verse can lead into a merely mechanical fluency? If you choose to write in 'free verse', why? How do you regard the line-break, and what principles lead you to break lines where you do? What sound-effects or textures do you consciously use or seek? How close is the rhythmical structure of your verse to the rhythmical structure of colloquial speech? Is the 'music of poetry', as Eliot claimed, a music latent in the speech of its time?

2. Syntax

Are you conscious of manipulating the syntax of your poems to achieve particular effects? If so, how is the syntax manipulated, and what expressive effects do you seek? Do you find that a particular syntactic arrangement reflects – or resolves? – a particular thought-pattern? In what ways does the syntax of a line co-operate with the rhythmical and/or metrical structure of that line? If you work in stanzas, is each stanza co-extensive with a unit of syntax, or do you run syntax over stanzas? For what reasons would you run a clause or sentence over a line- or stanza-break? Is your poetry inherently 'phrasal' (most syntactic/semantic work done by nouns, adjectives, and participles used adjectivally) or 'clausal' (most syntactic/semantic work done by finite verbs), or do you seek a balance between the two modes?

3. Lexis

What principles are at work in your choice of words? Do you ever consciously choose, say, native words (and native word-formation processes such as compounding) over Latinate/Romance – or vice-versa? Do you prefer the familiar to the rare, and if so, why? Do you ever employ 'nonce words' (new coinages)? Do you feel that certain words have some sort of phonaesthetic power? If you work in a rhymed form, how easy – or difficult – is it to 'find a rhyme'? In rewriting, what sense makes you reject or replace certain words?

Naturally, several of these questions overlap, and there are many points of relevance to the composition of verse (particularly, to the craft of verse-translation) not covered in them. Please include such points.

The tri-partite model for these guidelines is primarily drawn from a linguistic methodology, recognising not only the classic three-way interdependence of linguistic organisation (syntax, phonology, semantics) but also hinting that whatever constitutes a poet's craft may well be (I would argue that it is unavoidably) analogous with the 'craft' of language-use in general.

This hint at analogy bears directly on some of the doubts about the programme expressed by, for instance, Edwin Morgan: 'My first reaction on reading through the questionnaire which all poets were sent,' he writes, '. . . was that to many of the questions my answer was "I don't know", with the even stronger rider "And I don't want to know". It seemed to me that the whole exercise was misguided, and was a job for critics, not for the writers themselves.' Others expressed similar misgivings. Robert Wells questioned whether any 'personal answer' was possible, and pointed out that he (along with his fellow lecturers) seldom felt the need for critical terminology or procedures while writing: 'The reasons behind the choices made in writing a poem are largely unconscious; they have become second nature. It's a practical matter of seeing what will work, of knowing what is right or wrong in a particular set of circumstances which never exactly repeats itself.'

As different poets and critics have pointed out in different times and places,[3] it is not crucially necessary for a poet writing in, say, iambic trimeters, or for that matter in non-metrical verse, to have been trained in theories of Classical prosody, or to have passed examinations on the structure of the triadic device in Williams's poetry. Robert Wells's 'largely unconscious choices' evolve into persistence, ingenuity, instinct, and luck. Poetry is written, is made manifest, as it were in defiance of a critical programme: the line sounds and moves beyond its analysis.

Yet here, too, there are dangers: the validity of unconscious choices cannot legitimise irresponsibility either on the part of the writer or the reader. Charles Tomlinson writes of the 'misfortune' of those aspiring poets who might have attended creative writing classes where principles are ignored: 'the young poet... will too often be left to his own devices, composing in a free verse which cannot account for its procedures, with line endings which have no rationale and line lengths dictated only by the fact that it felt right that way at the moment of composition'. Douglas Dunn offers even stronger criticism: 'There are times when I even wonder if some contemporary poets were drawn into poetry by a gift, by a recurrent epiphany ... At times it can seem as if some poets have *chosen* poetry through a liking for it, or through education, or concern for poetry as a subject, or as a means to appearing in public, or as a way of getting regular, well-paid book reviewing'. And as Dunn goes on to say, 'Technique is to a large degree intuitive, but that should not be taken to mean that a poet is working entirely by chance or feel. Choices have to be made and decisions taken...'

It is useful here to return to the analogy between poetic craft and language-use. I would wish to argue that something significant can be said – and said by poets themselves – about the metrical, lexical or syntactic forms of poetry. Further, I think that 'something significant' reveals that analysis is not solely the concern of the critic, nor construction (still less 'creativity') the sole and rightful province of the poet. And although one of the distinguishing features of *The Poet's Voice and Craft* series was its mistrust of (or open hostility to) literary theory, it might be helpful here if I put the analogy between poetic craft and language-use into a theoretical framework.

It is salutary to remember that all for whom English is a mother tongue are inescapably creative. Following the pioneering work of Noam Chomsky,[4] one of the most important contributions of American and British linguistics not just to the study of language but also to theories of knowledge has been its insistence on the creativity of tongues, the fact that infinitely many new sentences are created infinitely many times every day. Studies in the acquisition of language by children, in particular, have revealed that this creativity is not primarily a matter of 'imitation'; rather, it seems to lie in the ability to inherit and learn a finite set of productive rules which will generate well-formed, new English (French, Spanish, Japanese...) sentences. Whatever the theoretical distinctions that have emerged between American and British linguists over the past thirty years, most would, I think, agree on the central tenet that language-use is rule-governed, and that these rules, themselves abstract and tacit in nature, enable creative communication.

Underlying this remorseless fecundity is a linguistic ability which Chomsky has called 'linguistic competence'. As noted above, this competence consists of a finite set of rules which enable English speakers to construct new sentences. These rules are not, to be sure, prescriptive dicta ('a preposition is something you never end a sentence with'), but consist of an abstract, limited set of instructions which enable their users to construct their relationships with the world in language. The description of the rules which form linguistic competence is, therefore, one aspect of a theory of knowledge. This theory rests on the assumption that language consists in 'rule-governed creativity'. Infinite ends (language use) proceed from finite means (linguistic rules); perhaps one proper study of mankind is language.

It will not need saying that this is hardly an unprecedented view – a basic linguistic textbook, any good account of structuralism, or, in a literary context, any encounter with the work of Roman Jakobson,[5] will confirm as much – nor that such a critical stance has its detractors. That there are problems in the analogy between 'normal' (perhaps a better term is 'normative') language use and the specialised use of language in poetry is readily apparent. In formal terms, to take but one example, poetry uses a constituent, the line, which is not used – at least not used systematically – in 'normal' discourse. In critical terms, one might want to claim that whereas vernacular discourse uses more or less appropriate words in the correct order, poetry must use the best words in the best order, as Coleridge's 'homely definition' stated. Those who believe (as I do not) that the English language is now in a perilous state of decay will then subsequently believe that one goal of poetry is a kind of purification, and adopt constructive, specialised poetic principles to that end. Yet these counter-arguments are circular: they only serve to emphasise the primacy of language, and the functions of language in all their guises, including what Jakobson called the 'poetic function'.

Just as we inhabit language, so many of us inhabit poetry. It seems to me that arguments which call on a poet's 'intuition', or inspired guesswork, are counter-productive. Nor, perhaps, should we relegate instinct to silence. Just as there exist rules which underlie our use of language, so there are rules – conventions – which underpin poetic composition. No one would wish to think of these conventions as an arbitrary, willed set of procedures, but the conventions exist, and crucially, they take their being from the normative rules of the language itself. Language patterns provide templates for poetic patterns.

Here it is useful to paraphrase David Lodge: 'the poet's medium is language: whatever s/he does, *qua* poet, s/he does in and through language'.[6] By placing the emphasis firmly on language, and inviting an analysis of what might be termed, following Chomsky, 'poetic competence',[7] the initial questionnaire which accompanied the *Poet's Voice* programme stands as a reminder that whatever gives poets the ability to write (and to re-write) poems may emerge, in the first instance, from the analysis of how poetic structures are manipulated from language. Further, such poetic competence may consist not only in authorial mastery, but also in a set of conventions for reading (or listening).

This prompts me to describe the two features of the series which helped to make it distinctive. One is the awareness of, and sensitivity towards, language which, without exception, every poet showed. It would be odd to insist on this point were it not for the fact that several current critical theories, while paying lip-service to the analysis of language (in particular the work of Ferdinand de Saussure), seem to me to misrepresent the analyses available. Moreover, several of these same theories have risked becoming synchronic, circular and introspective. Nor is it completely overwhelming to be told that the texts which constitute 'literature' are in dialogue not with ghostly tokens masquerading as persons but with other texts; as has long been recognised, the conventions which enable the production of texts also enable the production of other texts: poetry, as Northrop Frye put it, can only be made out of other poems. Again without exception, every poet contributing to the series recognised this, and emphasised the importance of reading. Douglas Dunn notes that 'a poet's critical acumen raises the questions triggered off... by intuition; and it is that same instinctive sense of what might be right, or wrong, together with a critical faculty nurtured by reading, which answers them.' C.H. Sisson concurs: 'No one will write verse of any quality who has not been a passionate reader of poetry, and has not acquainted himself, over the years, with more or less of the most accomplished work of the past; and he will be dumb indeed if this reading has not caused him to reflect on such matters.'

Behind this insistence on the importance of reading in establishing a recognition of serviceable or unserviceable convention, there was in the programme what I can only describe – setting it against the synchronicity and introspection of some critical theories – as an historical generosity, an intrigue of time and verbal potential. Robert Wells offers some strong testimony here: 'What strikes me about English – and other languages so far as I know them – is constancy rather than change. The language adds to itself, varies and shifts within itself, even contradicts itself, but it has a central nature which, if it changes, changes extremely slowly.' It follows for Wells (and I suspect most of the poets of this series would agree) that '[t]he language that is current is archaic too; a vast anonymity that we reach back into as soon as we speak. If we are aware of its ancientness we'll have a better sense of its precision as well.'

Structures, conventions, rules and history. Where these exist – and no one would, I hope, wish to deny that they are less intrinsic to poetry than they are to language – then they may be described. One central aim of the *Poet's Voice* series was to provide an entrance to such a kind of description, to make 'unconscious choices' manifest, a kind of witness. In particular, the project was not designed to elicit information about 'how to write poetry'; perhaps the interest of the project lies more in how poetry comes to be *re*-written or abandoned.

Having said this, each visiting poet interpreted the guidelines somewhat differently, as I had hoped and as each was invited and entitled to do. While the questionnaire directed its readers to conscious choices (e.g. 'How conscious are you of metrical considerations...?'), several poets could not resist looking more closely at those unconscious factors which bring any poem into being. In his essay 'Where do poems come from?', Grevel Lindop gives an intriguing glimpse of how the process of a poem begins: with a 'soup or stew of preoccupations, thoughts, feelings, mental pictures and scraps of sound', which requires 'a seed or nucleus to be dropped into it. This is what I call the crystal... Once this is present the poem can start to grow.' His account implies, surely correctly, that a poem cannot be willed, and it suggests that a poem is composed not in what Poe called 'an ecstatic intuition' but in a set of relationships which determine not only the crystal's ultimate size and shape but also its 'transitory brightness'. As Edwin Morgan notes, the process is an 'exteriorising, projective drama'. I also find it significant that Lindop's 'crystal' is formed by language ('a few words, a phrase or a line') – language at the roots of consciousness. It would seem that these fragments come loaded with rhythmical or thematic potential.

Such accounts of poetic genesis may, of course, be charming fictions – Morgan cautions that 'readers ought to be suspicious of authorial claims or attempts to lay bare the bones of their own creations' – but even if fictional, I find it striking that Lindop's metaphor of medium and crystal brings ready and significant corroboration from other contributors to the series (see Wainwright, pp.135-46 and Tomlinson, pp.10-25).

Beyond genesis, there is the line. Several poets devoted space to an analysis of the rhythmical and metrical structure of different line-units, relating their choice of structure either to some impulse derived from reading, or to the 'organic' demands of the poem of which a particular line or set of lines was to be a part. Both topics are highly relevant, but another and more basic question remains: what gives a line of verse its identity as a line of verse?

Donald Davie picked up this question: the integrity of the verse line, he writes, is 'something more than a metrical and typographical convenience'. This usefully indicates that however the verse line is actually performed, its identity may lie in the first instance at some deeper and more abstract level.

It is necessary to be careful about this, since the line is such a central concept. Its analytic centrality, as evidenced by the fascination with which both poets and critics (especially prosodists) approach the topic, seems to lie in the concept of difference. The rules which enable 'normal' discourse to take place, for example, structure along two hierarchies. One hierarchy is that of sound-structure (phonology): in ascending order, we might want to say that sound-segments (phonemes) are gathered into syllables, that syllables might be stressed or unstressed, and gathered into linguistic feet,[8] that these stress/syllable configurations then enter into larger phonological constituents, such as the intonational phrase, and that intonational phrases are then gathered into the largest phonological constituent, the utterance. Segment, syllable, linguistic foot, phrase, utterance are thereby all constituents of the sound-structure of English, constituents of its phonological grammar.

Turning to a syntactic hierarchy, we might want to observe that the smallest elements of syntax are morphemes. Whether these morphemes are nonlexical (as in the plural inflections /s/ or /ɪz/ – *cats, houses*) or lexical (= lexeme – *cat, house*), their function is to constitute words; words are gathered into syntactic phrases; phrases are gathered into sentences... and beyond the sentence, if we wish our hierarchical theory to account for reading as well as speaking and writing, we could include constituents such as the paragraph. But clearly, morpheme, word, phrase and sentence are again constituents of the syntactic grammar of English.

Although this is to some extent an oversimplified view of language organisation, it suggests one formal distinction between poetry and other forms of discourse. The distinction is this: poetry includes all the constituents named above (poets, as C.H. Sisson notes, cannot be exempted from 'the ordinary requirements of grammar'), but it also includes (at least) two other constituents, namely the line and the stanza. These are specialised to verse, including non-metrical verse, where they are used more or less systematically. Other forms of discourse (notably newspaper headlines and advertisements) do of course use structures reminiscent of the lines of verse – structures which might, in fact, function as lines of verse in a different context – but there they are unsystematically deployed. The concept of the verse line, beginning in formal difference, equally depends on its identity with or distinction from other lines in the same poem, a rhythmical and/or metrical equivalence. The line becomes Hopkins's 'figure of spoken sound', reiterated, parallelistic, productive.

This argument helps to account for the distinctiveness of the verse line, yet it cannot quite account for its identity. This identity is surely a matter of sound-structure and metrics, rather than an issue of performance (although Davie notes that he observes the integrity of the line by pausing at each juncture). If this view is correct, it follows that there must be some special relationships obtaining at the end of each line-unit which serve to demarcate each line as a constituent of the poem.

Such special relationships are (for once) empirically demonstrable in verse drawn from all periods and all languages. One simple example is Old English alliterative verse. Here, the half-line was the metrical prime: two half-lines are bound together in the long-line, and are bound by predictable patterns of alliteration. Drastically abbreviating the rules which enabled poets to construct half-lines, one could say that the half-lines were a minimum of four syllables in length, and that the vast majority included two chief stresses. And yet, of the possible combinations of syllable and stress-pattern, half-lines with stress-patterns such as / / x x never occur. Why? Precisely because special relationships obtained at the end of each half-line unit. These served to discipline and demarcate: half-lines could end on one fully stressed syllable (or its resolved equivalent), or on a stressed syllable (or resolved equivalent) followed by one, and only one, unstressed syllable. Effectively, this means that in Old English verse, half-lines could end in one of only two ways: a special relationship. This is not a matter of performance; it is a matter of abstract structure.

Another, perhaps more familiar, example can be found in the final, inevitable cadence of the Latin dactylic hexameter, a quantitative form whose final two feet are obligatorily / - u u / - - (*tegmine fagi*). It is noteworthy that it is only in this position of the line – the line-final position – where stress is allowed to reinforce quantity, main word-stress falling on the first syllable of the dactyl (***teg***mine) and the spondee (***fa***gi). Elsewhere in the line, stress and quantity do not obligatorily have such a reinforcing relationship; they are typically in tension. Again, a special, isomorphic relationship holds at the line-end.

Turning to the English tradition, and the pentameter, it has been argued, by the phonetician David Abercrombie among others,[9] that part of the identity of the pentameter line depends on its ending with a 'silent stress' – a line-final, rhythmically salient pause. The abstract, underlying metrical weight of the line therefore consists in five realised beats or stresses, followed by a pause, equivalent in weight to a silent beat. On this account, 'end-stopping' is not merely a matter of syntax, where phrases are co-extensive with lines; it is a co-operation between syntactic and metrical structure: silent beats occur at the end of lines whose termini are co-extensive with phrase boundaries. Where the silent beat is suppressed – because the demands of the syntax carry a phrase over from one line to the next – then the effect is one of enjambement. Enjambement is given a special name because it is a special effect, a departure from the normative structure. Handling the co-operation between syntax and metrics in terms of a theory such as this helps to explain not only our common terminology, but also our reading, instincts, and practice.

In this technical digression (whose terms by no means all would agree) I have tried to capture some of the features which emerged from discussions of contributions to the *Poet's Voice* series. The poets gave productive thought to questions of rhythm, metre and form – including the forms of non-metrical verse, stanzaic form, rhyme, half-rhyme and assonance. This concentration was at least half-expected. As Paul Fussell puts it,

> a comment of T.S. Eliot's can serve as a caution against the assumption that a poet's metrical decisions, because presumably instinctive and automatic, are somehow immune to criticism and even to analysis. Writing to Cleanth Brooks about an explication which Brooks had undertaken of one of his poems, Eliot observed: 'Reading your essay made me feel...that I had been a great deal more ingenious than I had been aware of, because the conscious problems with which one is concerned in the actual writing are more those of a quasi musical nature, in the arrangement of metric and pattern, than of a conscious exposition of ideas.' Which is to say that regardless of the amount and quality of intellectual and emotional analysis that precedes poetic composition, in the moment of composition itself the poet is most conspicuously performing as a metrist. And the same principle holds for the reader: at the moment of his first apprehension of the

poem he functions less as a semanticist than as a more or less unwitting prosodist.[10]

So the priority given to rhythmical and metrical matters, and to sound-structure and texture in general, was anticipated; nevertheless, I had not expected the testimony to be so significant or so distinctive. But 'to speak of one element in isolation is always . . . risky', and the rubric also asked for comment on the topics of lexis and syntax.

If there was a fairly general agreement about fundamental prosodic principles, there was less about lexis – 'words, words, words'. Several poets stressed the role of their formative reading, but beyond this, in the contexts of composition, there are lexical decisions themselves. Surprisingly, C.H. Sisson proved to be one of the more apparently relaxed commentators: ' "Prose: words in their best order; poetry: the *best* words in the best order." Those were Coleridge's "homely definitions", as he said. What kinds of words do I, the present witness, think best? Those words which come most naturally to me. What words are they? So far as I have succeeded as a poet, you will find them in my published volumes. Choosing the best words is of course a matter of the context: I should regard it as a strange aberration to choose them because they were of Saxon origin, or Latin origin, or because I thought they sounded nice . . .' Almost by contrast, several other poets testified to their struggle in reconciling the quotidian with the elevated, in finding an appropriate lexical variety. After giving an excerpt from his poem 'Fox Gallery', Charles Tomlinson notes: 'I like in writing this type of poem to keep options on diction open, going from the conversational to what might be called a higher style, as in the Latinate "deterred/ by habitation" . . . and also in the use of words like "disparate", "agility", "liquefaction". I'm not, as Williams does in certain poems, using an equivalent of the "stunned" idiom of workaday New Jersey, but trying for a variety of register of speech.' Alison Brackenbury also comments fully on this variety, specifically, the make-up of the English lexicon and its poetic potential:

> One of the deepest choices in the use of English is that between Latin and Anglo-Saxon words. There is a gulf here which our class and education system ensure remains deep and dark. What is the enduring role in English of Latinate words? It is no accident (Latin word) that the iambic pentameter, the metre of authority (Latin word) requires the writer to use longer Latinate words to articulate

it. And do we all need to know and use Latinate words to be articulate? Yes, I say regretfully. I would like to say no... But most abstract nouns in English are not of Anglo-Saxon origin...

Nevertheless, Brackenbury continues,

I believe that the Anglo-Saxon words are still the heart of English. They are strong, both because they are brief and because they often keep a strength of sound, a thickness of consonant, a breadth of vowel, which lends them power. When I hear reconstructions of the spoken English of the past, the long vowels of Chaucer, the still-broad vowels weighting a Shakespearean sonnet, I do not think we have progressed. If the grammarians have frozen our syntax, the mandarins have chilled our songs. In this instinct, hopefully, and beyond my control, my poems break back to their short final words. They risk becoming, as Latin would have it, inarticulate.

Robert Wells was another who insisted on the interplay and interconnection of the different lexical strata of English: 'in English poetry it happens time and again that elaboration is needed to come at plainness. The elaboration frames and sets off the plainness, and the one wouldn't be possible without the other... I'm always conscious of the division between the Anglo-Saxon and the Latinate elements in English, how they balance in what I write, and how those metaphors contained within words of Latin derivation fit the surrounding sense.'

Robert Wells's mention of metaphor indicates something of the conscious generosity and sensitivity with which contributors to the series appropriated the lexicon. In many ways it seems to me that the testimony offered by the series approached an almost Augustan ideal – what Donald Davie, in his *Purity of Diction in English Verse*,[11] summarises as the re-vivification of dead metaphor – an ideal of contextual precision aligned with etymological propriety. Jeffrey Wainwright, for instance, speaks of 'deliberate lexical loading': 'I tend to be more interested in the familiar than the rare. I have been fixated with mining familiar phrases so as to explore how their reference can be extended or carry an ironic or pathetic weight.'

The lexicon is inextricably linked with the syntax which carries it, a kind of interpenetration. Is the role of pronouns in a poem, for example, primarily a lexical or a syntactic matter? Surely it is both – lexical to the extent that choice of pronoun has a thematic relevance (to do with point of view, topicalisation and intertextuality), has a provenance which governs the overall diction and tone, and syntactic to the extent that categories such as mood, tense, and verbal aspect are all associated with some head (pro)noun and serve to bind the poem in a web of cohesive relationships. Fleur Adcock gave considerable attention to this point, confessing that point of view was one of the problems she continues to be confronted with. The question, as she sees it, is '[H]ow should the speaker's point of view be grammatically expressed?' The first person pronoun runs the risk of confession and embarrassment – something several contributors related to the 'confessional' poetry of the 1960s, finding this a difficult and even rebarbative model. Grevel Lindop, for example, writes that embarrassment

> is a force to be reckoned with . . . A poem may be embarrassing to the poet for two main reasons – either because it reads oddly, or because it reveals something uncomfortably personal about oneself, or (worse) about someone else. Fear of embarrassment is thus a major obstacle in writing, and makes itself felt as a pressure to write in ways that are familiar and safe. Clearly, any technical innovation risks looking odd; any degree of honesty risks the personal . . .

I suspect that English poetry in general, reacting as always against the models of the past, is currently unsettled about the validity of the first person. Within the series there were conflicting views. As Douglas Dunn puts it, '[t]o be any sort of writer at all, then at some point early in your life you have to make a leap from reticence into an artistically and socially acceptable candour that will be hospitable to both mischief and responsibility. Poetry insists of those who try to write it that they have the courage of their joys and melancholies. You also need to possess the courage of the present tense and the first person singular.' Yet others record strategies designed specifically to avoid the first person – Fleur Adcock writes that during the late 1970s 'I simply couldn't bring myself to write "I" yet again. As a result there are several poems from that period where the syntax is unusually contorted, in order to exclude pronouns as far as possible and to accommodate what was actually a first-person viewpoint without the use of "I". . .'

If I detect a general unease here, I also think that such unease might be related to the spread of more formalist writing (particularly in America[12]), almost a 'metrical revival' were it not for the fact that metrical verse has always been current, if not, in the twentieth century, always fashionable. The interest now shown in formal modes of writing is arguably impelled from three sources: difficulty with point of view, and resistance to topicalisation of the first person; a period of metrical retrenchment, engendered by the fact that 'notions of versification are in confusion' (the clause is Sisson's) and where this occurs, it is at least likely that some relatively conservative, formal procedures will gain in constructive power; and third, a powerful reaction against the models of the recent past. Alison Brackenbury puts this clearly: 'Perhaps it was in reaction to the Sixties' misplaced trust in inspiration that poets of about my age seemed to have learned techniques so carefully, and tried so hard to practise them. I notice a masochistic desire to produce villanelles...'

Moving on, finally, to larger syntactic structures, the series provided some fascinating commentary on 'phrasal' and 'clausal' modes of writing. The covert model behind the rubric was that provided by Josephine Miles, in her *Eras and Modes in English Poetry*.[13] Looking for 'some descriptive principle of period sequence,' Miles found that 'neither diction nor metrics alone seems to provide a pattern regular enough to mark change; but that, on the other hand, both are closely involved with sentence structure, which does reveal a sequential pattern'. As she continues,

> [t]he distinction I have found pertinent in kinds of sentence structure is between the sort which emphasizes substantival elements – the phrasal and co-ordinative modifications of subject and object – and the sort which emphasizes clausal co-ordination and complication of the predicate. The first or phrasal type employs an abundance of adjectives and nouns, in heavy modifications and compounding of subjects, in a variety of phrasal constructions, including verbs turned to participles; it is a cumulative way of speaking. The second or clausal type emphasizes compound or serial predicates, subordinate verbs in relative and adverbial clauses, action, and rational subordination; it is a discursive way of speaking...
>
> Theoretically, there might be a third type between these two: not merely a scale of degrees between extremes, but a mode of statement characterized by a balance between clausal and phrasal elements... We have, then, three modes technically describable in terms of dominant sentence structure and emphasized by usage in meter and vocabulary; these I call... the clausal, the phrasal, and the balanced modes of poetic statement.
>
> Classifying the poetry written from 1500 to 1900 in accordance with this distinction, we discover a sequence which runs as follows: clausal, clausal, balanced; clausal, clausal, balanced; phrasal, phrasal, balaced; clausal, clausal, balanced. In other words, there are four groups, one in each century, each begun by an extreme

and terminated by a balance. No periods of extreme come immediately together, because each is followed by moderation in a balanced form.

   These four groupings appear to coincide closely with the four centuries...

If Miles's hypothesis is correct, and if the pattern is to repeat itself at the end of this century, it is clear what should be expected: a 'balanced' mode of expression, balanced not just in individual poems but across a range of writing. Such a balanced mode would follow, and react against, a different predominant mode or modes. I believe this would make a rewarding research topic, but the sample would of course need to be far larger than that provided by the *Poet's Voice* series. But my impression – an impression of tendency only – is this: that we are indeed entering a period of balanced mode, following from two periods where phrasal procedures were more common. Such phrasal procedures, with a heavier preponderance of nominal groups, are perhaps one consequence and function of non-metrical verse. One has only to think of Pound's 'In a Station of the Metro' to realise what effects are possible in this style: not for nothing is it called Imagist.

   Against this, Wainwright and Brackenbury in particular testified to their conscious elaboration of more clausal modes (pp.135-46, 182-200). But in surveying the work of the poets who contributed to the series, I also found a number of poets working in predominantly phrasal modes. It is difficult to generalise about this, if only because such a range of metres is available to poets: short lines of non-metrical verse are, for instance, usually phrasal, and cumulative, whereas longer lines, of ten, eleven and more syllables, lend themselves to a more discursive, clausal organisation. And it goes without saying that many poets use both types of scheme, sometimes in the same poem. Equally, the stylistic options now available mean that any poet may choose to abandon one mode, temporarily or permanently, and switch to another (the work of Thom Gunn provides an example of this productive kind of stylistic switching). Nevertheless, tendencies were apparent in the testimony. Charles Tomlinson's work is, I think, very largely phrasal: what finite verbs occur are often modals or auxiliaries, and the descriptive weight and thinking of his poetry is carried by nominal groupings. Anne Stevenson's work, likewise, is predominantly phrasal, tending (in later and recent work) to the balanced. The contrast is essentially between the following excerpts, respectively of earlier and recent work:

And why inhabit, make, inherit poetry?

Oh, it's the shared comedy of the worst
blessed; the sound leading the hand;
a wordlife running from mind to mind
through the washed rooms of the simple senses;
one of those haunted, undefendable, unpoetic
crosses we have to find.

Here, finite verbs are restricted to the copula and the perfect
auxiliary; other verbal elements show as either stem infinitives, or as
participles used adjectivally. The effect is nominal. Contrast the fol-
lowing, from 'Ward's Island':

Still, I caught the next ferry back.
A gaunt youth in a baseball cap and two burly men
settled themselves and their boredom
in the too hot cabin,
there to spread newsprint wings and disappear.
I paced the warmth, rubbing life into my hands.
The city advanced to meet us, cruel and dear.[14]

Iain Crichton Smith notes another relevant topic here: the influ-
ence of one language on another. Finding a 'fertile use of adjectives'
in his 'Deer on the high hills',[15] he relates this specifically to Gaelic
poetry: 'In Gaelic poetry, particularly that of the eighteenth century,
there was, perhaps derived from the Irish, the use of a battery of
adjectives to define the noun...' Yet elsewhere, in a quite conscious
attempt to break away from the longer line, Iain Crichton Smith
writes in a non-metrical verse which tends towards the clausal, as
here, from 'Bank Clerkess':

She builds
towers of silver, unbuilds.
Riffles
pound notes
like a card sharp,
wears
a large
cheap
white
ring...[15]

As he comments: 'You can see what I was trying to do. I was trying to write about individual things and beings of the day. This attempt was quite conscious. It meant that the language had to change and becomes less large and Latinate. It meant that lines became shorter, that there was no formal metre...' The contrast in styles is one reason why Iain Crichton Smith's work could be categorised as 'balanced'.

I should stress that my impression of balance (in Josephine Miles's sense) is still rather haphazard, but I believe that the tendency is there, manipulated as it is by conservative pressures (themselves maybe one product of the fact that more poetry is being published than ever before), a mistrust of radicalism and an unease concerning the personal.

I have tried here to indicate something of the scope of the *Poet's Voice* project. In concentrating on the major elements of the programme – metrical structure, the lexicon, and syntactic potential – I am conscious of neglecting other topics of large concern where testimony was given: these topics range from rhyme and half-rhyme to nationhood, translation, and poetic constituency. Equally, I have evaded one enduring and central question: as one member of the audience put it, 'what's the point of poetry?' To this kind of question, rigour and formal analysis, and a focus on the distinctiveness of verse, proves insufficient. But as I was preparing this work, I happened across the work of the distinguished British biologist, J.Z. Young. In *Programs of the Brain*,[16] Young argues that '[p]roper study of the organization of the brain shows that belief and creative art are essential and universal features of all human life. They are not mere peripheral luxury activities. They are literally the most important of all the functional features that ensure human homeostasis.' He goes on to suggest that

> [t]he activites that go to the creation and enjoyment of works of art are... quintessentially those by which the brain, working every day as a creative agent, synthesizes input from the world to make a satisfactory life. This is why I say that for human societies the creative aesthetic and artisitic activities are among the most important things we do... The creations and satisfactions of art include and symbolize both our individual acts of perception and the expression to others of what we perceive.

This comment finds a telling and specific support in contributions to the series.

Notes

1. Not all our visitors were satisfied with this title. Alison Brackenbury, for example, writes that 'I always worry if people tell me my poems are well-crafted. I don't care for the term "craft". Women in particular, it seems to me, have messed around with craft for long enough. It is time we moved on to art... If people have had time to notice craft, then they have not been dazzled or moved enough'.

2. *Agenda*, Vol. 10/4, 'Special issue on rhythm', Autumn 1972.

3. See e.g. Paul Fussell, *Poetic Meter and Poetic Form* (New York: Random House, 1965), especially chapter 9 ('Conventions and the individual talent').

4. Noam Chomsky, *Syntactic Structures* (The Hague: Mouton, 1957); *Aspects of the Theory of Syntax* (Cambridge, Mass.: MIT Press, 1965).

5. See e.g. Roman Jakobson, *Language in Literature* (London: Harvard/ Belknap), 1987), especially chapters 6, 7 and 9.

6. David Lodge, *Language of Fiction* (2nd edition. London: Routledge and Kegan Paul, 1984), ix: 'The novelist's medium is language...'

7. See also Jonathan Culler, *Structuralist Poetics* (London: Routledge and Kegan Paul, 1975), chapter 6 ('Literary competence').

8. The concept of the linguistic foot is very different from units of Classical scansion such as iamb, trochee, dactyl etc. On the linguistic foot, see Richard Hogg and C.B. McCully, *Metrical Phonology: A Coursebook* (C.U.P., 1987), chapters 2 and 3.

9. David Abercrombie, 'A phonetician's view of verse structure' in *Studies in Phonetics and Linguistics* (London: O.U.P., 1965), pp.16-25. See also the paper 'Syllable quantity and enclitics in English' in the same volume, pp. 26-34. The possibility of 'silent stress' has also been analysed by Derek Attridge, *The Rhythms of English Poetry* (London: Longmans, 1982). Another recent paper which discusses the thematic role of line-final salient pauses is John Haynes, 'Metre and discourse', in eds. Ronald Carter and Paul Simpson, *Language, Discourse and Literature* (London: Unwin Hyman, 1989), ch. 12.

10. *Poetic Meter and Poetic Form*, pp. 3-4.

11. Published London: Chatto and Windus, 1952. See especially chapter 3.

12. See e.g. Timothy Steele, *Missing Measures* (London: Univ. Arkansas Press, 1990).

13. Published Berkeley and Los Angeles: Univ. California Press, 1957. The quotations are from pp. 2-3 of the work.

14. 'Making poetry' published in Anne Stevenson, *The Fiction-Makers* (O.U.P., 1985). 'Ward's Island' in *The Other House* (O.U.P., 1990).

15. In Iain Crichton Smith, *Selected Poems* (Carcanet, 1985), pp. 23-35.

16. Published by O.U.P., 1978. See especially chapter 20.

The Rudiments of Verse
Donald Davie

Note: verse, not poetry. How to write poems cannot be taught; how to write verse can be – though not to every one. I've been doing it, off and on, for forty years. Learning how to write verse starts with learning how to *read* it, aloud. The reason: 'verse' is from *versus*, a turn – from one verse-line into the next. Hence my one and only subject on this occasion is line-endings[1]. And first in reading. Comes the cry: 'Oh you stop at the end of every line!' No, I don't; but I *pause*. Hearing me, you should know whenever I reach the end of a line. (It is astonishing how few readers, including poets reading their own poems, observe or try to observe this rule.) The objection: 'Oh, but that makes it jog-trot or sing-song!' Not so. For though we pause at line-endings, by no means is every pause equal to every other: the pause on a full-stop, on a colon, on a comma, and on no punctuation-stop at all – all are different (in *weight*, only partly in duration). And the interplay between these different pauses is what gives verse its *music*, a music vastly enriched when we remember that full-stop, colon, comma can occur in mid-line, and their presence there too must be honoured and observed by the speaking voice. Run and pause and stop and start-again – *there* is the music of verse, to which alliteration and assonance and rhyme or near-rhyme (not just at line-ends) are so many grace-notes. So I am tempted to say, but go too far; let's say rather that these devices contribute not to the melody but only to its orchestration.

Here comes the first digression, or implication, or elaboration: *punctuation* is of the first importance. And yet there are poets (among them some highly acclaimed) who do not punctuate at all, or punctuate only very lightly and inconsistently.[2] They are within their rights of course, but surely very ill-advised to throw away this battery of resources. Moreover, to ask poets to punctuate means – for the most part, not quite inevitably – that we ask them to write in

1

sentences. And yet not all of them do; some of them are so wide of the mark as to think that grammar, along with punctuation, belongs in *prose*, hedged around with conventions and inhibitions from which they are liberated as soon as they write in what offers to be verse. Again, they are within their rights to proceed like this; but it is self-defeating – they are once again throwing half their kit out of the tool-box before they start. For syntax is a part, and a main part, of prosody.[3]

Note that I am not expressing a preference, still less an ideology; as it might be traditionalist rather than experimental, prescriptive rather than liberal. These principles emerge from what verse *is*, by definition and etymology and as we know it from our experience of reading it and hearing it read. Let me say it again: all that I have to say is rudimentary.

The next phenomenon we have to note is *enjambement* (striding over). This occurs – to some purpose, or to none – when a verse-line ends without a punctuation-stop at a point where we've been led to expect such a stop. This is the case where the reading voice has to make the lightest of pauses. ('Lightest' does not mean 'briefest'. In practice, *pitch* has much to do with it – if the speaker's voice stays 'up', he signals that there is more to come, and thus holds the reader's or hearer's expectations over quite a protracted pause.) Nothing so immediately sorts out the men from the boys among verse-writers, the women from the girls, as the matter of how they handle enjambements. And note first that, to be effective, enjambement must be used sparingly: unless the reader or hearer has been led to expect an end-stopped line, there will be no drama when that expectation is disappointed. Secondly, an enjambement may be violent, or less than violent. Other things being equal, we shall experience an enjambement as violent when in the succeeding line a major punctuation-stop (full-stop or colon) comes in the first few syllables. And woe to us as verse-writers if we have contrived such a violent effect when there is nothing in the emotional temperature of the verse – in what the verse *says* – to justify such violence. That is simply incompetence. There are wonderful effects – silkier and more cumulative – to be achieved from making enjambements not violent at all: this is the achievement of Milton in the verse paragraphs of *Paradise Lost* – his blank verse lines are seldom end-stopped, except very lightly, and yet his enjambements are seldom violent. They have the effect of leading us always on, our expectations always kept alive yet never completely satisfied until the poet is ready, usually at the end of his paragraph. In any case the identity of the verse-line – its integrity as something more than a metrical and typographic convenience – must register for us; only if that integrity is recognised (and honoured by us in our speaking of it), can the violating of that integrity, as by the enjambement, have any significance.

The question may be asked: Is enjambement possible in unmetered as well as in metered verse? (Note that I abjure the expression 'free verse', heeding in this the injunction of the greatest British master of unmetered verse, Basil Bunting.) There are some kinds of unmetered verse in which enjambement is virtually impossible, for instance the very long verse-lines of Walt Whitman; but in other kinds of unmetered verse enjambement is abundantly possible, so long as the writer (and we, his readers) respect the integrity of his metrically unequal lines as we respect the integrity of the metrically equal lines, the pentameters, of Milton.

[At this point in his lecture, Donald Davie then illustrated his arguments by reading and commenting on some poems. No texts were given: as Davie put it, 'I make no apology for not having the texts set before you. For I have been wasting my time if I haven't conveyed my conviction that our uncertainty about these after all rudimentary matters has to do with our reading with the eye, not with the ear.'

In this format, however, it might be helpful to see the relevant texts. They are given below; Donald Davie's written comments are appended.]

(1) verses from Psalm 102, in the 'Old Version' of Sternhold and Hopkins, 1551, and the 'New Version' of Tate and Brady, 1698.[4]

> *Psalm 102*: Sternhold and Hopkins
> O Heare my prayers (Lord) and let
>   my cry come vnto thee:
> In time of trouble doe not hyde
>   thy face away from me.
> Incline thine eares to me, make haste
>   to heare me when I call:
> For as the smoke doth fade, so doe
>   me dayes consume and fall.
>
> And as a harth my bones are burnt,
>   my hart is smitten dead:
> And withers as the grasse, that I
>   forget to eate my bread.

By reason of my groning voyce,
    my bones cleaue to my skin:
As Pellican in wilderness
    such case now am I in.

And as an Owle in desert is,
    soe I am such a one:
I watch, and as a Sparrow on
    the house top am alone....

Psalm 102: Tate and Brady

When I pour out my Soul in Pray'r,
    Do thou, O Lord, attend;
To thy Eternal Throne of Grace
    Let my sad Cry ascend.
O hide not thou thy glorious Face
    In times of deep Distress,
Incline thine Ear, and when I call
    My Sorrows soon redress.

Each cloudy Portion of my Life
    Like scatter'd Smoak expires;
My shriv'led Bones are like a Hearth
    That's parched with constant Fires.
My Heart, like Grass that feels the Blasts
    Of some infectious Wind,
Is wither'd so with Grief, that scarce
    My needful Food I mind.

By reason of my sad Estate
    I spend my Breath in Groans;
My Flesh is worn away, my Skin
    Scarce hides my starting Bones.
I'm like a Pelican become
    That does in Desarts mourn;
Or like an Owl that sits all day
    On barren Trees forlorn...

Donald Davie comments: 'Whereas it is the received wisdom that Tate and Brady wrote better verse than their Tudor precursors ("smoother" is the term often used – but that begs all sorts of questions), trying to *voice* the lineations of the Old Version shows on the contrary that the distinction is between non-verse (Sternhold and Hopkins) and verse (Tate and Brady).'

(2)   *Via Negativa*: R.S. Thomas[5]
                   Why no! I never thought other than
                   That God is that great absence
                   In our lives, the empty silence
                   Within, the place where we go
                   Seeking, not in hope to
                   Arrive or find. He keeps the interstices
                   In our knowledge, the darkness
                   Between stars. His are the echoes
                   We follow, the footprints he has just
                   Left. We put our hands in
                   His side hoping to find
                   It warm. We look at people
                   And places as though he had looked
                   At them, too; but miss the reflection.

Here, Davie comments, 'the enjambements are violent to no purpose.'

(3)   *The Calling*: R.S. Thomas[6]
                   And the word came – was it a god
                   spoke or a devil? – Go
                   to that lean parish; let them tread
                   on your dreams; and learn silence

                   is wisdom. Be alone with yourself
                   as they are alone in the cold room
                   of the wind. Listen to the earth
                   mumbling the monotonous song

                   of the soil: I am hungry, I
                   am hungry, in spite of the red dung
                   of this people. See them go
                   one by one through that dark door

                   with the crumpled ticket of your prayers
                   in their hands. Share their distraught

joy at the dropping of their inane
children. Test your belief

in spirit on their faces staring
at you, on beauty's surrender
to truth, on the soul's selling
of itself for a corner

by the body's fire. Learn the thinness
of the window that is
between you and life, and how
the mind cuts itself if it goes through.

Davie comments that here, 'the enjambements are, though violent,
justifiable.'

(4)   *Christmas Syllabics for a Wife*: Donald Davie[7]
          When I think of you
          dying before or
          after me, I am
          ashamed how little
          there is for either
          one of us to look
          back upon as done
          wholly in concert.

          We have spent our lives
          arming for them. Now
          we see they begin
          to be over, and
          now is it too late
          to profit by what
          seems to have been a
          long preparation?

          The certainty that
          many have scaped scot–
          free or even praised
          sets the adrenalin
          anger flushing up
          through me as often
          before, but can we
          wait now for justice?

Horace says, Be wise
broach the ripe wine and
carefully decant
it. Now is the time
to measure wishes
by what life has to
give. Not much. So be
from now on greedy.

Davie: 'Whereas English syllabics, usually in lines of either five or
seven syllables, require a great number of weak endings (see discus-
sions by Yvor Winters explaining this[8]), even in this special case a
pause can be made after syllables so weak as "a" or "to", if the verse
has been well enough written.'

(5) from *One Times One*: E.E. Cummings[9]
Davie: 'Of this I give the text... because the point is precisely that
whereas the eye reports it impossible to pause at line-ends, the voice
and the ear can, if they sufficiently trust the poet's lineation, make
such pauses; and moreover, only by doing so, will they apprehend
the poet's tone of voice: at once mourning and exasperated.'

XIII

plato told

him: he couldn't
believe it (jesus

told him; he
wouldn't believe
it) lao

tsze
certainly told
him, and general
(yes

mam)
sherman;
and even
(believe it
or

not) you
told him: i told
him; we told him
(he didn't believe it, no

sir) it took
a nippponized bit of
the old sixth

avenue
el; in the top of his head: to tell

him

Notes

1. Compare the essay by Charles Tomlinson here, where the concept of the line-break receives special attention.

2. C.H. Sisson comments in his essay that 'I have in my time been arraigned by Donald Davie for a shortage of full stops and other marks of punctuation.' Sisson counters with the observation that 'the lines themselves are units of punctuation, of a sort... Read the lines one at a time and it will be clear where a longer or a shorter pause is required.'

What is at stake here is not altogether a merely orthographic quibble: it is the textual status of the line. Both Sisson and Davie would, I think, argue that the verse-line has its own integrity (Davie claims this explicitly later in his essay), and agree that this integrity is more than what Davie calls 'a metrical and typographic convenience'. The verse-line, that is, functions as a metrical (or non-metrical) constituent, Hopkins's recurrent 'figure of spoken sound', entering into relationships with other constituents of an equivalent length and/or prosodic or syntactic structure. The difference in emphasis between Davie and Sisson centres on how the textual status of the line is made manifest: Davie argues that punctuation helps to realise the graphic, phonological and syntactic features of the line; Sisson argues that such definition is not always necessary ('Why should not the reader do a little work?'). But underlying this difference in emphasis is a larger question: if 'given' marks of punctuation (authorial or editorial) help to define verse-constituency, then does 'the text' become a prescriptive artefact?

3. It is significant that Davie's long-held view of the interrelationship between syntax and prosody has received linguistic corroboration. The word- and phrase-stress rules of English, which we share as parts of our linguistic competence, are sensitive precisely to syntactic structure. A simple example is the difference in stress between phrases and compounds:

compound nouns such as *yellowhammer* (bird) bear strongest prominence on their initial syllables: their syntactic structure is [[yellow]$_{adj}$[hammer]$_N$]$_N$ – where 'N' = Noun. Phrases, on the other hand, such as *yellow hammer* (hammer which is yellow), bear strongest prominence on the tonic syllable of their rightmost lexical word: their syntactic structure is e.g. [[yellow]$_{adj}$ [hammer]$_N$]$_{NP}$ – where 'NP' = Noun Phrase. The rules assigning stress must therefore be able to scan syntactic constituents – in this instance, the difference between compound nouns (outermost brackets labelled 'N') and phrases (outermost brackets labelled 'NP').

4. The texts used in editing Donald Davie's contribution were as follows: *The Whole Booke of Psalmes collected into English Meter by T. Sternh(old), I(ohn) Hopk(ins), W. Whittingham and others, conferred with the Ebrue, with apt notes to sing them withall* (1581. Printed in London by John Daye ('dwellyng ouer Aldersgate')); and *A new Version of the Psalms of David, fitted to the Tunes used in Churches* (1696. Nahum Tate and N. Brady. Printed in London by M. Clark for the Company of Stationers).

5. From *H'm; Later Poems 1972-82* (London: Macmillan, 1983), p.23.

6. From *Laboratories of the Spirit* (London: Macmillan, 1975), p.50.

7. From *Los Angeles Poems* (1968-9); *Collected Poems* (London: Routledge and Kegan Paul, 1972), p.218.

8. See especially Yvor Winters, *The Function of Criticsm: Problems and Exercises* (London: Routledge and Kegan Paul, 1962), p.79ff. ('The audible reading of poetry'), and footnotes there.

9. From E.E. Cummings, *Complete Poems 1913-62* (New York: Harcourt Brace Jovanovich, 19XX), p.553.

De La Musique Avant Toute Chose
Charles Tomlinson

The following account of poetic form and poetic metre largely concerns my own practice. But it begins by touching on an aspect of these in earlier traditions and on the changes affecting them in our own century.

The relationship between poetic form and poetic metre must lie at the heart of any poet's literary biography. Pope 'lisped in numbers, for the numbers came.' The numbers were chiefly the iambic pentameters in rhymed couplets that were the hold-all form of the day. A later poet, Rimbaud – virtually the inventor of free verse in a poem like 'Marine' – wrote at the age of fifteen a translation of Lucretius' address to Venus. He, once more, could turn to a hold-all form that had dominated a great deal of previous French poetry, the rhymed couplet of the alexandrine. Much of his maturer work still adhered to the alexandrine, often in quatrains symmetrically rhymed *abab*, and however he might depart from tradition in terms of diction, enjambement, subject matter, his metrical base had been laid far back in literary history. In the twentieth century, with the explosion and extension of prosodies, things grow more complicated for the young poet, and if he has the misfortune to pass his formative years in creative writing classes, he will too often be left to his own devices, composing in a free verse that cannot account for its procedures, with line endings which have no rationale and line lengths dictated only by the fact that it felt right that way at the moment of composition. Rhyme comes on the scene accidentally. I once remarked to a young writer at an American university that, unlike his confrères, he actually used rhyme – not at the end of lines, it is true, but hidden away within the line, so that it cropped out in unexpected places. His reply was that he had done this without noticing it.

My own generation was more fortunate than his. At the provincial grammar school I attended, we were taught scansion of French,

English and Latin poetry. In reading English verse, I found that iambs, trochees, pyrrhics, spondees were, like the policeman of these days, my friends. Unfortunately, once I actually began to write verse, I allowed myself to become distracted by the long lines of Whitman and of Blake's prophetic books. I had somehow to find my way back to the bounding wiry line Blake speaks of and which he uses in *Songs of Innocence and Experience*. This occurred by accident when Peter Russell, the editor of *Nine*, showed some of my compositions to G.S. Fraser and the latter, after an unnervingly silent perusal, said, 'Why don't you use a shorter line?' So I tried octosyllabic quatrains and found myself back with traditional metres. It was some time, however, before I could make them work for me instead of my working for them (twenty-five sonnets proved a particularly exhausting episode). I needed also to work away from them towards a more personal metric and that too is part of the story.

I have retained a single example of my very early poems in *Collected Poems*,[1] namely the first one in the book, simply entitled 'Poem'. It begins:

> Wakening with the window over fields
> To the coin-clear harness-jingle as a float
> Clips by, and each succeeding hoof fall, now remote,
> Breaks clean and frost-sharp on the unstopped ear.

I had soon found that among those friendly terms listed above, I felt a particular affection for the spondee with its double accent. In this stanza there is a tendency towards spondees all over the place: coin-clear, clips by, hoof fall, breaks clean, frost-sharp. I say 'tendency towards spondees' because the iambic pattern often forces a would-be spondee like 'frost-sharp' back into the ti-tum rhythm of the traditional line. That is clearly what happens with

> Breaks cléan and fróst-sharp ón the únstopped eár.

The predominating pattern there makes 'and-frost-' into an iambic foot, with a heavy stress on 'frost', so that 'sharp' loses the fuller stress that a spondee would have outside the iambic pattern and this passes to the preposition 'on'.

Spondees held my imagination because, in combining two words, they seemed to produce maximum power. A spondee always seemed to have something of the kick of the verb, even though it might be purely adjectival, with its packed energy perfect for expressing counterstress in a chiefly regular line. One day during this early intoxication with tum-tum instead of ti-tum, I bought myself *A Selection of Poems* of Ezra Pound. My copy to this day bears anxious pencilling which tried to discern the principle of scansion in the following passage from 'Mauberley':

> For three years, out of key with his time,
> He strove to resuscitate the dead art
> Of poetry; to maintain 'the sublime'
> In the old sense. Wrong from the start –

I liked the movement of this – particularly the enjambement, a device I would variate on more and more as I gradually discovered the role of syntax and the extended sentence. I tried to scan the lines and realised it could not be done on any principles I knew. But again one thing that caught my attention was the effect of the spondees, which gave the lines a syncopated lilt. They were everywhere in this stanza: three years, dead art, old sense, and glancing down the page, I saw there were more of them: lee-way, half-savage, men's memory. I didn't realise then that Pound was doing what I had naïvely wondered whether you could do when I learned about the different lay-out of French and Latin scansion – that is, bringing over effects of syncopation into English from another language, in this case from what he'd learned from Greek metre (something that Thomas Hardy was also to achieve).

Before I could handle anything like the sort of syncopation Pound was using, years passed and I read Hopkins who also rejoiced in the spondee and had invented a stress metre of his own. Hopkins, as the general reader well knows, even had a whole theory of stress,[2] linking it to the energies of the universe via the energies of God's creation, so that in a metre based on an irregular disposition of stresses within the line, he could feel that language re-enacted and came into relation with the divine energies which, as he says, *in*stress the universe and the human soul. Without necessarily taking over Hopkins's metaphysic, I certainly admired the sharp energy in his poems with their stresses sometimes side by side with several unstressed syllables pulling counter to the normal iambic line. I also linked one of his more regular poems, 'Spring', for its unexpected placement of rhymes, besides those at the line ends. Here was an early lesson in aural structure that was to be reconfirmed later on by Austin Clarke's Englishing of traditional Irish rhyme patterns[3] and also by what Basil Bunting calls his own 'completely undisciplined use of

[Welsh] cynghanedd.' By this I take it he meant that, instead of obeying the strict rules of cynghanedd concerning the relation between accent and caesura and those governing the specific patterns of rhyme, alliteration, assonance and consonance, he was aiming for a similarly intricate effect more suited to the propensities of the modern ear, where aural attention would ensure delightful and unpredictable linkages of sounds. This kind of intricacy I first came upon in youth in Hopkins's 'Spring':

> Nothing is so beautiful as spring –
>> When weeds, in wheels, shoot long and lovely and lush;
>> Thrush's eggs look little low heavens, and thrush
> Through the echoing timber does so rinse and wring
> The ear, it strikes like lightnings to hear him sing.

A lot stayed with me from this – particularly those chimings between 'lush' and 'Thrush's' (the rhyme nicely deflected by the <s> – phonemically, the /ɪz/ – of the possessive), the close sound relationships in 'strikes like lightnings' (the 's' in 'strikes' once more aurally functional and the discord between 'like' and 'light-' clearly audible); there were the chimes between 'echoing', 'wring', 'lightnings' 'sing', all carrying on, of course, from the first rhyme word, 'spring'. There were the simple and satisfying internal rhymes in that final line of 'ear' and 'here', and the woven pattern of vowel sounds whose threads went from 'beautiful' to 'shoot', 'weeds' to 'wheels', along with the unifying effect of alliteration. I liked too the concision brought about by the suppression of articles in 'Thrush's eggs look little low heavens, and thrush . . .' I knew at once that there was a lesson in all this and that it was largely a question of the music of poetry – music kindling energy and transcending any preconceived message by begetting meanings as the melody unfolded.

One phrase in particular from Hopkins – 'does so rinse and wring / The ear' – lodged in my own ear. In the way things do, it got associated in the mind with a phrase later on in Pound's 'Mauberley', where Pound refers to the way Odysseus, in order to sail past the sirens, had his men put wax in their ears so that the sirens' song should not tempt them, whereas he had himself tied to the mast, without wax, so that he could hear the song and not dash overboard lured by it. The Poundian phrase was 'Caught in the unstopped ear.' With the passage of time, both Pound and Hopkins somewhere in the background, I found myself writing the line in 'Poem' in that already quoted stanza,

> Breaks clean and frost-sharp on the unstopped ear.

I felt my own ear was gradually unstopping as I learned to play with stress in the use of spondees, and to syncopate the normal iambic line while speaking 'counterstress' at the conclusion of this same poem:

> To cóunterstréss the lílting hóof fall as it bréaks.

I was simultaneously counterstressing the iambic pattern and, instead of using the normal ten-syllable line, getting here the effect of a French alexandrine of twelve syllables. All the way through this early yet, for me, initiatory poem, one is within hailing distance of the pentameter, as in 'Breaks clean and frost-sharp on the unstopped ear', and again the first line of that same stanza,

> Wakening with the window over fields

is iambic with a trochaic inversion of the first foot. I hear 'Wakening' as three syllables – no shortening of the word to 'Wak'ning'. The second line,

> To the coin-clear harness jingle as a float

has a hypermetric unstressed first syllable. The third line,

> Clips by, and each succeeding hoof fall, now remote

is an alexandrine with a reversed first foot. The final line homes back to pentameter form, though bristling with potential spondees. Already I was both saluting the traditional line and drawing away from it. It was not until 'Fiascherino', the last poem in my second pamphlet of verse[4], that I found myself at last establishing my own kind of hold-all form, to be used along with varying forms in other American-influenced poems, a topic I shall return to. 'Fiascherino' tried to reflect the movement of the sea where I was living in Italy, and its stress-based form, with muscle and backbone, or so I hoped, permitted me to use impressionist colour and light effects without letting the verse become fragmentarily impressionistic:

> One leans from the cliff-top. Height
>> Distances like an inverted glass; the shore
> Is diminished but concentrated, jewelled
>> With the clarity of warm colours
> That, seen more nearly, would dissipate

> Into masses. The map-like interplay
> 　　Of sea-light against shadow
> And the mottled close-up of wet rocks
> 　　Drying themselves in the hot air
> Are lost to us. Content with our portion,
>
> Where, we ask ourselves, is the end of all this
> 　　Variety that follows us?

I wanted here to bind the description of flux – the shimmer, the sheen, the changing light – to a firm formal basis where syntax, frequently roving over stanza breaks, gave added malleability. Reconciliation of the shifting and the stable was the first big problem I had to overcome. That whole question – the fact that we live in a world of time and change and yet long for forms that last (in art, in our own lives) – opens the way to some of the more sombre themes (ruins, death, political violence) that subsequently enter my poetry. Early on in my new metre – a basically four-stress line with variants of five and six, besides allowances being made for the weighting effects of stops within the line – the sense of tragic waste and wreckage appears in poems like 'The Ruin', 'The Mausoleum', 'The Hall at Stowey' from *Seeing is Believing*.[5]

In these poems and others I was in search of a verse whose beat was variable as to position in the line and a variety of discriminated sound patterns, less rich than Hopkins's, but owing something both to his word-music and his sprung verse:

> I have lived in a single landscape. Every tone
> 　　And turn have had for their ground
> These beginnings in grey-black: a land
> 　　Too handled to be primary – all the same
> The first in feeling.

The four-stress beat gradually establishes itself here and so does the union of syntax and enjambement. 'Lived' and 'single' ask the unstopped ear to discriminate their slightly acid discord, 'turn' grows out of 'tone', 'land' finds an internal rhyme in 'handled', and 'The first in feeling' moves alliteratively towards the positive side of the poem which, working its way past several obstacles, builds to a climax through five lines of enjambement, a freeing effect, though the climax still retains something of the acidity of 'lived' and 'single':

> The cows stand steaming in an acrid wind.

After the long sentence which delivers that ambiguous vista above the Potteries, the poem can now quietly settle its account through a rhymed couplet:

> This place, the first to seize on my heart and eye,
> Has been their hornbook and their history.

In the final line of this concord we have a four stress line which could also be read as an iambic pentameter, the final syllable of 'history' suggesting a ghostly stress if one hears it iambically, just as in some twelve-tone music – Berg's violin concerto, say – one is suddenly ushered into a key.

Word-music is a suspect term – my own teacher of English thought 'cellar door' the most beautiful sound in the language. But there is surely a possibility for the reconciliation of discriminated sound ('music') with syntactical articulation whereby the term is rescuable. When the theme of music itself has entered my poetry it has sometimes been affected by the fact that the house I live in is situated on the bank of a stream. Together with word-music, an active syntax can attempt to gather up into its own momentum the movement of that stream in images of succession, spacial continuity, song, even Rossinian aria. In a poem, 'Programme Note',[6] I imagine Rossini or Donizetti taking on a not particularly promising libretto which then flows

> Out from his musician's mind, not
> As the Gesammtkunstwerk (let that dragon sleep),
> The streambed's deep self-inspection,
> But the purest water where reflection
> Pooling for a moment, is drawn along
> Over drops and through recesses, to emerge
> Strong though contained, a river of song;
> You feel that you could leap it from side to side:
> Its dazzle and deftness so take hold,
> They convince the mind that it might be
> Equally agile, equally free:
> Are you the swift that dips here, or the course
> Of sheer, unimpeded water, the counterforce
> Of rock and stone?

These images seem to me to be given structure by an intricate and extended syntax that parallel the effect of sung melody, the sense reaching forward over the line-endings as the melody flows from bar to bar. I hoped also that the reader's ear would catch the ripple of alliteration, the light-hearted and irregular appearance of end-rhymes, the syncopation of rhyme between the accented 'course' and the less accented final syllable of 'counterforce'.

The same metre I used here I also used in two poems of political violence, 'Prometheus' and 'Assassin', both dealing with the event and aftermath of Bolshevik take-over in Russia. In going back to the French Revolution, in some ways a try-out for the latter event, I found after much struggle that my hold-all metre would certainly not hold the occurrences stemming from 1789. I began in my four-stress measure a poem on Charlotte Corday – a good assassin to balance the 'bad' assassin in the poem of that name, but the material itself actually resisted any such imposition of the form. I underwent precisely the same experience in writing about other protagonists in the French revolutionary period – Marat, Danton and Jacques-Louis David, the painter.[7] In working on 'Charlotte Corday', I found more and more the poem was turning into iambic pentameters. The subject seemed to demand the metre. The more I moved, imaginatively speaking, among these people who saw themselves as living after the high Roman fashion, the more the heroic line shaped by Marlowe and Shakespeare, Milton, Dryden, Pope demanded to be used. Charlotte Corday carried on her person, whether in muff or reticule I do not know, Plutarch's *Lives of the Great Romans*; David painted heroic subjects from Roman history; all of these characters were living on a vast political stage where they were consciously re-enacting the events of republican Rome, killing Caesar and renovating the Roman virtues of stoicism and plain living. With that high Roman theme in mind, how could one avoid the poetic line that had served Shakespeare in his Roman plays? Once one came to think about rhyme schemes, an element of variety entered in. 'Marat Dead', though, obeys a very relentless rhyme scheme in touch with Jacques-Louis David's use of history in his painting of the assassinated Marat for the purposes of propoganda. But in writing 'For Danton' I found, at first, that I was rhyming in a rather desultory way, often within the line and not simply for closure. But as the situation of the poem falls under the sway of necessity, and the consequences of political action more and more threaten Danton himself, rhyme takes charge and clinches the end of the lines:

> . . . He must come back to rule and Robespierre.

> Not yet. This contrary perfection he
> Must taste into a life he has no time
> To live, a lingered, snatched maturity
> Before he catches in the waterchime
> The measure and the chain a death began,
> And fate that loves the symmetry of rhyme
> Will spring the trap whose teeth must have a man.

So in these poems I found myself going back to a metre which twenty-five years before I had to break out of to find new tunes. Perhaps once I had found them, my new tunes in some way permitted me to write iambics quite different from those I might have written if I had never broken with that metre.

The break, as I have explained, was facilitated in part by Hopkins, but further extended by the example of the Americans, Marianne Moore and William Carlos Williams. Miss Moore's example was less metrical than a lesson in diction and subject matter. I tried to imitate Williams's famous three-ply layout in which he fragments sometimes long phrases into their constituent parts – into what Robert Creeley has called 'contentual emphases'. The content being emphasised by the repeated triadic device operating across the normal architecture of the sentence or phrase, concerns the minutiae of linguistic structure and intonation that tend to be absorbed and blunted by traditional metric. Williams in his use of these spatial recurrences – an attempt to make 'the ear and the eye lie/down together in the same bed' – was thus able to bring out the tension in grammatical constructions and rhetorical pauses.[8] Curiously enough, it was in a poem addressed to Marianne Moore, 'Over Brooklyn Bridge', that I feel my early pupillage to Williams issues in one of its better moments, the theme of bridging and reaching out towards a fellow artist finding a lucky parallel in the lineation of the verse:

> And what I like
>   about the bridge
> was the uncertainty
>   the way
>   the naked steel
> would not go naked
>   but must wear
>   its piers of stone –
> as the book says

> 'stylistically
>   its weakest feature.'
> I like
>   such weaknesses, the pull
>   the stone base
>   gives to the armature.

Williams once commented on a poem of mine and its 'generosity towards the American idiom'. Its 'generosity' was really towards his three-ply measure rather than any specific idiom. Williams's obsession with what he called 'the American language' momentarily blinded him to the fact that I was writing as an Englishman, though deriving my structure from an American example. The truth of the matter is that my work intersected at certain points with his concerns, but I was not a native of New Jersey and 'Williams', as I have said in my book *Some Americans*,[9] 'had to face out a sense of cultural deprivation and overcome alienating forces very different from the day-to-day experiences of a European.' What ultimately seemed to matter in Williams was less this triadic device than the ability he had in running a long sentence through comparatively short lines, producing an effect of almost breathless excitement while keeping the units of the poem clear and unconfused (though often the theme of confusion entered into what he was talking about). I liked onsets such as that of his 'Young Sycamore':

> I must tell you
> this young tree
> whose round and firm trunk
> between the wet
>
> pavement and the gutter
> (where water
> is trickling) rises
> bodily . . .

– and the poem presses on, taking parentheses in its stride, without a single full stop (even at the end, where its energies like those of the tree are still reaching out to the world about it). The question is not specifically one of the American idiom but of a skill in breaking lines just where the break counts for ear and voice, letting the meaning leap the gaps between the quatrains as if it were all simply one long line. This kind of movement, with what Ezra Pound calls Williams's 'jerks, balks, outblurts and jump-overs', which surges on yet is directed by the narrow channel of the lineation, is perfectly suited to transferral to English English. Of course, Williams, or any other influence, offers no simple recipe for writing verse, but the American sense of language and form, where form directs our attention to the smaller units of language including the syllables themselves, suggests new possibilities. Williams says that place is the true core of the universal. For him physical place is an anchorage against easy transcendence and abstract universality. And so is the language of verse and its existence as typography. Topography or place becomes typography, the place of the poem where the physical lay-out of print must now sharpen ones's ability to see and hear through the unfolding of lines, through pauses and enjambements, the meshing of rhyme, the sense of closure or the refusal of closure. In my own work there is a debt to the flexibility of the modern American line, variable, consciously using eye- and breath-pauses at the end of lines, but also (I trust) something of my own – something irreducibly English – in poems like 'The Fox Gallery':

> A long house –
> the fox gallery you called
> its upper storey, because
> you could look down to see
> (and did) the way a fox would
> cross the field beyond
> and you could follow out, window
> to window, the fox's way
> the whole length of the meadow
> parallel with the restraining line
> of wall and pane, or as far
> as that could follow the sense of all
> those windings. Do you remember
> the morning I woke you with the cry
> Fox fox and the animal
> came on – not from side
> to side, but straight
> at the house and we craned
> to see more and more, the most
> we could of it and then
> watched it sheer off deterred
> by habitation, and saw
> how utterly the two worlds were

disparate, as that perfect
ideogram for agility
and liquefaction flowed
away from us rhythmical
and flickering and
that flare was final.

I like in writing this type of poem to keep options on diction open, going from the conversational to what might be called a higher style, as in the Latinate 'deterred/by habitation' here, and also in the use of words like 'disparate', 'agility', 'liquefaction'. I'm not, as Williams is in certain poems, using a equivalent of the 'stunned' idiom of workaday New Jersey, but trying for a variety of register of speech. In a humorous poem like 'The Rich',[10] I try to run the changes on diction through contrasting and sometimes slightly ludicrous ranges of speech, beginning with

I like the rich – the way
they say: "I'm not made of money"...

but elevating the vocabulary side by side with expressions from everyday speech where my rich happen to be 'good socialists':

But are they daft or deft,
when they proclaim themselves
men of the left, as if prepared
at the first premonitory flush
of the red dawn
to go rushing onto the street
and, share by share,
add to the common conflagration
their scorned advantage?

Those last two lines, along with 'first premonitory flush', stretch the language upwards into a sort of mocking humorous discrepancy, though a linguistic gamut of this sort need not necessarily be either mocking or humorous: I like to play on the full keyboard.

As to pronunciation, 'daft', in 'are they daft or deft', is not 'darft' as south of the Trent, but the good old Midland sound of William Shakespeare. 'The Rich' rides next to 'Class' in my *Collected Poems* and that title also asks for a more northerly intonation than people give it in London literary circles. 'Class' is the story of my losing a job because my employer, Percy Lubbock (in his youth a friend of Henry James), could not tolerate, although he proclaimed himself 'a bit of a Bevanite', what he took to be the demotic note in my speech. I've already spoken of 'discriminated sounds' and the sounds I discriminate when the Midland *a* is in question go back to those early beginnings in the 'single landscape' of Stoke. Thus, in 'A Dream', another humorous poem, where I dream that I am at a poetry reading with Yevtushenko and Voznesensky, I talk about riding the tide of cheers that greet their expressive performances,

> breasting effortlessly
> the surge of sweat and plaudits to emerge
> laurelled in vatic lather, brother, bard...

Here I want a decidedly short *a* in 'lather' to coincide completely with the short *a* of 'vatic'. When in 'The Way In' I describe the wrecking of our cities in the post-war years, I want 'A century's lath and plaster' to have the whip lash of my native *a*'s, given added asperity in their alliance with *th* and *st*. I am sure that this kind of thing affects the delivery of much of my poetry: I count on an attention to clearly pronounced syllables (we Midlanders would give the 'ing' of 'breasting' full treatment) and a refusal to swallow one's phrases as they do in the south. Vowels must be full and not turn into the miaowling diphthongs of the south-eastern counties. I find support in some of these matters from Charles Carrington's account of Greek and Latin metres in his introduction to *Kipling's Horace*, where he states:

> Both Latin and Greek were inflected languages, abounding in long words in which every syllable was pronounced and almost every vowel given its true tonal value, while our uninflected English is built on strong Anglo-Saxon monosyllables around which cluster pronouns, prepositions, auxiliaries, that are rarely stressed and sometimes mute. While this wealth and variety of long and short words provides our language with its adaptability and charm, it encourages our lazy habits of speech, our corrupt vowel-sounds, our irrational spellings and the vulgar habit (seemingly cultivated by broadcast announcers) of dropping the voice at the end of a sentence.

Though inflection is no longer a part of our grammar, may it flourish (one is tempted, as a Midlander, to say) in our thinking about the full value of sounds and syllables in relation to the verse line. Basil Bunting's first recording of *Briggflatts*, the tape of which was long thought lost, but has been re-issued by Dr Richard Swigg of Keele Tapes, provides an ideal example of the way the educated northern voice (and ear) can respond to the sonic range of English. Of course, one can overdo this kind of thing, and Bunting's final recording of his magnificent poem sounds as if he wanted to give his northernness an almost Scottish resonance. Far more healthy was his reaction to Hugh MacDiarmid's 'When we get independence, we shall take back Northumbria.' – 'No you won't, you bugger.' Rather than let the matter slide into petty Balkanisation – something Scottish and Welsh nationalists with whom I have spoken seem unhealthily prone to – suffice it to say that we hear things differently up there. I doubt if any southerner could have written Bunting's

> Decay thrusts the blade,
> wheat stands in excrement
> trembling, Rawthey trembles.
> Tongue stumbles, ears err
> for fear of spring...

As a reader of poetry and a writer of it, I warm to these lines and their invitation and challenge to hear clearly. One must not exaggerate the virtues of locality in pronunciation (there are some hideous local slovenlinesses) and it is in a passage like this that Bunting, hearing with a northern ear, achieves something that poetry is always doing in focusing our auditory sensibility anew. The challenge was accurately summarised by Hugh Kenner, writing soon after the publication of *Briggflatts* and before English critics had made up their minds about its excellence. 'We are meant to discriminate,' he says, 'the sound of four monosyllables "ears err for fear", hear them bracketed by assonantal "tongue" and "spring", and trace the sound of the interposed "stumbles" back through "trembles" and "trembling" to a root in the terminal syllable of "excrement".'[11] If this is free verse, its approaches to the richness of cynghanedd are hardly 'completely undisciplined', nor is its artistry merely 'organic', that buzz-word with us ever since Romanticism. 'I have never supposed a poem to be organic at all. I don't think the thing grows, it's built and put together by a craftsman,' as Bunting has said in one of his numerous interviews.

I have passed to another artist who illuminates for me experiences I had had a decade before the composition of his masterpiece.

Perhaps it is no accident that he, too, had felt the influence of the Americans and was accounted by his friend Louis Zukofsky a member of the Objectivists' group in which Williams moved. Bunting was an artist, moreover, who even anticipated Williams's triadic device in his poem 'The Orotava Road', combining it there with a sense of quantity reminiscent of Latin metre in the line 'Its ill-roped crates heavy with fruit sway'. We are back with the spondee once more.

I have mentioned three kinds of verse in my own work: the iambic, the sprung line, and short-lined, so-called free verse measures. To dwell on the varieties of invented forms I have used (quatrains with variable line lengths, freely rhymed sonnet forms, five stress non-pentameter lines, the six line narrative stanzas in 'Of Lady Grange') would be tedious for the reader. There remains only one further statement of artistic debt to be made and this, too, is related to the theme of a verbal music, intricately crafted, and opposed to the lazily 'organic' – the casual free verse that wanders so often into print. I mentioned earlier on the name of the Irish poet Austin Clarke, a name in danger now of being forgotten and one that is excluded from a recent Faber anthology of Irish verse edited by Paul Muldoon. At the very moment I discovered my four stress 'hold-all' metre, I came upon (thanks to my friend Donald Davie) the poetry of Austin Clarke, with its extraordinarily copious rhyming. The forms were derived from ancient Irish and included also reverse rhymes, such as 'bough top' with 'cup now', among 'the delicate and dancing interlacing [and] love knots' (the phrase is Christopher Ricks's[12]). Clarke is again a poet who makes us listen – certainly made *me* listen and expand my own aural range at a given period. Ricks once more: 'The consonants and vowels owe their place primarily to the emphases and qualifications which Clarke can enforce by sound.' When John Montague says of Clarke that 'he has opened up the Gaelic tradition, for Irish writers in English',[13] I would like to steer that statement away from its proud nationalism to add that for one English poet at least a world of new tonal possibilities opened up when I came to read him. 'De la musique avant toute chose' – or almost 'toute'.

Notes

1. Published by O.U.P., 1985. Charles Tomlinson's *Complete Poems,* 1955-89 are also available in cassette from the University of Keele. The Keele cassettes include Basil Bunting's first recording of *Briggflatts.*

2. Hopkins's own account of his theory of prosody may be found in eds. W.H. Gardner and N. Mackenzie, *The Poems of Gerard Manley Hopkins* (London: O.U.P., 1967), pp.45-49. This forms Hopkins's Preface to *Poems* (1876-89). A further useful monograph on the subject is Marcella Marie Holloway, *The Prosodic Theory of Gerard Manley Hopkins* (Washington: Catholic University of America Press, 1947; rpr. 1964). Hopkins's lecture notes on 'Rhythm and the other structural parts of rhetoric', and on 'Poetry and verse', may be found in ed. H. House, *The Note-books and Papers of Gerard Manley Hopkins* (London: O.U.P., 1937), pp.221-51.

3. The brief essay on Austin Clarke in Michael Schmidt, *A Reader's Guide to 50 Modern British Poets* (London: Heinemann, 1979), pp.173-80, is a useful starting-point. This work also includes a bibliography of work on Austin Clarke.

4. From *The Necklace* (1955); *Collected Poems,* pp.12-13.

5. Published New York: McDowell, Obolensky (1958). *Collected Poems* includes the second, British edition of this work, pp.15-56.

6. In *Collected Poems,* pp.331-33.

7. From *The Shaft* (1978). *Collected Poems,* pp.273-312.

8. Williams's techniques of versification are usefully discussed in Walter Sutton, *American Free Verse* (New York: New Directions, 1973), chapters 9-10. A brief and good summary of Williams's early career is given by David Perkins, *A History of Modern Poetry* (Cambridge, Mass.: Belknap/ Harvard, 1976), chapter 22. Tomlinson's own memoir of Williams (along with Wallace Stevens and Marianne Moore) is given in *Some Americans.*

9. *Some Americans.* Berkeley: University of California Press, 1981, p.19.

10. *Collected Poems,* p.249.

11. Hugh Kenner, 'Never a Boast or a See-Here', *National Review* 31 October 1967, pp.1217-18.

12. Christopher Ricks, *A Tribute to Austin Clarke on His Seventieth Birthday.* Dolmen Editions, 1966, pp.18-19.

13. In Christopher Ricks (fn.12); see pp.8-11.

The Best Words in the Best Order
C.H. Sisson

The trouble about asking poets to talk about their voice and craft is that they will always – almost always – say something. I am no exception: I have of course to prove that I did not accept this invitation under false pretences. But I do not under-rate – and I ask you not to under-rate – the difficulties and dangers of the situation.

The ways of the human race are, I am afraid, very devious. I have been watching them for some time. I have also been one of them myself, for longer than I care to recall. Take warning! There is not one of you, I imagine, who would take at its face value what you heard from a politician who was asked to talk to you about the wonders of his activities. Poets, you will say, are different. So they are. And we live in a world all the time re-echoing with the noise of politicians giving answers which are only partly true to questions so often so ignorant and absurd that it is virtually impossible for them to give sensible replies. I do not have that excuse. The questions proposed in this series[1] are quite knowledgeable, and leave the speaker entirely at liberty to answer or not, and to attempt to deal only with such aspects of them as the speaker feels he knows something about. That is exemplary behaviour but it leaves a heavy responsibility on the respondent. He has no excuse for pretending to know more than he does – though it may be difficult to avoid a bit of that. Poets as well as politicians – and with less excuse – are under a standing temptation to be plausible.

It is, I take it, the design of this series to elicit information about the practice of a variety of contemporary writers of verse, rather than to establish a set of rules about how such writing ought to be done or even – though this is a more hopeful proposition – about how not to do it. Variety of practice there certainly is. And of course there should be. We work in different ways. There have been ages, however, when a certain uniformity of practice was recommended, or

26

even insisted upon, by distinguished poets and critics, and it should not be too readily assumed that they were off their heads. Our own prejudice in favour of variety – going under some such utterly mis-leading title as individual freedom of expression – is at least as ques-tionable. Much depends on the state of the language at the time. The state of our own, in the 1990s, is pretty confusing. We should at least reflect on that. It is, however, no part of my scheme of things to propose new rules for the correct writing of verse. All I propose to do – as invited – is to try to say something about my own practice. Those of you who are fortunate enough to hear or read the whole series of lectures will be better placed to consider the question whether there *are* legitimate bounds to variety of practice, and where they might lie. But whatever you hear or have heard or read, I hope you will not be so impressed by any of it that you forget, even for a moment, that in poetry, as in all human activities, the proof of the pudding is in the eating. Never let critical theory take over.

That goes for the poet as well as for the reader – or, to put it more modestly, it goes for the poet who is now addressing you. I am not suggesting that what is said by acute and judicious critics about such matters as metrics and sound-structure, about syntax and the choice of words, is of no interest to the poet himself, nor that it may not properly have a bearing on the way he does his work, only that such things are of interest to him as a *reader* rather than as a writer. No-one will write verse of any quality who has not been a passionate reader of poetry, and has not acquainted himself, over the years, with more or less of the most accomplished work of the past; and he will be dumb indeed if this reading has not caused him to reflect on such matters. All I am saying is that I do not see theoretical analysis as having any direct and immediate part in the actual process of com-position.[2]

I cannot avoid trying to say something about the nature of this process, as it appears to me, but I am aware of the extreme difficulty of accurate reporting from so confused and obscure a battle-ground. We are in the unreliable field of self-observation, and the observation of moments when the mind is fully engaged in a quite different form of activity. I do not know how to describe that activity – the process of composition – better than by saying that it is a process of listening rather than of speaking. The words emerge. In the perfect case, for a few lines at a time, they may be interrupted. More commonly, a line, or a few words only, come to the surface: there are intervals of distraction which, in relation to the poem itself, are merely intervals of waiting. The essential thing is to recognise the words of the poem as, so to speak, they come in through the door. There are cases of mistaken identity; one may scribble a few words, only to see at once that one has made a mistake, cross them out, and wait again. How does one recognise the words of the poem? That is the inner secret of the art. It is not a secret one can tell – not because of any caginess about revealing trade secrets, but because it is a trick one has to learn for oneself. None the less, I will try to give some indication of the process as it appears to me. I would say that what I am most conscious of recognising is the continuation of the rhythm.[3] That leaves a lot of questions unanswered, but we shall come to some of them later on. Continuation of the meaning is essential too, of course, but that cannot be allowed a conscious priority. The poet (the same one, I am afraid) has to trust the rhythm to deliver the right words at the door. If I write what I think to be a good poem – the only real sort of poem – I am usually surprised when I discover, when I come to read it over, what the meaning was. It is a commonplace of criticism that the poet may not be aware of all the meanings of his own poems.

It follows from what I have said that all my poems are in a sense determined by the rhythm of the first line, which comes unasked and often when one is least expecting it. It is commonly followed by other lines, whether by one or two or by a whole poem. I am very relaxed about this. Nothing more may come than this fragmentary manifestation. It is important not to go on deliberately – wilfully making up, as it were, for the failure of the natural process. To know what one is going to say is a sign that one has nothing to say – nothing, that is, that needs a poem to convey it. If there is a poem there, it will present itself. I have found that poems continue themselves when they want to. They will not be bossed. A short poem will usually continue itself in a few hours or in the odd day or two. With a longer poem, I have more than once had the experience of thinking it had ended, even quite satisfactorily, only to find that weeks or months later, when one's mind is on something quite different, it goes on without one realising, as one writes or even for a little time afterwards, that it is another part of what one has written before, and to all intents and purposes, put out of one's mind. It picks up the rhythm without being ordered to do so, as it were in reproof of all conscious intentions. This is surely a phenomenon which tells us something about the nature of poetry. It is as if poems formed themselves, somewhere beyond the poet's control or awareness, and the poet had only to allow their appearance.

Of course this is not the whole story, only the final chapter. It suggests that this process – perhaps something like what Keats had in mind when he spoke of 'negative capability', or asserted that 'if poetry comes not naturally as leaves to a tree it had better not come at all' – is an essential one, but it certainly does not follow that poets need not bother themselves with thinking about verse, or about anything else they can apply their brains to. I believe that the main influences on a poet are involuntary. By that, I mean only that they are not willed by the poet, not that he is therefore excused all the usual exercises of consciousness, including using his brains on practical and intellectual problems and accepting his laborious part in the ordinary social responsibilities. So it is with verse. The main influences on a poet's technique – as on his whole work – are those he has absorbed by the mere enjoyment of other people's poetry. A certain width of experience, an openness to contrasting forms of writing and to the practice of several centuries and preferably to more than one language, is necessary to give him any serious competence. Very little of any practical use has been written about the technique of verse, but some knowledge of metrical analysis, of the principles of accented and quantitative verse is desirable, and is likely to be picked up by any literate reader. There should be no need to insist on that here, and the poet, certainly, ought to know something about these things and if he does not, the quality of his reading, and of the skills it should give him, must be deficient.

I need hardly say that excellent verse has been written, in various times and places, by people who had no idea of these analytical distinctions, and one has to admit, therefore, that such knowledge is not essential. I would not, however, encourage anyone's ignorance or laziness. The English language is now in such confusion that it can do without anyone helping it to more: notions of versification are in confusion. People even talk of metrical verse – Americans of 'metred verse' – as if there were some other kind, though no-one has ever explained to me exactly what it is.[4] Of course there is verse of varying degrees of metrical regularity, fading away into writing which is indistinguishable from prose. (This is often called *poetry*, but we will not go into that.) If one is to use the term *verse*, there must be some metrical reference – to accent, quantity, or number of syllables. Pay no attention, in this context, to the sort of declamation which has no other distinction than that it does not reach the right-hand side of the page.

It is my own practice – I have to remind myself again and again – that I am supposed to be talking about, not the universal laws of poetry. You will find, in my published work,[5] a considerable variety of metrical practice. You have to take my word for it that when I was at school – and I am not talking merely about my sixth-form days – I could write competent 'rhymed and metered' verse, as my American anthologist calls it. In my sixth-form days I even wrote a series of sonnets, after what I had been taught to call the Italian model, though I did not produce them for official inspection. When at the age of seventeen, I left school, I had – just – encountered the work of T.S. Eliot, and the verse I wrote as an undergraduate – not too much of it, I am glad to say – was therefore modernist. As is recorded elsewhere,[6] I gave up writing poetry at the age of twenty, and did not start again 'til nearly ten years later. That is where my *Collected Poems* begin. The earliest poems there are not regular, in metre or in length of line, but I think I can say that they are such as could not have been written by anybody not familiar with the long-established habits of English accented verse, which of course has long accommodated itself to lines of irregular length. The poems certainly have marked rhythms. There are odd rhymes or half-rhymes, and the last of this group of poems even feels its way forward to almost regular octosyllabic quatrains, with the second and fourth lines rhyming. There was then a further gap of four to five years in which I did not write any verse. When I began again, it was in fully-rhymed quatrains, not because I made any deliberate choice to write that way, but because that is how the poems chose to present themselves. A certain variety set in after that, but none of it is in verse which could be called 'free', if by that is meant verse having no clear metrical reference, or moving towards prose. I had written prose – including two novels – so I knew the difference.

In the matter of syntax, one can probably get away, in verse, with some deviations which are hardly serviceable in prose. That has to be said with reservations, if one keeps Joyce in mind – though Joyce, it must be added, did not start his peculiar tricks until he had mastered, and long practised with great elegance, the art of prose as more commonly understood. A poet whose sentences never got anywhere would be of very limited interest. Subjects, finite verbs and, where appropriate, objects are the basis of ordinary speech, and they must surely be the basis of poetry. No odd turn of phrase can be excluded, on merely a priori grounds: the poet's voice may trail away into uncertainty, like anyone else's, and in the right context, that may add a grain of meaning. There may be occasions for nouns or adjectives, or nouns *and* adjectives, on their own, but anyone who finds such expressions suitable for a staple diet is probably weak in the head, which on the whole I think poets have no particular licence to be. Anyone who flatters himself on the power of his lovely phrases is almost certainly on the verge of being cracked. Some allowance, however, must be made for the fact that we are all slightly cracked. There may well be points in a largely coherent discourse in which the mind, trying to express itself, is filled with uncertainties and some tentative, unfinished expressions may be necessary for completeness. The arbiter, as I have said in talking about the process of composition, will be the rhythmic life which binds one phrase to another.

I have in my time been arraigned by Donald Davie for a shortage of full stops and other marks of punctuation. I am not in general averse to them, nor to the ordinary requirements of grammar. Nor was it a case of some mechanical defect in my typewriter. The volume which occasioned this reproof was *Anchises*.[7] There are some poems in that volume which have a proper outfit of punctuation – 'Marcus Aurelius', for example – but any lover of commas and full stops might be appalled by, say, 'Saint-Rémy', 'Sillans-la-Cascade' or 'The Corridor'.[8] No doubt I did not punctuate them fully because it was too difficult. That is quite a good reason. Why should not the reader do a little work? I don't think any even mildly qualified reader would attempt to read the poems without pauses of varying lengths. I would say that the lines themselves are units of punctuation, of a sort, and this can be effective where no grammarian would dream of putting a comma, as where a word of one line – and that word a subject – is followed at the beginning of the next line by its verb, thus:

> Tears
> Are not always there for the danger of having them.

The emphasis, it seems to me, is inescapable. Read the lines one at a time and it will be clear where a longer or a shorter pause is required. So I allege at any rate. Of course the poems where I indulge in this trick – or despairing lack of tricks – are of a peculiar kind. They are less forms of speech which would be adopted by one person addressing another than solitary meditations. You are invited into the obscurities of the poet's mind. Certainly that sort of thing can be overdone. You may not want to be there; on the other hand, you may find that the outlines of what is passing are clear enough to tell you something you would not otherwise have apprehended. That is a good enough reason for reading a poem. Why doesn't the poet tell us clearly what he means? Because what he means, for the duration of the poem, is what it says there, and not some clearer matter for which he could have provided an equivalent more to your taste. I would say that, as usual, the poet has said what he had to say as clearly as he could. Like it or lump it.

At the risk of casting you into further darkness, I will tell you something about the composition of 'The Corridor'. I was feeling an itch to move on to different rhythms – different, I suppose that is, from those of the Provençal poems I had been writing. It was a question of taking a pick-axe and breaking them up. It did not occur to me that the intervention of consciousness, or at any rate of deliberate intention, could go much further. I started jotting down words – any words – which broke away from the rhythms I felt were beginning to come too easily. What those first words were I no longer know. Anyway the exercise was followed – over several weeks if I remember aright – by other bits; I did not think much about them, certainly not about their import, and I cannot have listened continuously with all the discrimination the writing of a poem requires, for what I was left with, in the end, was a good many pages of verse and non-verse, sense and nonsense. I wondered whether to throw the whole lot away, or to rescue some of the small poems I thought I could see embedded in it. It was David Wright who perceived that what was embedded there, like a vein running through rock, was a long poem, and with his connivance I extracted 'The Corridor', adding nothing, that is to say, but taking away all that did not seem, rhythmically, to be part of it. This sequence of events is unique, so far as my experience goes. But the essential operation corresponded with what has always been my practice. Some people, I am told, produce innumerable drafts of poems and improve them as they go along. I have never had much luck with such proceedings and my normal practice has been to make deletions from the original draft but not to add to it. Of course one is tempted sometimes to change a word or two, even a line or two, and I am not pretending that such repairs can never be made. But more often I have found, when preparing a final copy of a poem, that it is more profitable to go back to the original draft, in search of first thoughts – perhaps crossed out – which are so often better than second thoughts.

'The Corridor' is a poem in what I suppose would be called free verse, though I have expressed my reservations about that term, and perhaps I should make it clear that what I have said about later corrections, and the authority of first drafts, applies equally to verse in stanza form, which some people, I have discovered, suppose must be the product of a different sort of deliberation. It is true that, in writing, one may sometimes have the impression of being held up for a rhyme, but it is a line or a phrase that one is waiting for; the acceptable one will come with its sounds as well as its rhythms. The process, in a sustained poem with a regular rhyme-scheme, should not be essentially different from that one experiences in a poem which allows only occasional rhymes, half-rhymes, or none at all. The poem itself has to decide where it is going.

I am afraid that to some of you this will seem to be a very irresponsible statement, and one which evades most of the questions I was invited to answer here. It does evade some of them, but I am asked to give evidence, and this I am doing to the best of my ability. To me the writing of poetry appears to be a psychological trick, or perhaps I should say rather a disease – a *dis*-ease, as it literally is – something which happens to one rather than something that can be learned.[9] It is something quite different from a *verbal* trick, which can be learned. It can and does make use of much that is consciously learned, including the verbal trick of writing verse. It can and does use anything and everything absorbed by the mind and this is its importance, and the reason why poetry is the central part of all literatures and an indispensable part of the human record. But to come to my excuses. Because the writing of poetry has in it a large element of the involuntary – in the ordinary sense of that term – there are many questions about poems which are as well, or better, answered by the reader than by the poet who wrote them. Such questions as, 'How is the syntax manipulated?', 'In what ways does the syntactic arrangement reflect – or resolve – a particular thought-pattern?' are in this class. The author himself, at the time of composition, will not have had his mind on such matters; the reader, who comes fresh to the completed poem and is baffled by some of it, may have a real motive for considering them, though I hope he will not do so until he has first enjoyed the poem and let it sink into his mind. So with such questions, also, as why the lines break where they do. And so, certainly, with the choice of words.

'Prose: words in their best order; poetry; the *best* words in the best order.' Those were Coleridge's 'homely definitions', as he said. What kind of words do I, the present witness, think best? Those words which come most naturally to me. What words are they? So far as I have succeeded as a poet, you will find them in my published volumes. Choosing the best words is of course a matter of the context; I should regard it as a strange aberration to choose them because they were of Saxon origin, or Latin origin, or because I thought they sounded nice. I have, ordinarily, no sense of addressing a particular audience, but merely of addressing whomsoever it may concern. My conception of the matter rather is that I should say what I have to say as directly as I can. How simple that proves to be must depend on what I have to say, in a particular poem. The reader has to take me as he finds me, and what he will find, inevitably, is the reflections of the man whose story is told, rather laconically, in *On the Look-Out*.[10] I was born in 1914: naturally I do not write like somebody born in 1934, or 1954, or 1964. If, in conversation, I venture for a moment into current slang, or into one of those awful malapropisms which are continually used and promoted by the media, it is with an inflexion which indicates that they are not part of my language. You must expect nothing better from me in prose or verse. Not that I am sniffy about the spoken language: on the contrary. If you have read – as you should have done – my *English Poetry 1900-1950*,[11] which was written twenty years ago, you will know that the opening section makes the point that all writers of verse 'have an inevitable relationship with the talk of the period.' The book also says: 'The penumbra of the twentieth century stretches back into the nineteenth – as far as you like, in fact.' The poet – once more I am pointing to myself, as the invitation I received entitles me to do – will feel an irresistible interest in following the language into the past, and will certainly not stop at the nineteenth century. The past is where all but the most superficial elements of the language comes from, and the poet will feel none of that absurd snobbery about the present which is now so widespread. He will also want to know something, at least, of other languages, in which there have been parallel developments, or which have made their own contributions to English. Even a little knowledge of these matters is better than none and all will contribute to the clarity with which the enquirer sees his own language, and to the clarity with which he can express himself.

I cannot conclude without saying something about the subject of translation, an activity in which I have indulged myself more than most.[12] Not everyone has been grateful. I have recalled, at the end of *On the Look-Out*, a reviewer who alleged that I believed myself to have *composed* three plays of Racine, 'together with the works of Virgil and Dante.' I cannot make out why he stopped at that modest total. However that may be, I have no doubt of the benefit of the exercise for the poet, or indeed for anyone who wants to extend his capacity for writing his own language, as well as to improve his acquaintance with a foreign original. My own concern has been mainly with verse translation, but there is much to be learned also from translating prose, and indeed that is almost – but not quite – where I began. Immediately after the war, when I was trying to re-orient myself in various ways, I was asked to translate four short stories by Jules Supervielle for a volume of 'new short stories from France' selected and introduced by Denis Saurat. The commission was tremulously undertaken, but to my relief thought to be successful. Certainly I learned a lot from it and I was able to go on, shortly afterwards, to write 'One Eye on India', which was too good for publishers at the time and has only just seen the light of day.

The problems of verse translation are more complicated. I had already made my first attempts, with Heine; one of my two major exercises in the 1960s was with the *Eclogues* of Virgil. I had for several years been brushing up my sixth form Latin in order to read more of the Roman poets: or rather, I had begun to nibble at the Roman poets – starting with Catullus – and had to brush up my Latin in the process. The problems of verse translation are less in establishing what are called literal meanings – a process in which plenty of scholarly aids are available – than in finding a form.[13] There one passes out of the realm of deliberation and into the involuntary realm of poetics. I remember how the rhythm I was to adopt for the *Eclogues* descended upon me like a hawk. I understood at once that all the elaborations of Virgil could not be accommodated in these octosyllabics. Yet the translation – which can be faulted for its omissions by anyone with a crib – does give the drift of the poem, I would maintain, something of the shape of each eclogue, and of the subterranean content of the whole. It is in fact still a poem when the translator has finished with it, and of how many translations can this be said?

If this sounds rather arrogant, I think on this occasion I must stand my ground. I am not trying to contend that what are called literal meanings should be treated in a cavalier fashion, only that, for the poet-translator, it is the poet who must have the final word. The impulsions of rhythm and other involuntary constituents are rarely as powerful, with a translation, as in the case of the author writing an original poem, except perhaps where what is in question is part adaptation, or where the translation fades into what may in fact be an original poem. In my 1984 Jackson Knight Memorial Lecture on 'The Poet and the Translator'[14] I illustrated from Campion and Samuel Johnson the marvellous effects which have sometimes been achieved in this way. These are not wilful effects but a genuine form of the poetic process. Perhaps I may quote here the conclusion of that lecture:

> What we call a translation is no more than a reading, in one time and place, of text from another age and another language. It syphons off something from the original, but as much only as we in our different world are able to take. A successful translation –

the concrete embodiment of a reading – does not preclude other attempts, it invites them. All are partial, all give the original a particular twist. That is why, beside the word 'translation', which implies the removal of something from one place to another, we should set the word 'version', which emphasises the twist.

Twisters are rightly suspect, but a recognition by the operator of what he is up to should be beneficial rather than otherwise. The danger comes when the operator is so pleased with his own cleverness that he reckons himself above his text. The perfect translation would give way entirely before the text, but that is impossible. The translator remains stubbornly himself, like it or not – like him or not. Of course critics from heights towering above those of Parnassus itself, will continue to demand the impossible. But for the poet it is a consolation to have made a readable book in the English language.

Such books I would claim to have offered to the world – if that is not too grand an expression – in my translations of Catullus, Lucretius, Dante and Virgil's *Aeneid*, all of which stick closely to the matter of the original, so far as it can be given in the language of our own day. And since the matter of poetry matters, this is something.

There are those who maintain – it can only be, I think, without due reflection on the process or on the practice of the great translators of the past – that the translator should follow the verse forms and rhyme schemes of the original. For my views on Dorothy Sayers see the introduction to my version of Dante.[15] For the Latin poets there is Milton's translation of Horace's Ode I. v, 'rendered almost word for word without Rhyme according to the Latin measure, as near as the Language will permit,' as he says himself. That this is immensely accomplished goes without saying, but his own description of what he has done at least contains the essential admission that the language will not permit everything the scholar would wish. There is more to it than that. Milton's contemporary, Fanshawe, produced a version which has some advantages over Milton's. Fanshawe saw more clearly than the youthful Puritan what sort of girl Horace had in mind. The general point is that the great translations of the Roman poets have to be in accordance with the genius of the English language, not of the Latin. One need only mention Dryden. All translations have to be in the verse the poet can best manage, for a particular occasion. He may well increase his metrical range, and his skill with language, by his exercises with foreign poets, but that does not mean he can adopt any pattern he likes. He cannot produce a translation of any poem he likes. It is only when the first lines of his translation come involuntarily into his head, as the beginning of one of his own poems might, that the rhythm and the tone of his translation are determined. It may be added that a poet is better occupied – and learns in time far more about the writing of verse – when he undertakes a translation than when, for the sake of practice in verse, he attempts to write a poem of his own without having anything in his mind which insists on being said in verse. At least he is not pretending to think when he does not: instead, he is feeling for the matter of another mind, in another time and place. The voice must still be his own; the matter is another's, and has to be assimilated as he proceeds.

That, I am afraid, is about all I have to say about the poet's voice and craft. I do not suppose I have made anything very clear. Throughout, I have tried to say what it is like to drive a car, rather than to lay down a highway code for incipient poets to follow. And the way you should drive a car – as you all know – depends upon the road and on the state of the traffic and on a whole range of changing perceptions. It is only the bad driver who thinks he knows exactly what he is going to do next and is determined to do it. In that respect, at least, the parallel with writing poems is exact.

Notes

1.   See the Introduction.
2.   A point often repeated in this series. The sternest voice is perhaps that of Edwin Morgan: '[I]t is not healthy for poets to become so acutely self-conscious about their work. I cannot imagine anything more likely to inhibit them from writing their next poem, and that, after all, is their function'.
3.   See also those notes on the primacy of the underlying rhythm by Adcock, Dunn, and Scupham.
4.   Some relevant issues are touched on in the Introduction.
5.   C.H. Sisson, *Collected Poems* (Carcanet, 1984).
6.   See the Foreword to *In the Trojan Ditch* (Carcanet, 1974).
7.   Carcanet, 1976.
8.   See e.g. the opening lines of 'The Corridor' (*Collected Poems*, p.227):

> Nothing is what I have done
> Where I have been
> These long years

> No such thing
> As metaphysical
> Escape
> There is a safe
> Kind of body begins
> With the toe
> Continuing through
> The bones of the foot...

9. A useful supplementary work, and significant in a reading of Sisson's poetry – especially in view of his comments on form – is Herbert Read, *Form in Modern Poetry* (1932, 1989), section II: 'What is suppressed in consciousness may be found reactive in the imagination...', (p.25).

10. *On the Look-out: A Partial Autobiography* (Carcanet, 1989).

11. Published by Hart-Davis, 1971; reissued by Carcanet, 1981.

12. Some selected translations appear in the final section of *In the Trojan Ditch*.

13. See also Fleur Adcock's comments on this problem.

14. University of Exeter. Reprinted in *In Two Minds* (Carcanet, 1990).

15. C.H. Sisson, *The Divine Comedy* (Carcanet, 1980).

Where Do Poems Come From?
Grevel Lindop

As soon as the question is asked, two kinds of answers, equally unhelpful, jump into the mind. On one side, a clamour of voices offering quick, plausible solutions: 'Poems come from the unconscious. From the gods. From society. From the language. From other poems. Perhaps even from the poet.' From the other side, a drier, more pedantic voice insists that the question is unanswerable and therefore meaningless.

To ask about the origins of poetry may seem out of place: I realise that the brief here is to talk about craft, about the shaping of poems. But if we are to look at the hammer-and-chisel aspect of making, the carving and polishing of the poem, it seems reasonable also to give some thought to the quarry from which the marble comes. And in fact this aspect of the question forced itself upon me when I was asked to say a little about the 'willed' aspect of poetic work – the element of conscious choice, decision and planning involved in writing poems. For as soon as one takes a look, one realises that one cannot often tell the difference between choice and chance, between conscious and unconscious. There are no sharp boundaries. Will, purpose and choice shade off into murky depths like marine rocks, sharply-defined at their exposed tops but fading into cloudy, wavering and finally invisible masses down in the water.

This situation makes self-deception not just likely but unavoidable, and we ought to bear in mind the real possibility that papers like these, where people talk about their own creative processes, are simply a catalogue of delusions: that we may be relating a series of fantasies that we have about writing, whilst the poems are getting themselves written in some quite other way that we know nothing about.

In particular it seems impossible to say much about anything except the *verbal* formulation of the poem. In reality the words embody something else: what Sidney Keyes usefully called 'some inkling of the continual fusion of finite and infinite, spiritual and physical, which is our world'.[1] To talk about how this dimension of the poem originates, focuses itself and gathers language about it would be supremely valuable; certainly it seems to have been possible in the past, and perhaps it will be again one day; but the present state of our poetic culture doesn't lend us the means to do so. All we can do is to start from what looks clear and gradually feel our way back into the darkness until things become too vague or confusing.

As it happens, the clearest thing about the way I write is that the work has to be done in small hardbacked notebooks with lined pages measuring roughly six inches by eight. Ever since I started trying to write consistently some twenty years ago, I've been using such books and although if necessary I can write on anything, the only blank page I can bear to stare at for any length of time is one of these. Pages this size look inviting but not intimidating. There's room for a fair bit of writing – twenty-odd lines – yet one soon fills a page, if only with crossings-out, and so has the illusion of making progress. Clearly there's something childish about this, an indication that one is trying to co-ordinate one's rational self with other selves that are moody and whimsical and insist on being humoured in small ways.

So much is clear, but one more step takes us over the threshold, into the inner world, where nothing has a firm outline any more. For when I sit down to face the notebook and work on a new poem, two other things are needed, and these things have no names. Yet I have to refer to them, and so I'm going to call them 'the medium' and 'the crystal'.

By 'the medium' I mean a kind of soup or stew of preoccupations, thoughts, feelings, mental pictures and scraps of sound all of which are swirling around some matter or other. I can write a poem only when I find that some preoccupation has been vaguely fermenting away in my mind for months or years and has collected this sort of medium around it. I don't mean by this that the subject has been coherently thought about. On the contrary, poems normally seem to come from a cluster of vague notions – something seen or heard, something else dully speculated about, a feeling of sadness or warmth, perhaps a pictorial image or two that seem somehow associated with it all. But in due course one becomes aware that, loosely swirling around somewhere in the mind, there is this mental soup which has, vaguely, a flavour, but no particular coherence. I call this the 'medium' because it is the medium in which the poem will grow, as a seed grows in earth or a tadpole in pondwater.

Yet as these similes imply, the medium can do nothing on its own. It requires a seed or nucleus to be dropped into it. This is what I call the crystal, and it consists, normally, of a fragment – a few words, a phrase or a line – which at some point seems simply to pop out from nowhere. Once this is present the poem can start to grow. The process is like that of growing actual crystals, which you may have done as a child, at school. You get some water into which you've previously dissolved a lot of some soluble powder – say copper sulphate – to the point where no more will dissolve: the solution is saturated. Then you get a small piece of solid copper sulphate, fix it on a thread, and hang it in your jar of solution. At once, from the solution, solid copper sulphate begins to coalesce around that little piece and in time a large, nicely-faceted crystal grows. The liquid, in a sense, was ready to crystallise, but the molecules didn't know how to arrange themselves until you put in the right kind of nucleus to show them. Once that's there they begin to line up and build.

The conception of a poem seems to be rather similar. There is the medium – that incoherent mental stew of preoccupations washing around at the back of the mind. At some point there comes into one's awareness the phrase, line or more – the crystal. As soon as the two come together, the poem starts to grow, to precipitate. The sounds, rhythms, images or associations present in the crystal start pulling towards them material out of the medium.

Both crystal and medium are absolutely necessary. Scattered through my notebooks are dozens of apparently 'good' phrases and lines which led nowhere because there was no medium ready to receive them. On the other hand, for years various concerns and preoccupations have been with me about which I should like to write poems, but the crystals for these have never presented themselves, and so nothing can be written.

There is one other element which may or may not be present in the mind when a poem begins. This is a kind of visual image of the finished poem which appears sometimes when the crystal comes into my mind, and sometimes before that, as soon as I feel that I would someday like to write a poem on a particular theme. I tend to see in my mind's eye a white page with a shadowy patch on it, the shadowy patch being speckled with brightly-coloured areas which represent images. The shady patch represents the general shape of the poem: if it is a certain kind of square, I know that the poem will be a sonnet or something similar; if it is tall and thin with a smooth right edge it will probably be in octosyllabic couplets; if the right edge is ragged, it may well be in free verse, and so on. The finished poem on the page is often, but not always, the same shape as this visual foreshadowing, and the visual image seems not so much to precede or follow the choice of a poetic form, as to be a part of the process of choice. It is part of the process of realising that a poem of a certain sort will look right if it is a particular shape, or cast in a particular form.[2]

But the critical element in the construction of the poem as a text is the crystal itself – the few words which seem to be 'given' and whose production is involuntary and unconscious.[3] Usually this will have a certain intensity about it, and will feel as if it ought to be either the first or the last line. Generally I know which: a first line seems to involve some problem or uncertainty that needs working out; a characteristic last line will have a solid, resolved or static quality about it.

To give specific examples, I can point to the first and last lines of a long poem[4] I wrote over a period of several months, where the whole process happened several times, and there was more than one 'crystal'. The first crystal that appeared was a line: 'They talked about great art, and the cafés...' This seemed a bit of a cliché. Who were 'they'? And what did they mean by great art, anyway? It clearly couldn't be a last line, and had a string of rhyming couplets not followed almost instantly it might not have stayed as a first one either. But it so quickly brought with it other lines that began to make sense of it, that it turned out to be quite appropriate as a starting point (though I never found out who 'they' had been). Not long afterwards another line presented itself: 'The unmarked page is pure, and hard as stone'. Equally clearly, this was a last line. It seemed rounded and decisive, and it seemed to come up against an immoveable object.

I may have given the impression that the growth of the poem from the crystal is a straightforward business. In reality, of course, once a suitable crystal has appeared a long messy process of trial and error usually starts. Odd lines and half-lines may follow the crystal promptly. There will also be single words, which may belong quite elsewhere in the poem. If the poem is in rhyme, or feels as if it will be in rhyme, there may be rhyme-words chiming with things already written down or appearing in pairs or big clusters. All these I note down anyhow on the page and begin playing with them as with the pieces of a jigsaw puzzle, trying to fit them together, trying synonyms and substitutes, and trying to fill the gaps between what already seem parts of the poem. As I do this I am alert for ambiguities in the words I am writing down. Are there, by apparent coincidence, metaphors emerging or puns cropping up which, if emphasised a little, will point in some consistent direction and help to hold the poem together by giving it a permeating subtext?

When I get stuck there are various strategies available. If I'm lost for a rhyme, I will sometimes go through the alphabet putting every possible letter in front of the sound I want to see if there's an appropriate word I've missed and listing all possible combinations in the notebook. I observe a strict taboo on rhyming dictionaries and *Roget's Thesaurus*,[5] but I feel that any amount of browsing in the OED is permissible. On occasion I have invented words I wanted to use, and afterwards looked them up to see if they existed – they did, of course, and indeed it's almost impossible to invent a monosyllabic word that doesn't already exist in English; though the meaning when you find it may not turn out to be one that you can use. (At one time, incidentally, I used to try deliberately to use in each new poem at least one word I had never put into a poem before, in the hope of keeping the vocabulary fresh and expanding. I no longer bother with this, though because I systematically scrutinise every word I use for its main meaning, its range of associations, and its sound, I hope the vocabulary remains reasonably alive.)

If I simply cannot discover what comes next in a poem, I pretend to myself that the complete poem already exists and begin reading (usually aloud) from the first line. When I reach the break I try to hear with the mind's ear what is going to come next, or even to speak it aloud. Sometimes this works; if it doesn't, I often find myself drawing rhythmical shapes in the air with my arms rather like a conductor encouraging a diffident section of an orchestra: parts of poems tend in any case to come first as a kind of rhythmical wave within the body,[6] and I often prowl the room trying to coax the pattern up from the level of bodily posture and gesture to that of inarticulate grunting sound and thence into actual words.

These are ways of dealing with gaps or silences, where gap or silence doesn't seem to be what the poem wants. There's another way of being stuck, when you write a passage but it keeps coming out as nonsense: tangled or incoherent or just sounding completely wrong for the poem it's supposed to belong to. At such times I find it helpful to take a step back, as it were, and write out in prose as nearly as possible what it is I'm trying to say. This generally reveals that I've been trying to say two or more incompatible things at once; acknowledging this often involves also admitting that I wasn't being altogether honest in what was being written. Some doubt is being suppressed; bringing it to the surface enables the poem to go on, and makes it better but also, often, more embarrassing.

Embarrassment, as a matter of fact, is a force to be reckoned with, and it's become a private maxim of mine that most good poetry, when new, has something embarrassing about it. A poem may be embarrassing to the poet for two main reasons: either because it reads oddly, or because it reveals something uncomfortably personal about oneself, or (worse) about someone else. Fear of embarrassment is thus a major obstacle in writing, and makes itself felt as a pressure to write in ways that are familiar and safe. Clearly, any technical innovation risks looking odd; any degree of honesty risks the personal. One can wholly evade embarrassment only at the cost of dull and dishonest writing. The situation is not made any easier by the fact that there are closely allied kinds of embarrassment that need to be treated with respect – the embarrassment caused by simply clumsy writing, and that caused by sentimentality. To differentiate between the kinds is difficult.

These statements are in the present tense and may suggest that my ways of writing don't change. This is very far from the truth: the writing of poetry is a quest or journey which undergoes a continuous evolution and in sense even perhaps has a goal, though I can't conceive of what that might be.[7]

As soon as one starts trying to write seriously, the need for continuous self-criticism and self-training becomes obvious. Of course, that perception isn't steadily acted on, because self-training requires effort and the mind invariably shrinks from effort, finding a prolific supply of excuses not to make it. But from time to time I try to pull myself together and say, 'Right, come on, if you were giving advice to someone else who'd written what you've written, what would you tell them to do?' When I can do this and actually take the ensuing advice, the results are always rewarding in some way. Very often the advice is to make a conscious study of technique in some area of writing: for example, I've sent myself off to read the whole of Pound's poetry systematically in the hope of improving my free verse and my sense of rhythm generally – something I might never have done for pleasure, though it became a pleasure once the taste was acquired. At another time I set myself to read and study the work of a range of sonnet-writers, trying to understand and feel their use of structural principles, in order to improve on my own rudimentary handling of the form.

Looking back, I can see that a hankering to improve my technique has had a large effect on the kind of poems I've written. For a long time I've felt that a poet should have as wide a range of technical mastery as possible – that he should ideally be at home with the main kinds of verse which form part of his tradition, just as we would expect a musical composer to understand harmony and counterpoint and be familiar with the basics of composing in pentatonic, eight-note and twelve-tone scales and the usual range of time- and key-signatures. And I've never seen any problem in regarding the various kinds of free and metrical verse as equally valid parts of the reper-toire, to be used as occasion requires. It seems slightly odd that some poets have a doctrinaire adherence to one or the other, as if a painter should consistently refuse to use a certain part of the spectrum – though I accept that for certain kinds of work or at particular periods such a refusal might legitimately become an artistic principle in itself – a constraint within which the artist chose to work.

Poetic form started to become a central element in determining what I wrote after 1981, when I decided to write a series of poems to accompany twenty-one wood engravings by the eighteenth-century Tyneside engraver Thomas Bewick.[8] Twenty of the poems were in free verse, but for the twenty-first I decided to address Bewick directly and to do so it seemed natural to use a form he would have understood. The heroic couplet would have presented too stark a contrast to the other poems, so I chose blank verse (which Bewick would have known from Milton, Thomson and Cowper) and wrote a forty-seven line poem to him, acknowledging my debt and includ-ing a few phrases from Bewick's own brief autobiography.

The poem was a real gesture of gratitude because leaning on Bewick's pictures had given me the nerve to write an extended sequence. It had got me over my fear of breaking out of the limita-tions of the short lyric, and I realised now that I needed to write on a larger scale than the single short poem offered. One reason for this was, and still is, that I have never been able to recognise a distinctive poetic 'voice' in my own work. When other writers talk about finding a 'voice' I blush and keep quiet, because I'm not sure that I ever have found mine. I seem to write poems of different sorts in dif-ferent styles, and for a long time this worried me. When I was put-ting together my first book, *Fools' Paradise*,[9] I tried to plan it with a roughly symmetrical structure, separating poems with similar tones and placing them apart, to try and attain a kind of balance. The effect, I now think, looked like a random distribution and prevented the book from having any apparent coherence or sense of direction. Like badly hung paintings in an exhibition, each one was 'killed' by its neighbours.

The Bewick poems showed me that I needed, often, to write

poems in groups or sequences. If I changed styles or voices in between, that didn't matter: a group of poems was large enough to establish its own context and stand up against the pressure of other poems. And the range of voices could be a virtue, an exploration of different parts of the spectrum.

The Bewick sequence had other consequences. Having chosen blank verse for the final poem, I found that I liked that metre and wanted to use it at greater length – partly, in a way, because I wanted to get rid of it. I couldn't see myself writing in blank verse for ever, but I could also see that there was something addictive about it. Write a poem in blank verse and you soon find yourself thinking in it. It can be very hard to stop. So I thought, right, let's do one long poem in blank verse to get it out of our system, then we can move on to something else. The idea floated around in my mind for a while and got mixed up with the medium or stew of ideas that was starting to swirl around memories of a visit to Bali which I'd made with my wife some years before. I started jotting down notes – little travel sketches – and they came out quite naturally in blank verse. The poem changed its focus in due course but kept the same form and became the title-poem of my second book, *Tourists*.

I felt I had extricated myself from blank verse, but behind that lurked another opponent. Somehow the process of working in blank verse over some months had started to turn my mind towards the notion of the rhyming couplet. I wasn't sure I wanted to get involved with the couplet, but the idea drifted around in my brain and somehow got itself saturated in the medium which was beginning to collect around my reading of the German (or rather Bohemian) poet Rilke. I'd translated a couple of his poems and something about the quality of his mind had attracted me and yet slightly repelled me. I pondered the idea of writing a poem about him, and eventually the idea spilled over like boiling milk from a saucepan and I risked writing down a few lines. I found I couldn't stop, and large tracts of a poem began to emerge written in rather rhetorical rhyming couplets. I didn't try to interfere because Rilke himself always kept to a somewhat high style and had a great fluency with rhyme. It seemed appropriate enough, and I told myself that at any rate once I'd finished the poem I could consider that honour was satisfied as far as the couplet was concerned and write no more.

Things weren't as simple as that, however, because about the time the Rilke poem was finished I started to find the notion of the sonnet was getting into my head, and in a particularly virulent form, for somehow once the idea of the sonnet had arisen, the idea of the sonnet-*sequence* wasn't far behind. And if the sonnet-sequence, then why not (as the object of the exercise was only to get the sonnet out of my system once and for all) – why not an *interlinked* sonnet sequence, the sort where the last line of one sonnet becomes the first line of the next and so on, with the fourteen repeated lines being collected to form a fifteenth sonnet at the end? This seemed to be approaching the outer limits of sanity but for some time I felt quite safe, as I couldn't see any proper subject or 'medium' for such a poem.

There was vaguely present in my mind a notion, from several years back, of a group of 'suburban sonnets', poems which would look at various aspects of daily life in the inner-city suburb where I live – things like gardening and supermarkets and cats. But this didn't seem a very exciting idea. Nevertheless it recurred from time to time. Another more hopeful project that I kept turning over was that of a poem about patchwork. I had a friend who specialised in making patchwork quilts and it had often struck me that this would be an enticing subject for a poem: patchwork would provide a nice metaphor for the construction of the poem itself, there would be plenty of scope for colourful imagery and there must be interesting opportunities for formal innovation – for somehow the shape of the poem ought to match the patched and pieced nature of its subject. I couldn't for the life of me see how this was to be done, however, until one day I was in town shopping. Thinking vaguely for the thousandth time about suburban sonnets and patchwork poems I went into a café and as I was lowering myself into a chair the two ideas suddenly overlapped with an effect like the sliding into focus of the two pictures in a stereoscope. I saw that the suburban sonnet sequence and the patchwork poem could be the same thing. Each sonnet would be one square in the patchwork, the repeated lines would be the seams between them, and any number of patterns of tone and colour could be produced. To represent the different textures and patterns of the scraps of fabric fifteen different rhyme-schemes could be used (not difficult, since the Petrarchan sonnet alone has at least seven recognised variants). The 'Patchwork' title would justify the most miscellaneous range of subjects, and the whole could be unified by a running metaphor of textiles; the names of fabrics and sewing terms are countless and most of them have other meanings, so that there would be generous scope for wordplay. These thoughts, together with the materials that had accumulated around the two original ideas, meant that a 'medium' for the sequence was immediately available, and at the same time the 'crystal' appeared too: the line 'Rooms in a house, leaves from a calendar' presented itself. I managed to resist forming any more of the opening poem until I had some paper available and could guide it into the appropriate rhyme-scheme.

Work on this sequence is still in progress and I hope I haven't blighted it by talking about it before it's finished, but there are only two more sonnets to write and they are in many ways determined by their place in the sequence, so I suppose they will get written. Then I shall be able to face, with relief, a future without sonnets. But already demonic whisperings are starting again; I've recently been hearing about the constrained forms devised by the French OULIPO group. There is, for example, the series of poems which must be written using only the ten most frequently-used letters of the alphabet plus one other, no letter to be re-used until all the rest have occurred and the eleventh letter changing from poem to poem. Possibly this too will have to be faced eventually, and if madness does not supervene first it may later.

All this suggests that a fascination with poetic forms may involve some sort of compulsion neurosis, like the habit of doing everything three times or avoiding the cracks in paving-stones. But the compulsion is not altogether dominating and I find that in between working in strict forms I feel a need to write in much looser forms both for relief and to keep a certain flexibility. When I first started writing in couplets, I found it a pure and rather guiltily-indulged sensuous delight like eating bag after bag of chocolate creams; yet once I'd been using the form for several months I began to promise myself the pleasure of writing a poem in really irregular free verse the minute I'd finished the job in hand, as one might promise oneself a nice cup of tea after some taxing manual task.

One difficulty, though, is that the form of a poem has to mesh with the subject – in a sense, the form always needs to be part of the subject. As a result one sometimes finds oneself devising new forms for particular poems. In 1983, for example, I wrote a poem called 'Summer Pudding'[10] based on a recipe, the idea being that the pudding itself epitomised memories of summer, it really *contained* summer rather than just fruit, and hence also that the pudding was the poem. I needed to convey a lot of information in the poem and sensed the need for a strong framework to hold it together and avoid rambling. I considered rhyme, but taken with the recipe element it would have made the poem seem too comic, too much a piece of light verse. I needed a metre but not a tight one and not the predictable alternative, blank verse. The first line was already in my head –

'Begin with half a pound of raspberries' – and it was a five stressed line (as I, a Northerner, pronounce *raspberries*, anyway) so I decided simply to alternate five-stressed lines like that with longer, seven-stressed ones. That created an ebb-and-flow movement to give interest to the poem, it was firm and clear, yet not constricting, and allowed much information to go into each line.

(This tendency to write poems about domestic matters like patchwork and recipes, incidentally, has unexpected consequences: when I arrived to read at a Swiss university I was greeted with some hilarity because the students who'd been reading my poems, getting no clue from my name, had assumed I was a woman.)

At about the same time I wrote a poem about a migraine-attack, and decided to use syllabics. Many excellent poets will tell you, with logically irrefutable arguments, that syllabics are pointless,[11] that they cannot give structure to a poem, that because the ear can't hear the syllable-count one might as well use free verse, and so on. I agree that the logic looks unbreakable, but the plain fact is that they do work. On the few occasions I've used them they've enabled me to write as I could not otherwise have done. I readily admit that the effect they produce, because it ignores the usual verse-making elements of stress and quantity, is harsh and slightly inhuman. But then if you want to give a harsh and inhuman texture to a poem, syllabics are what you need. In particular they provoke the poet into breaking the line in odd places – between article and noun, for example. I would find it very difficult in any other kind of verse to end on 'a' or 'the'; in syllabics it seems far easier.

But deciding to use syllabics is only the first of several necessary decisions. How many syllables to the line? How many line-lengths? In the end I decided to use lines of two lengths, seven and nine syllables,[12] both short so as to give a constricted effect, and to alternate the line lengths, putting bigger and bigger blocks of nine-syllable lines between each pair of seven-syllable ones to give the effect of increasing pressure as the migraine progressed. I hope the effect of these bigger and bigger groups of longer lines alternating with the single short ones conveys the sense of a wave pattern, like the ink-trace of an electro-encephalograph with longer and longer bursts of disturbance interrupting the normal pattern. I would hope that this is felt intuitively by readers who don't ever consciously notice the syllabic structure of the poem. These are examples of some of the forms I've played with. Mostly I write in far simpler forms, and increasingly in very simple traditional ballad-stanzas, or quatrains. It's refreshing to come back to these after getting involved in more elaborate forms.

But what goes into these patterns? One of the highest priorities when I start work on a poem is to remain concrete: never to let go for long of sharp and vivid sensory images. Sometimes I open a poem with generalisation – 'Forgotten desires fulfilled/Are the best kind' – but find myself immediately following it with images which engage the visual and tactile imagination and begin to substantiate the opening statement:

> Her yellow silks uncrumpled
> By the wind,
> Out of their furred green case
> The Welsh poppy now
> Unplanned, unasked, displays...

To have followed the opening proposition immediately with any more reflections on memory and desire would have been dangerous – it would have amounted to telling rather than showing, and poetic truths should always seem to be discovered rather than asserted. I tend to visualise my images very clearly: I sit and gaze mentally at them, and when possible try to touch or taste or smell them too. It's been pointed out to me that there are a great many references to feet in my poems: this is true and derives from the fact that to prevent imagined scenes from becoming too weightless and etherial I often include a reference to the contact of the footsole with the ground to stimulate the reader into a sense of bodily presence in the imagined place.

These perceptions naturally embody themselves in sentences, and the nature of the sentences varies with the process by which the mind arrives at them. A sudden clear seeing will result in a sharp, simple sentence. The process of investigating a situation or idea or object and trying to get to the bottom of it, to make sense of it, produces long, intricate sentences, with lots of subordinate clauses. I admire Edward Thomas's use of these elaborate, thought-tracing sentences and I think something of his technique has unconsciously been borrowed by my own writing – I didn't realise how much until I found that in reading certain poems aloud I was running out of breath in mid-sentence. I was transcribing a rhythm of thought rather than of speech, and I began to be more wary of it. Sometimes, though, I deliberately let these sentences develop, if there are special conditions that seem to require it. In 'Echoes', for example, where I try to describe the perceptions and flight of bats, I happily let one or two sentences run riot because of the peculiar nature of the subject.[13]

Connected with this is a certain liking for complicating the conclusion of a poem, allowing it to withdraw itself into ambiguities, uncertainties or negations. This is a way of setting the poem free by letting it be seen as a verbal structure that points beyond itself, rather as a landscape painter might at some point lead the viewer's eye into a series of receding vistas that leave him at last unsure whether in the remotest distance there is something or nothing, a suggestion of further objects or merely an abstract texture of paint.

Negative endings, in particular, have this tendency pleasantly to pull away the carpet from under the poem. I enjoy them in other people's poems – some of my favourites are Stevens' 'Nothing that is not there and the nothing that is'; Auden's 'Nor would they thank you if you said you were' at the end of 'The Managers'; Larkin's 'Words at once true and kind/Or not untrue and not unkind': all of them invite careful thought; all of them, by avoiding positive statement, seem to cut the thread that holds the poem to the poet and let it go, like a balloon whose string has just slipped through one's fingers. My own use of this device may be excessive: looking through the last lines of recent poems I find 'Towards the hills she doesn't know are there'; 'For subtleties I had already missed'; 'We are perhaps neither accidental nor alone'; and 'I don't know, I don't know.'

Talking of closure, two general matters perhaps need to be added. One is that the writing of a poem seems normally to be a process of coming to understand something better. Often I find myself thinking that a poem is finished, but being compelled to return to it hours, days or weeks later to add to it or change it. Invariably the root cause is that something else has been seen – usually something disturbing or embarrassing, which I had not earlier wanted to recognise as part of the subject. Once that new understanding has come – and it comes as a verbal entity, not as an 'idea' for which words have to be found – the poem is usually finished; and I do have a sense of a poem as 'coming right' rather than merely being abandoned at a certain stage.

The other is that (despite the title of this project) having a poetic 'voice' may not always be such a good thing after all. The poem is always the voice of something else – a problem, a tradition, a physical object, another person – speaking to or through the poet. I find nothing incongruous about the idea that a poem might embody the speech of a waterfall, a piece of wood, a bird, or a person dead or not yet born. There is an element of mediumship – in the spiritualist sense – about poetry[14]. The poem records, not the poet doing something, but the impact of something else on the poet's linguistic instrument. The poet's responsibility is to open fruther and further depths and sensitivities of that instrument to what may come.

Notes

1. Sidney Keyes, 'The artist in society'. Quoted in M. Meyer, (ed.), *The Collected Poems of Sidney Keyes* (1988), xv.

2. Both Adcock and Scupham share this view, although in differing degrees. Adcock calls the poem on the page 'primary . . . not merely a text for performance', although nevertheless this primary text 'must . . . be capable of being read aloud . . .'. Scupham goes further: the poem, for him, is both 'aural and optical'. On the last, he continues: 'All poems are concrete, an optical patterning . . . I found, and still find, a sensuous satisfaction in the caress the eye gives to a long and short, indented shapeliness . . .'

3. Almost all poets writing here share this view. As Sisson puts it, 'The words emerge'; as Adcock puts it, 'I have to rely on what I can only call inspiration for the genesis of a poem'.

4. 'Meudon', in *A Prismatic Toy* (Carcanet, 1991).

5. As Adcock puts it, 'discoveries are no fun if you've been led to them by a guide'. The poets represented here seem to have barred themselves from using rhyming dictionaries or thesauri; at least, none admitted such use.

6. In some works on rhythmic production and perception, various scholars at various times have claimed that rhythm is primarily a physical entity. Perhaps the first to develop such a view was the great German metrist, Eduard Sievers, now known largely for his work on the prosodies of the Germanic languages (*Altgermanische Metrik*, 1893). In a later work, however, Sievers claimed that 'every specific psychological condition of motion is capable of being projected outwardly in the form of an associated curve pertaining to bodily activity'. The nature of such curves, he continued, expresses 'the specific nature of that working-off of psychological tension which is at the bottom of all human behaviour and therefore of speech'. Sievers went on to describe a series of 'measure-content curves' which, crudely-speaking, describe the relationship between musical measures and the rhythms of speech. ('Aims and methods of Schallanalyse', two lectures delivered by Sievers in 1922; unpublished English translation by Angus McIntosh.)

Sievers' views anticipate, although do not directly underlie, more recent work on the phonetic of rhythm by e.g. Stetson (1951) and Abercrombie (1965), both of whom claimed that the production and perception of rhythm is primarily a physical matter, whereby muscular contractions in the thoracic cavity produce linked series of pulses corresponding to stressed syllables.

7. Whether the production of poetry – in any culture and time – is teleological has been usefully discussed by the eminent biologist J.Z. Young, *Programs of the Brain* (1978). In that work, Young argues that 'Proper study of the organization of the brain shows that belief and creative art are essential and universal features of all human life. They are not mere peripheral luxury activities. They are literally the most important of all the functional features that ensure human homeostasis . . .' (p.231). He develops this idea – particularly the notions that art symbolises the continuous creative activity all humans share, and that art exists as a set of symbolic satisfactions – in ch. 20, 'Enjoying, playing and creating', pp.231-50.

8. In *Tourists* (Carcanet, 1987), pp.47-70.

9. Carcanet Press, 1977.

10. *Tourists*, pp.30-1.

11. Adcock calls syllabics 'a pointless form if ever there was one'.

12. This choice of syllable-count is interesting in so far as odd-numbered syllabic lines seem to resist metricality more easily than even-numbered syllabic lines, which seem to be ghosted by those duple constituents, iamb and trochee (or spondee, or pyrhhic). Perhaps, as Lindop argues, syllabics 'do work' (when well-handled) precisely because they are an evasive strategy, an attempt to break away not only from the august metrical past, but also from the rhythmic shape of the language itself, where stresses tend to fall on equally-spaced syllables (e.g. *Simon must have been in this Department*, where the rhythm is strictly alternating, or trochaic, or again, *The man my mother married comes from Leeds*, etc.).

13. See *A Prismatic Toy*, pp.78-9.

14. See Inglis, *The Unknown Guest*; cf. with fn. 3 of Fleur Adcock's essay.

The Poet's Voice and Craft
Edwin Morgan

My first reaction on reading through the questionnaire which all poets were sent, and asked to investigate and comment on, was that to many of the questions my answer was 'I don't know', with the even stronger rider 'And I don't want to know'! It seemed to me that the whole exercise was misguided, and was a job for critics, not for the writers themselves. If I may quote Barnett Newman: 'Aesthetics is for the Artists like Ornithology is for the Birds.' As I see it, it is not healthy for poets to become so acutely self-conscious about their own work. I cannot imagine anything more likely to inhibit them from writing their next poem, and that, after all, is their function. Our labour and devotion are to create, to produce, to deliver the goods, not to analyse how the goods came to be made.

My first, basic objection, then, is that it is not any part of the duty of a writer of poetry to make a detailed examination of his own work. Perhaps that should be rephrased as 'to *try* to make a detailed examination of his own work', since the question arises immediately, how far it is *possible* to make such an examination of the creative process as we were asked to do. Supposing I believed it was worth while (which I don't), could I do it? The possibilities of rationalisation after the event are endless. Either out of a desire to please the enquirers, or carried along on a wave of enthusiasm for one's own past ingenuity in having solved creative problems as they arose, the poet could well present an apparently persuasive account, but how much trust would you place in it? Edgar Allan Poe's essay on 'The Philosophy of Composition'[1] stands as a warning. This bouncy, step-by-step putative recollection of how he came to write his poem 'The Raven' is really a sort of charming imaginative fiction of how a mad rationalist might go about the task, rather than a true memory of the creative process. Poe gives seven steps of deliberate creative choice: (1) the length of the poem (short); (2) main impression

54

to be conveyed (beauty); (3) the tone (sadness); (4) the constructional keynote (a refrain); (5) the word in the refrain which would best convey the sadness of the tone ('Nevermore'); (6) speaker of the refrain, human or animal? (raven); (7) topic or theme (death of a beautiful woman – bringing together sadness, beauty and universal poetic feeling). Well, poems are not written like that, and Poe knew it. He very interestingly, in the same essay, gives the game away in a passage quite apart from his description of the evolving of 'The Raven'. He is talking about poets other than himself, those who do not share his claimed ability of total recall of the creative process. He mocks them, but in doing so, despite himself, he gives what is in fact a strong and true evocation of the real creative state of affairs: it emerges gradually out of the mockery until the mockery disappears, and it is clear that in this paragraph he is genuinely recalling, in terms that any poet would recognise, the messy and imperfect, but intense and devoted business of creation:

> Most writers – poets in especial – prefer having it understood that they compose by a species of fine frenzy – an ecstatic intuition – and would positively shudder at letting the public take a peep behind the scenes, at the elaborate and vacillating crudities of thought – at the true purposes seized only at the last moment – at the innumerable glimpses of idea that arrived not at the maturity of full view – at the fully matured fancies discarded in despair as unmanageable – at the cautious selections and rejections – at the painful erasures and interpolations – in a word, at the wheels and pinions – the tackle for scene-shifting – the step-ladders and demon-traps, the cock's feathers, the red paint and the black patches, which, in ninety-nine cases out of the hundred, constitute the properties of the literary *histrio*.

What is remarkable about that passage – and Poe, for all his persiflage about 'The Raven', was a real poet and had things to say – is the honesty of its generalisations: the 'elaborate and vacillating crudities of thought', the 'true purposes seized only at the last moment', the 'glimpses of idea' that never came into full view, the apparently mature and ready imaginative touches 'discarded in despair as unmanageable'. I would underwrite all these ideas, and I'm interested too in the imagery that underlies them: (1) suggestion of large complex bulky oscillating machines, (2) sense of a hunt or chase, (3) a vision which keeps tantalisingly appearing in parts but not as a whole, and (4) kinetic sense of something fully made but unwieldy being thrown away... These visual, tactile, and kinetic images seem to me to be very much to the point, and their understatement is in nice contrast to the full-blown dramatic images of the last part of the quotation, where the previous struggle of the poet to manage the growth of the poem is now identified with the theatrical preparations to stage a play – the wheels and tackle, the ladders and trapdoors, the paint and feathers – the poet himself becomes the *histrio*, the actor in his own drama, and by 'his own drama' I do not mean the interior drama of his own soul but the exteriorising, projective drama of the poem he is gradually, painfully, yet also joyfully dissociating himself from as he completes it. When the poem is finished, *finita la commedia*, he stands back, his part is over; and the general public and the critic can then step in.

In citing Edgar Allan Poe, I wanted to suggest that a mighty struggle with intangibles, a drama of conflicting moods, is what goes on in the composition of a poem, rather than a series of conscious choices to produce certain effects as is suggested by the questionnaire. If this idea of a struggle or drama has any truth in it, it would in fact be difficult for any poet to work himself back into the frame of mind he was in when he was writing the poem, since that frame of mind would have had a very active subconscious element, virtually irretrievable. As Shelley wrote in his *A Defence of Poetry*:

> Poetry is not like reasoning, a power to be exerted according to the determination of the will. A man cannot say, "I will compose poetry." The greatest poet even cannot say it; for the mind in creation is as a fading coal, which some invisible influence, like an inconstant wind, awakens to transitory brightness... This instinct and intuition of the poetical faculty is still more observable in the plastic and pictorial arts... and the very mind which directs the hands in formation is incapable of accounting to itself for the origin, the gradations, or the media of the process.

Shelley's phrase about the mind being 'incapable of accounting to itself' for the creative process might be questioned by someone who had read Henry James's prefaces to his own novels, which don't show any apparent 'incapability'. Yet even there, what you discover is that the preface is not necessarily very helpful or relevant; the account he gives of how a story began may or may not be truthful, and is never the whole truth; he often fudges, playfully and tantalisingly, some crucial point of character or action; and in fact what he is doing is giving you a little ancillary work of art which you may or may not find easy to attach to the story – like the blindfolded man with the donkey's tail.

This would suggest that readers ought to be suspicious of authorial claims or attempts to lay bare the bones of their own creations. Either in the case of apparently (but not really) highly co-operative authors like Henry James, or in the case of highly reluctant authors like myself, there may well be some underlying protective mechanism at work, in the sense that literary creation is a 'mystery' in both senses of the word, i.e. it is a skilled craft or trade or profession as the word implied in medieval and Renaissance times, and it is also the delivery of a mysterious object, not reducible to full analysis whether by the producer or by anyone else, the link between the two meanings being the fact that every trade has its secrets, from the magic ingredient in Coca-Cola to the sound of a Stradivarius. It's a question of where the creative power resides. When Delilah found out that Samson's hair was not just an ordinary head-covering, she cut it off. Is there a lesson there? Perhaps not! The creative spirit is fairly strong, and indeed is made to overcome obstacles (witness Hopkins and Milton). But I have a strong feeling – and I don't know what other speakers in this series have said or written, but I imagine it must be quite a general feeling – that the persistence of the mysteriousness of poetry, which even critics cannot dissolve, though it is part of their duty to try to, ought to be important to poets themselves, if they want to go on writing it. Pasternak has a poem called 'Definition of Poetry' which begins:

> It is a sharply discharged whistle,
> It is a cracking of squeezed ice-blocks,
> It is night frosting leaves,
> It is a duel of two nightingales.[2]

A critic, especially a Formalist critic, would be overjoyed to be asked to analyse what that stanza told him about how a poem begins to emerge, and he would have no shortage of topics, from anaphora to onomatopoeia, to discuss. Yet the stanza seems almost designed to ensure that the poet himself would say 'pass' if he was asked the same question. Unlike Pope in 'An Essay on Criticism', who tells you exactly how to produce the effects you want, Pasternak makes an immediate imaginative leap into regions beyond technique. Only a high-powered technique could have produced the stanza, but the poet's real concern is to push himself, and us, into startling and unexplored contrasts of sound and silence ('whistle' and 'night'), isolated and seasonal happenings ('whistle' and 'ice-blocks'), and single and double or dialectical voice ('whistle' and 'duel'). He himself, I'm sure, would not want to say even as much as I have said in that last sentence. Mandelshtam has an interesting comment on that poem and others like it from Pasternak's early period. In his essay 'Notes on Poetry' (1923)[3] he does first of all make a gesture of relating the force of this poetry to something specific – Pasternak's fresh use of what he calls the secular Russian vernacular – but very soon he falls back on metaphor – 'falls back' is the wrong phrase, he 'mounts up' on metaphor – in his attempt to convey how Pasternak's power emerges:

> When a ship stops coasting along the shallows and moves out into the open sea, those who cannot stand the rolling return to shore. After Khlebnikov and Pasternak, Russian poetry is again moving out to the open sea, and to many of the customary passengers the time has come to say goodbye to the ship. I can see them already, standing with their suitcases at the gangway leading down to dry land. And yet how welcome is each new passenger stepping onto the deck at this very moment!... This 'burning salt' of certain kinds of speech, this whistling, crackling, rustling, glittering, splashing, this fullness of sound, fullness of life, flood of images and feelings, leaps out at us with unprecedented force from the poetry of Pasternak... To read Pasternak's poetry is to clear your throat, to strengthen your breathing, to restore your lungs: poetry like this must surely cure tuberculosis. We have no poetry that is more healthy at the present time. It is *kumys* after tinned milk.

That passage of prose could itself afford a nice prospect of analysis to a critic! The point I want to make is that Mandelshtam was himself a poet, and figurative language seems to him the best or perhaps the only means of re-presenting the creative process.

What I have tried to put forward so far is the grounds of doubt or objection regarding this project. Obviously this does not mean that I think the 'craft' of poetry is a misnomer. Poetry may succeed in spite of faults or weaknesses of craft (as with Spenser's *Faerie Queene*), and even in spite of apparent over-indulgence in craft (Hopkins's 'The Wreck of the Deutschland'), but it is certainly true that poets have to have an apprenticeship in the craft side of their writing. What is important to remember, however, is that the other side of writing, the inspirational or imaginative, is equally necessary and may loom large. To meet, to woo, to tempt, to attract the inspirational and imaginative spirits, no amount of craft will help, and the mind of the would-be poet must at all costs be prepared to be open and tentative and exploratory, open above all, even at times to the edge of passiveness:

> He [i.e. the poet] will watch from dawn to gloom
> The lake-reflected sun illume
> The yellow bees in the ivy-bloom,
> Nor heed nor see, what things they be;
> But from these create he can
> Forms more real than living man,
> Nurslings of immortality!
>
> (Shelley, *Prometheus Unbound*,
> Act 1 – 4th Spirit)

Because there is this *given* element in poetry, the concept of craft becomes a variable. I'd like to discuss the balance between craft and givenness from some examples of my own poetry. This is outside the terms of reference of this series, which concern the structural components within the poem, but it relates to it by bringing to bear elements which the terms of reference omit.

At one end of the scale are some poems which are largely or almost entirely given. These in the nature of things will tend to be short; they are always surprising because they are totally unpremeditated; and they almost write themselves, with very little working on, very little applied craft. The first one I'd like to give here was written on a train, a long-distance train, after I'd been looking through the window in a desultory sort of way at a rather dreary greyish landscape going past, not thinking of anything in particular, when suddenly the lines of this poem began to come into my head one after the other, and I wrote them down on a scrap of paper, feeling immediately excited and involved with the words, jolted out of my lackadaisical mood. Without any intention whatsoever of writing a poem, I was writing a poem. I called it 'The Sheaf':

> My life, as a slant of rain
> on the grey earth fields
> is gathered in thirsty silence, disappears.
> I cannot even guess
> the roots, but feel them sighing
> in the stir of the soil I die to. Let this rain

> be on the children of my heart,
> I have no other ones.
> On the generations,
> on the packed cells and dreaming shoots,
> I send this drop to melt.[4]

The grey fields and the rain came from the landscape I had been look-
ing at, but why at that particular moment I should have had that
sharp emotion, mixing a sense of mortality with the hope that the act
of writing – in this case a mere 'drop', a short poem – might reach
and stimulate future readers as the rain stimulates the growth of
plants, I have no idea. Nor do I want to know. To me, the event is
all that matters, and I pass it on to you as a thing in itself which you
may find interesting, and might even want to think about further,
and which you could not guess from the poem as it is printed.

Another rather similar example of the given element is one that
struck me even more forcibly. I was lying in bed, with the light out,
getting ready to go to sleep, but with the mind very active, as often
happens in that situation (it's the opposite of the experience in the
train, when my mind was lying fallow), and again very suddenly,
with no warning and no preparation, and with no follow-on as far as
I am aware from anything I had been thinking about during the
evening or seeing on television or reading, the first four rhyming
lines of a sonnet came strongly into my head with a sense of great
urgency, and I put on the bed-light and wrote them down on the
telephone pad; at once the further development of the sonnet became
clear, and again this unforeseen poem took shape, in this instance
almost against my will, because of this terrifying subject – I felt that
if poets were prophets, as they are sometimes thought to be, this was
a fearful poem to be writing. The area just north and west of Glas-
gow contains the largest concentration of nuclear weapons and
installations in these islands, so that in the event of a major conflict
the Glasgow conurbation, with about two and a half million people,
would be a prime target. I called the poem 'The Target':

> Then they were running with fire in their hair,
> men and women were running anywhere,
> women and children burning everywhere,
> ovens of death were falling from the air.
> Lucky seemed those at the heart of the blast
> who left no flesh or ash or blood or bone,
> only a shadow on dead Glasgow's stone,
> when the black angel had gestured and passed.

> Rhu was a demons' pit, Faslane a grave;
> the shattered basking sharks that thrashed Loch Fyne
> were their killer's tocsin: 'Where I am, watch;
> when I raise one arm to destroy, I save
> none; increase, multiply; vengeance is mine;
> in no universe will man find his match.'[5]

What was perhaps surprising in that poem, as compared with 'The Sheaf', is that the structure of metre and rhyme was itself a given, whereas 'The Sheaf' was in free verse. There was something almost frightening, though also thrilling, in this revelation of the power of the subconscious mind to erupt, not formlessly but with order, into full consciousness. I remember I was shaking, and wondering if these midnight creative excitements which I had scribbled down would really survive the cold light of morning. But they did; they still seemed good; and the poem did not need much working over. The thing that made my hair stand on end was the fact that these first four lines had roused me wide awake from near-sleep and forced me to write them down.

Perhaps the other extreme from these two poems would be a poem where the exercise of craft was so continuous and so demanding that the danger would be that not enough space, not enough interstices, might be left for the spirit of inspiration to slip in. Some concrete poems, if they depend on a largely mechanical or rigorous rearrangement of their component words or letters or sounds, run this risk unless the poet allows an element of strangeness, like the deliberate asymmetries of the best oriental carpet design, to break the expectations – or alternatively, unless he allows his chosen basic pattern to be only the impetus for some freewheeling, so that the poem can develop in a partly open way. An example of this latter point would be my poem 'Opening the Cage',[6] where the overall conception is very strict, a fourteenfold variation of the fourteen words in John Cage's definition of poetry ('I have nothing to say and I am saying it and that is poetry'), but I allowed the rearrangements of the words to come as they suggested themselves to me line by line and not within a prearranged grid – so that the accidents, inspired accidents one would like to call them, of connections from line to line, and even a certain narrative quality, could emerge and make the poem more interesting:

> I have to say poetry and is that nothing and am I saying it
> I am and I have poetry to say and is that nothing saying it

I am nothing and I have poetry to say and that is saying it
I that am saying poetry have nothing and it is I and to say
And I say that I am to have poetry and saying it is nothing
I am poetry and nothing and saying it is to say that I have
To have nothing is poetry and I am saying that and I say it
Poetry is saying I have nothing and I am to say that and it
Saying nothing I am poetry and I have to say that and it is
It is and I am and I have poetry saying say that to nothing
It is saying poetry to nothing and I say I have and am that
Poetry is saying I have it and I am nothing and to say that
And that nothing is poetry I am saying and I have to say it
Saying poetry is nothing and to that I say I am and have it

In another poem, not concrete, I had a different mixture of the deliberate and the open. This poem is in Scots, and is called 'The Birkie and the Howdie'; it's a dialogue or flyting between a young man and an old woman.[7] It is one of a group of imaginary computer poems, in this case one of the computer's first attempts at dialect, Lowland Scots. The mechanical part of its composition comes from the fact that I culled from the glossary of Robert Burns' complete poems (in Kinsley's big three-volume edition[8]) the most Scottish, the most ethnic words, like a computer programmed to spot and spit out everything non-English.[9] Out of this bizarre list of words I then made up the little story of the poem, allowing both meaning and sound to suggest what they could, within their limited provenance, the result being somewhat like what the Scottish language might be if it had had a complete development away from English:

A dorty, vogie, chanler-chaftit birkie
brattled the aizles o the clachan chimlie,
glunched at his jaupin quaich o usquebae,
scunnered red-wud at the clarty lyart howdie
snirtlin by the ingle-neuk sae laithron and tozie,
and gied the thowless quine a blaud wi his gully
till she skreighed like a cut-luggit houlet and dang her tassie
aff-loof at his unco doup, the glaikit tawpie.
The skellum callan goaved at her fell drumlie:
'Ye tocherless wanchancie staumrel hizzie,
ye groazlin, driddlin grumphie, ye awnie ferlie,
deil gie your kyte curmurrings o scroggy crowdie,
and bogles graizle ilka ramfeezl't hurdie
till aa your snash is steekit, ye duddie hoodie!'

– 'Ach, I hae warlock-briefs, stegh the collieshangie!
Aa your ier-oes sall gang sae muckle agley
they'se turn to blitters and bauckie-birds, and in a brulzie
they'se mak their joes o taeds, aa thrang and sonsie,
snowkin in aidle whaur asks and clegs are grushie:
yon is an ourie pliskie!'
                              Wha wan the tulzie?

The majority of my poems come somewhere between these four
examples of the extremes of givenness and craft, and I would only
add that in any ordinary poem, craft must lead to givenness at some
point, and often the best parts of a poem are those lightning dis-
coveries that fly into the mind, unplanned, from sources that may
seem to be remote from the ongoing discourse of the poem. Doubt-
less everything in the universe has a cause, but in the heat of compos-
ition the causes, the concatenations, are like a chain that melts *into*
being instead of out of it. And there are few things stranger than
that. If we lose sight of the strangeness, we lose sight of poetry.

What I have been saying may apply with less force to poetic trans-
lation, of which I've done a good deal,[10] since by its nature transla-
tion is a more conscious and deliberate art, and many initial or early
decisions may have to be made on purely technical matters: whether
the general structure or metre of the original poem is to be retained
or imitated, whether rhyme is important, whether imperfections are
to be improved or smoothed out, whether difficulties are to be left as
difficulties, whether faithfulness or paraphrase seems the best
approach, and so on: a series of reconnoitrings on the intellectual
level before translation properly begins.

Yet even here it is important to let the poem float into or through
your mind on a much more emotional and imagistic level, as a series
and also a cluster of impressions which you must store up and even-
tually combine with the more consciously worked-out ideas you
have about the status and nature of the language-transfer. I try to
sum up the general appearance of the poem, its symmetry or rugged-
ness, length of line, close or open texture, curious or common voc-
abulary, even such basic things as shape and length. In the end one
has to be faithful to these first shocks and splashes of impact, repre-
senting as they do one's first sudden glimpse of the foreign poet's
world, the poet's foreign world, which one is about to enter. For
example, when I began translating the Italian poet Montale, long
before I really understood his often quite difficult poems, I watched
his poetic 'world' stirring and revealing itself: a shimmer, a play of

light on water and on crumbling buildings, a face glancing in a mirror, an accordeon being played in the twilight... Absorbing this atmosphere is a step in comprehension, and one grasps at this point not only the tone of the particular poem but the signature of the author's style, if he has an identifiable style. Of course the semantic plod, phrase by phrase and line by line, has to be undertaken too. But in so far as translation aspires to the state of poetry, as it ought to do, it must not keep its nose continuously to the grindstone, as the books on translation always assume; it should be able to look up suddenly and see the whole poem, like a cloud or a constellation or a lighted city, twinkling within its form, even slightly changing its form, somehow active rather than passive, pulsing, something alive, something beyond grammar and lexis though obviously containing these. I again, you will notice, refer to indefinable things, and use simile and metaphor to indicate the power I believe these indefinables have. Perhaps the best test of this is when you have to translate into a sister language, say from Scots to English or English into Scots. The temptation would be simply to find the nearest dictionary equivalent for individual words, keep the syntax and figures of speech just as they are, and produce as a result a version which looked something like the original out of focus. An example would be William Kean Seymour's translation of Burns into English. In Scots, 'To a Haggis' begins 'Fair fa' your honest sonsie face...'[11]; Seymour's version of the opening line is: 'Good luck to your plump honest face...' Something more thoroughgoing is required. The whole passage or poem has to be re-felt, re-seen, re-created, bringing out, if possible, the differences between the two languages as idiomatically used. I made this attempt in a Scottish version of a scene from Shakespeare's *Macbeth*, Act 1 Scene 5, when Lady Macbeth has received her husband's letter about the witches' prophecy that he will be king hereafter. Since her soliloquy (broken only by some words from the Messenger, telling her Duncan is coming to the castle) is a fairly well-known passage, I thought I might here instance the Scottish version, to give some idea of this attempt at wholly re-experiencing the speech in terms of a Scottish Lady Macbeth. I hope you will find it, therefore, both familiar and very unfamiliar.

> L.M.
> Aye, ye are Glamis, ye are Cawdor, and ae thing mair
> ye sall be, ae thing mair. But och, I traistna
> sic herts as yours: sic fouth o mense and cherity:

ower-guid for that undeemous breenge! Ye'd hae
the gloir, the gree, the tap-rung, but ye want
the malefice the tap-rung taks. Ye'd hae
the pooer, gin pooer cam by prayin; ye carena
for fause pley, but ye'd win whit's no won fair.
Yon thing ye'd hae, gret Glamis, that caas 'Dae this
to hae me, or hae nane' – and then yon thing
that ye mair fear nor hate to dae. Come ye,
come ye, I maun unfauld, maun speak, maun whup
wi this tongue's dauntonin aa thing that hinners
your progress to thon perfit circumgowdie
aa thae wanearthly warnishments and weird
shaw as your croon to be.

[Enter a castle carle.]

>   Ye bring me news?

C.C.
This nicht ye hae a guest – the king.

L.M.
>   Are ye wud?
Your maister's wi the king. I'm shair he kens
we maun mak preparations for the king?

C.C.
My leddy, it is true. Ye'll see erelang
oor laird hissel. The message cam fae him:
wan o his men run on aheid, tellt me it
aa pechin and forfochten.

L.M.
>   Tak tent o'm,
his news is guid. *[Exit castle carle.]* Pechin? The gorbie itsel
micht hauch and rauch to tell me Duncan's come
like a deid man in-through my castle-waas.
Cwa sichtless cailleachs o the warks o daith,
transtreind my sex, drive into ilka sinnow
carl-cruelty allutterly, mak thrang my bluid,
sneck up aa yetts whaur peety micht walk furth,
that nae saft chappin o wemen's nature shak
my fey and fiendly thocht, nor slaw my steps
fae thocht to fack! Cwa to thir breists o mine
you murder-fidgin spreits, and turn their milk

> to venim and to verjuice, fae your sheddows
> waukrife ower erd's evil! Cwa starnless nicht,
> rowed i the smeek and reek o daurkest hell,
> that my ain eident knife gang blinly in,
> and heaven keekna through the skuggy thack
> to cry 'Haud back!'

The translation is obviously not word for word, but it is accurate in the sense that what is in Shakespeare is there, including the difficulties, which have not been shirked or fudged.[12] But it has been done along the lines of what I have been saying throughout this paper – the craft, in this case the accuracy, is not the be-all and end-all but must keep itself open to the lyrical oestrus of unexpected, 'given' solutions. 'As kingfishers catch fire, dragonflies draw flame.' I hope that in not answering the questions proposed in this series, I have nevertheless set a perspective on them which you will find suggestive and (in its *lucus a non lucendo* way) useful. I am very willing to investigate the poetry of other people, but as far as my own work is concerned, my slogan is: Poetry to the Poet – Criticism to the Critic!

Notes

1.   Edgar Allan Poe, 'The philosophy of composition' (1846), reprinted in James A. Harrison (ed.), *The Complete Works of Edgar Allan Poe* (1965), Vol. XIV, pp.193-208.
2.   Compare here the most recent translation of Pasternak's 'Definition of Poetry' by Andrei Navzorov (*Second Nature: Forty-six Poems by Boris Pasternak*. London: Peter Owen, 1990, p.28).
3.   A useful translation of Osip Mandelshtam's 'Some notes on poetry' can be found in Jane Gary Harris (ed.), *Mandelstam: The Complete Critical Prose and Letters*, trans. Jane Gary Harris and Constance Link. Ann Arbor: Ardis, 1979, pp.165-9.
4.   In Edwin Morgan, *Collected Poems* (Carcanet, 1990), p.181.
5.   *Collected Poems*, p.452.
6.   From *Concrete Poems* (1963-9); reprinted in Edwin Morgan, *Selected Poems* (Carcanet, 1985), p.19; *Collected Poems*, p.178.
7.   *Collected Poems*, p.276.
8.   James Kinsley (ed.), *The Poems and Songs of Robert Burns*, 3 vols (Oxford: Clarendon Press, 1968).
9.   See also here Douglas Dunn's analysis of the distinctions (and the similarities) between English and Scots.

10. See e.g. Edwin Morgan, *Rites of Passage: Selected Translations* (Carcanet, 1976).

11.
>   Fair fa' your honest sonsie face,
>   Great chieftain o' the puddin-race!
>   Aboon them a' ye tak your place,
>   Painch, tripe, or thairm:
>   Weel are ye wordy o' a grace
>   As lang's my airm...

12. It might be useful to compare the following version of Lady Macbeth's speech:

> ... The raven himself is hoarse
> That croaks the fatal entrance of Duncan
> Under my battlements. Come, you spirits
> That tend on mortal thoughts! unsex me here,
> And fill me from the crown to the toe top full
> Of direst cruelty; make thick my blood,
> Stop up the access and passage to remorse,
> That no compunctious visitings of nature
> Shake my fell purpose, nor keep peace between
> The effect and it! Come to my woman's breasts,
> And take my milk for gall, you murdering ministers,
> Wherever in your sightless substances
> You wait on nature's mischief! Come, thick night,
> And pall thee in the dunnest smoke of hell,
> That my keen knife see not the wound it makes,
> Nor heaven peep through the blanket of the dark,
> To cry "Hold, hold!"...

Morgan's translation is reprinted in *Rites of Passage*, pp.82-3.

Poetic Practice

Peter Scupham

Metrics, syntax, lexis!

'A poet,' said Larkin, 'is about as welcome in a University as a cow at the Headquarters of United Dairies.' Or Hindquarters, or United Diaries, which says something about lexis, which I'll come back to. And now the cow is supposed to contemplate its navel, or omphalos, and describe the functioning of that decorative and, after the birth-pangs, non-functioning object.

In the subdivision of Stephen Potter's *Gamesmanship*, expanded into *Lifemanship*, the art of controlling situations by subterfuge and cunning from a basis of incompetence or ignorance, there is a section of 'Carmanship'. 'There's a child behind that ice-cream van,' says the back-seat driver. The driver's reaction should be instantaneous. He pulls the car to the side of the road, switches off the ignition, and stares at his adviser. 'Do you mind?' he says. 'You have brought to the conscious mind something a lifetime of practice has made uncon-scious. I do not mind bad manners, but I do mind death. Thank you.' The journey, and the poems, continue in the usual silence, exile and cunning. So you will allow, the initial question having been put and accepted, the existence of dubieties, subterfuges, cover-ups and con-tradictions. If I knew where I was going and how to get there, I'd start from somewhere else and hope to read the signposts back-wards.

Metrics, syntax, lexis. Things can be said, but a poem, or one's experience of it as reader or writer, is a totality; the eggs can't easily be unscrambled from the omelette, and since poems for me are cloudy mysteries being coaxed into lucid mysteries, I shall have to start with the hinterland of early experience in which metrics, syntax and lexis first made their impact on me. I am in the 1930s, and my grandfather is reciting, not reading, in a delayed, Victorian Lincoln-

shire: 'Under the village chestnut tree/The village smithy stands/
The smith a mighty man is he/With broad and sinewy hands/' – or
The Ballad of Barbara Frietchie: 'Shoot, if you must, this old grey
head/But spare your country's flag, she said./' I am in the garden of
white and blue flowers and I am learning from him 'ifaka iaka':

> Ifaka iaka hadaka a-aka neckaka likeaka swanaka
> Iaka wouldaka giveaka allaka theaka goldaka Iaka
> hadaka inaka myaka purseaka.

At six I am learning the 1920s' words on my mother's dance records,
and singing to myself:

> I wonder what's become of Joe,
> I'd give all the world to know,
> How I'd love to see him smiling again,
> Like he used to when
> He was my friend; I loved him so dearly . . .

Syncopation, rhyme, urgency of rhythm. My father was one of F.R.
Leavis's first students at Cambridge in the 1920s. It didn't really take.
How do you cure first love? My father's was Swinburne. I must have
been very young when I felt the magic of his voice reciting 'Atalanta
in Calydon':

> When the Hounds of Spring are on Winter's traces,
> Mother of months in meadow and plain,
> Fills the shadows and windy places
> With lisp of leaves and ripple of rain

or calling downstairs, 'I'm looking for the Ogo Pogo/To put him in
the Lord Mayor's Show'. His almost photographic memory could
launch into huge chunks of *The Lay of the Last Minstrel*, and, since he
was a Lincolnshire man, Tennyson's 'Northern Farmer: Old Style',
and Donne's *Holy Sonnets* or Sitwell's 'Façade'.

And what does all this mean? It means that I was deeply coloured
by sound, by the urgency and strength of half-understood words,
by the arbitrary bracketing of the wildest sense and the wildest non-
sense, and by the cut and thrust of loved words tumbling first on the
ear and only secondarily off the pages of a book. And the heady gar-
lic of swingeing rhythms – Masefield, Kipling, Noyes, Newbolt,
George Sim's parlour ballads – a kind of aural intoxication – was
with me by the time I was eleven or twelve.

When I went up to Cambridge I sneaked into the Sheldonian at Oxford in a borrowed scholar's gown to hear Auden giving his inaugural lecture as Professor of Poetry: *Making, Knowing and Judging*.[1] We had one thing in common; both of us, as young children, had been given Walter de la Mare's anthology *Come Hither* to plunder. No bad poems, many very good ones, much song and incantation, a puzzling introduction and a discursive About and Roundabout of miscellaneous information at the end of the book. And so, to recapitulate, the child was formed by an olla podrida or pomander of verbal sensations, the habits of being read aloud to. De la Mare's *Peacock Pie* was also an intoxication, and being left to follow my own devices and nose in a world where some people loved words and kept their judgements to themselves.

And so to the second wave. The reader somehow turned into a writer, and for this project I've fished out an ancient folder and looked at what that writer was doing at seventeen. Since the child is father to the man, there must be some degree of consanguinity between the adult and the adolescent. At seventeen the early, casual, undemanding indoctrination of the early years has been transposed, but there is a recognisable umbilical cord uncut. I was not writing heavily introspective verse, wandering in an aching cosmos with a misunderstood heart; I was testing out my admirations in pastiche, parody and translations from the French – Jammes, Verlaine, Rimbaud. I was playing, inexpertly, what Auden calls 'the game of knowledge'. I was trying pattern and cadence, in such unpublished and unvisited-before fragments as this, from Paul-Jean Toulet:

> In Arles, along the ancient avenues,
> When the shade is red beneath the roses
> And the air is still,

> Beware of the sweetness of things
> When, causelessly, you feel your heart
> Beating too loud,

> And when the doves are silent.
> Speak softly, if it is of love,
> Beside the tombs.

I was writing triolets, villanelles, sapphics, playing with Donneish conceits, and generally hanging round words, translating Baudelaire's 'Une mendiante rousse' or bits of Desnos or Queneau as formally as I could. It was never really what was being said that mattered; it was the fascination of being a basket-weaver or cage-maker, and though the vocabulary was sentimental and sub-Georgian and I had nothing particular to say, the baskets were pretty good baskets and if anyone had put logs or apples in them the bottoms wouldn't have fallen out. I was fond of the Wits, of Vers de Societé, of Praed, Calverley, Thomas Love Peacock, of emotions held at a distance, sprightly, mannered; and I'll always find a good word for an Austin Dobson, a J.K. Stephen, a Locker-Lampson.

And then came the business of life, and a huge hiatus, until the pressure built up again, and I buckled down to trying to make the stuff seriously that I'd always dumbly assumed was the most important stuff for me to make. The equipment was now some actual experience of life; the poetic hinterland was an old and very traditional magic, and a versatility in the forms in which that old and traditional magic had been put. Of literary fashion, who's in, who's out, court news, I had no real inkling. I'd read most of what I cared about in two years' National Service before going up to read English at Cambridge. I had my elective affinities before Cambridge got at me, and I was unbudgeable on them: Hardy, Thomas, Graves, John Crowe Ranson, MacNeice, James Reeves, Norman Cameron, Herrick, Herbert – the fastidious, the metrically inventive – and the theologies of Leavis's Great Tradition and *Scrutiny* I sidestepped, as I sidestepped Pound, Bunting and later would sidestep Plath, Sexton, Hughes, Lowell and Berryman in favour of Richard Wilbur, Anthony Hecht, John Heath-Stubbs, Marianne Moore. There are no prescriptions for a writer; I feel no oughts, no guilts. Kipling and Housman are in my bones; every cat to his own catmint. How right Stevie Smith was, when criticised for failing to be 'contemporary', to reply that since she was alive, the times would just have to enlarge themselves to make room for her.

No, my problem was to somehow make personal and individual, bring into some kind of order and acceptability to my peers, a lyrical, romantic, evocative tradition without becoming a living anachronism; to modify those strong rhythms without denying their power and validity; to extend the sensuous, romantic range to cope as well as I could with the darker places and the bric-à-brac – and this has also given me a slant away from the Larkin spell, which can, to my taste, fall into the negative and the quotidian too easily for its own good. I am a theme-plotter, moving the books forward from the bones and stones of the first, *Prehistories*, through history in *The Hinterland*, the natural world in *Summer Palaces*, war and darkness and its attendant numen in *Winter Quarters* and *Out Late* to the mythos of a child's world war in *The Air Show*,[2] using such metrics, lexis and syntax as I can lay my hands on to explore time and eternity as interconnecting geologies, layers, levels, in sequences and themes, lightening the impact of dense, textural experiences by lyrics in which I hope to retrieve something of the grace of mentors.

So, let us return to our sheep, and consider metrics and structures. Whatever free verse is, the only freedoms I am at home with are those conferred by discipline, whether the traditional disciplines of my earlier models, less frequently used now, or the modifications I can make to them by various arbitrary rules. One of the biggest problems in making any valid comments on my structures is that the organic changes one's psyche makes as one grows older and more ignorant affect in an only dimly understood way the patterns and the breaks and disconnections in the patterns from book to book. Before the detail, a little more generalisation.

Poems, for me, are aural and optical constructs. At the simplest level, I dislike a poem of, say, six-line stanzas which leads to a verse travelling overleaf, hanging on a page two-thirds empty as if it were a codicil. The blank book on which poems are written is in some sense the page format which Oxford University Press provides me with, and I am now conscious, by second nature, as to how many lines each page can accommodate.[3] Was it Jarrell who said, 'The strength of a genie comes from his being confined in a bottle'? I believe this as an article of faith, it is the strength of the lyric tradition, and in a way the page itself dictates the size of the bottle, and all poems are concrete, an optical patterning. The poems which first enticed me by their shaping were the baroque poets of the seventeenth century, and quite apart from the emblematic shapes of an 'Easter Wings' or 'The Hourglass' I found, and still find, a sensuous satisfaction in the caress the eye gives to a long and short, indented shapeliness. I like their vital statistics! I am offended by out-hanging, dropped lines, trailing words. If I see a poem in two blocks on a page, one block of eleven lines, the next of twelve, I am annoyed. I can detect these misfeaturings without counting, and a typical *Outposts* poem of say, three lines followed by eight lines, followed by four lines will not, on those grounds alone, lead me to fall in love with it. My own work has certainly developed in complexity of substance, become more chunky with age – the first OUP book, *Prehistories*, now looks to me nervy in its couplets and triplets; the sense of almost too much jumpy air flowing between the old stones; but this again is a psychic problem. Sometimes one feels the theme or one's nature is to build a fairly substantial, close-packed dry-stone wall; sometimes one feels the need to build nets with a wider mesh to let the air and light in. *Summer Palaces*, a formalised book with the natural world as its theme, has optical, visual interstices and crevices; light lines, breath-cadences; a kind of shot-silky open look to me when I turn its pages. *Out Late* and *The Air Show*, night and war, have clenched some kind of fist on this spaciness; the lines are longer and have impacted themselves more densely. Black holes are grave things which pull in gravity. Since I would certainly call myself a formalist, my problem is to marry as natural a speech-rhythm to my formal structures as may be, but here again comes a problem. As someone said of Yeats – 'perhaps Theatre is his deepest form of sincerity' – what is the talking voice? For me it is not necessarily the demotic, the hesitant, the interrupted, the um-er-ishness of conversation. Is Yeats's prose the 'talking voice'? Well, that depends on how one talks, and I talk, unfashionably, in sentences. Let us call it a formalised talking voice, instinctively attempting to walk the tightrope between what might be said by human beings and what might be said by educated angels! I talk in sentences and think in dangerous and specious analogies. I think that's probably what my poems do. My masters were strongly stressed rhythms, falling back into heartbeat iambics; I still use them. But, in this digression, let's come back to shape, and the nature of the arbitrary. I think that Houdini had a good idea – apart from asking someone to punch him and dying of a ruptured appendix, was it? – he thought you could create a good impression by loading yourself with chains then getting out of them. To load oneself with poetic chains, like being hanged tomorrow, sharpens the mind wonderfully. In *The Air Show* I picked an arbitrary form, the sestina, then made it more complex by introducing a different Shakespearean quotation including the word 'toys' into each stanza. I think the result is, to me, formally satisfactory and *says something which could be said no other way*. Saying something which could be said no other way seems a good idea. Why is the contour of any game defined as it is? The contours of the game I play are my arbitrary shifting of goal-posts, changes of measurement in the width of the court. Each one leads to *saying something that could be said no other way*. In one of my favourite games, the sequence, I have played the Hungarian game: fifteen sonnets, the last line of the first fourteen makes the fifteenth; each sonnet's last line gives an impetus towards the last sonnet. Is this merely a piece of finnicking nonsense, as Colin Falk said in a review ('The sort of thing that gives poetry a bad name')? No; the sonnets contain real deaths, a commemoration of the dead of the First World War, acts of family pietas, tributes – and the material is not voulu; in fact it had been teasing me for a year or more. Was the writing contrivance? No, I wrote the fifteen sonnets in about three and a half days, and when I was writing I felt that I was bringing the whole thing together simultaneously. I was not, as Stanley Spencer is said to have done in painting, starting at the top left corner, finishing it, and working on from there. I did not think of my last lines first and begin by writing the concluding sonnet. I've no doubt there was tinkering, but I was working from warm, not cold, whatever the result, and producing something important to myself, testing my perceptions inside an astringent and demanding form. But if chess-players can play fifteen games simultaneously, blindfold, and win some, and composers write symphonies, why should such simple skills as a Hungarian sonnet-sequence arouse either naïve cries of admiration or cat-calls of 'Cheat, fake – it can't be for real'? I confess to being completely baffled at the idea that such simple skills elaborated into more complex ones should in some way be seen as the enemy of poetic truth. It is important to me that in my *Midsummer Night's Dream* sequence[4] the arbitrary decision to write the substantial sections on Lovers, Court, Mechanicals et al. with thirty-four lines to a section, a quotation from the play itself acting as a central hinge in each section and with the word *oak* as an image of England and time and much else coming in each section, should give a solidity and anchored shapeliness to what I felt was worth the saying. And when I hold the pages to the light I like to see the last lines of those sections registering exactly with each other. Perhaps I am a scholiast – I've always liked the patterning of the medieval cosmos, and any model of order is a prophylactic against the chaos without and the chaos within.

Metrics? At first I was a good counter; I played with syllabics, worried about the consonance between my decasyllabic lines, iambic pentameters and five-stresses, played my tunes too carefully. One of my correctives was learning from pastiche and parody, catching the tone of a Ransome, a Frost, a Marianne Moore – see the group of pastiches in *Out Late*.[5] Doing this gives the freedom of these poets in the way one has conferred on one the freedom of a city; rehearsing another language is one way of finding one's own, and such paradox, or wearing Welchman's Hose, as Robert Graves puts it, is to me the most vivid approach to the kind of truths to be found in poetry. And while I am on optics, which are a part of metrics, I am conditioned, physically, to taking poems apart letter by letter and reassembling them: the Mandeville Press, which I have run for fifteen years, has been printing poetry, including pamphlets by John Fuller, Anthony Hecht, Geoffrey Grigson and Joy Scovell in mono-type letterpress, hand-set, and the half-conscious, half-unconscious physical labour, making poems physical in their own terms as phys-ically substantial as an alphabet of lead slugs, endlessly re-formed and dispersed, has certainly given me a sharp sense of the weight and texture of poems and the art of placing them as objects into the frame provided by a white page.

What I have been talking about, loosely under the heading of met-rics, may seem to be at some variance with those early, primal aural experiences, those rituals – are they poetry? – of singing 'run, rabbit, run, rabbit, run, run, run', the delightful circularities of an uncle chanting 'It was a dark and stormy night, and the three brigands were gathered together in a cave...', a mock-solemn grandfather dandling me to 'A wise old owl lived in an oak, the more he saw the less he spoke...' These, though, are more basic, nearer to the heart of anything I write than anything I have learned later in Academe. Aural patterning is second nature to me, and is one of the pair of equally yoked horses that draw my farm-cart or chariot. Everything I write is aurally tested. Pope said that the difficulty of writing poetry is the true management of the letter 's' and I would agree with that. I have done a fair deal of acting, a fair amount of Shakespearean pro-duction work with children and adults; I am very aware of the shape sounds make on the ear, and I am faintly baffled at the prosaic, stumbling unpatterns many poets make when reading in public. As Yeats says: 'It has given me a devil of a lot of trouble getting these words into verse, and that is why I *will not* read them as if they were prose.'[6] Inside my formal metrics I think I have an open ear and an open mouth for assonance, speech cadence, and accuracy of intona-tion. I feel that since words like ritual, celebration, rite, have deep meaning for me, the shapeliness of words in their acts of naming should be a delight, as to my ears 'Façade' is still delightful. I rejoice in Edith Sitwell's 'the golden planets Calliope, Io, Pomona, Antiope, Echo and Clio' – poets might do worse than practise tongue-twisters – or Tennyson's 'the snowy-banded, dilettante, delicate-handed priest'; and though I do not, in general, make purely musical con-structs, the music of Victorian voices, often minor ones, a Lord de Tabley, John Meade Faulkner, Thomas Lovell Beddoes, seems to me still a lyrical directive that can be built on. I think, being prescrip-tive for myself, that one of my difficulties has been to free my stan-zaic forms from too closely-punctuated, too stanza-stopped and line-stopped a style, to allow my song-lines more freedom to link my cadences onward; to create streams and rivers rather than lakes and pools. But to ally formal structures with open cadences and a through-line is a pleasure to me, and seems, whether the actual poem is memorable or not, a gesture towards the concept of memorability. I was brought up in the tradition of knowing by heart, and I should feel the poorer without lines in my head, and less ambition if I eliminated the idea that it might prove possible, *deo volente*, to write lines worth remembering or not easily forgotten. To emphasise all this I'll here give a complete poem, the epigraph to *The Air Show* ('Under the barrage'), in which, I hope, lyric is used to an entirely serious purpose through the lightest of textures. The poem is an epitaph for the victims – a huge theme – from a child who was there, and who imagines himself again in his barricaded city house as the sirens sound their alert.

Schlafe, mein Kind
In your mother's bed
Under the barrage.
The soon to be dead

Will pass you over;
It's not your turn.
The sheets are warm
But they will not burn.

In your half-dream
Sirens will sing
Lullay, lullay,
Lullay my liking.

A saucer of water
For candlestick:
The night-light steadies
A crumpled wick

In a house of cards
In a ring of flame;
The wind is addressed
With a different name.

Schlafe, mein Kind
In your mother's bed.
Under the barrage
The soon to be dead

Lie as you lie,
And will lie on
When the dream, the flame
And the night are gone.

I doubt, deeply, whether I am ever very far away from the essentially lyrical measures; as I have said, my problem is to find a dynamic, to move away from an over-heavy reliance on end-stopping, a rather punctilious litter of colons and semi-colons. I would now rather underpunctuate a little, risking more parenthetically, and trusting myself to think in coherent images and sentences without marking them up too tightly.

Yes, I regard the line-break as a break in duration and find it impossible to close my lines on a 'to' or an 'and' where no break is possible in the speech-flow. A line-end is, for me, a break in the transitiveness of things, and this probably is instrumental in making my poems rather more phrasal than I might like; they tend to hang on participles rather than drive on under the lash of verbs. But I'm working on it, and certainly have sympathy in theory if not in practice with the belief that the adjective is the enemy of the noun.

So, sound patterns come easily, perhaps too easily. And at this point I think I'll throw in some general observations on my practice. I am basically a thematic kind of writer and I usually find that each book has a thematic centre and that the poems I'm writing group themselves about a particular set of puzzles, half-understood sensations. It is particularly easy to see this with *The Air Show*; the rumours and pressures of an adult re-experiencing a wartime child's sensations left little space in my head to go off for strolls in other directions. For a couple of years everything I wrote hung in the air of 1939-45; all my madeleines were old cartridge-cases and deserted air-strips. I am attentive to the theme of the year and do not deflect myself much from it; I have no capacity to see all the chance *rencontres* and passing events as so many poems waiting to be written; I work conspiratorially with time and lower myself into its waters, allowing it to give me a purpose and mental set until the next book temporarily exorcises a set of ghosts – though the ghosts come back again and the pudding gets richer and fuller of sixpences as the years go by. Themes have their own times for surfacing, but I see my practice as kind of quest backwards and forwards in time securing different areas of my world, colonising my experience – not as the repetition of a certain way of looking at things.

My next book, *Watching the Perseids*,[7] centres on my mother's death at Christmas two years ago and is shaping itself into acts of pietas, family-fabling – I have sometimes felt that my landscapes were, like Paul Nash's, somewhat stripped of human beings; it now seems psychically right to remedy that deficiency, to fill out my theatrical and historical canvases with more human flesh and blood. The poetic and the human progress is to me very closely linked. Also, I have certain practical prescripts. I leave very little indeed unfinished, and usually bring my poems to their abandoned conclusions within a couple of days of starting them. I have no notebooks of unrealised possibilities, homeless phrases. I have a habit of completion, and whether a poem or not seems to be working as a construct, I carry on with it, having learned that cold trails and puzzles are quite as fruitful as a feeling that things are all going swimmingly, and a cold *donné* or suggestion from someone else may produce as effective a poem as one which seems to start with an internal pressure – pressure, inside my thematic limitations, can build from almost any source, and a poem in the making may be protean, a real shape-changer, starting as a scrawl, as prose, as one metric, and becoming something quite other as the work proceeds.

Often I will work from an image which for some days has been present with me, writing quickly, allowing the words to breed themselves without applying judgement, filling in pauses with gobbledygook or gibberish to keep the flow going. Out of that quarry I will find my figures, clearing away the chippings and detritus. Eventually I am happy to tighten, pare, focus. I am a sculptor, releasing the figure, rather than a modeller, working by addition and accretion, alert to suggestions, levels, geologies of time and experience. I do not see time as linear, but simultaneous – sympathetic to the idea of palimpest, over-writing which reveals the writing behind itself. I like the approach of a David Jones, using the specifics of different periods shifting behind gauzes to make one period, the period of the poem. In this sense, my poems are like the house in which I live; I am not happy unless I live in a multi-layered choc-a-bloc environment where bric-à-brac from all historical periods and styles forms a homogenous and heterogeneous *mélange*, beach-pebbles, seventeenth-century books, Peruvian pots, what have you? I am responsive to 'kinds'; if, as in 'Horace Moule at Fordington',[8] I am using a Victorian theme, I will instinctively use such verbal and metrical structures as the period would understand. It makes a kind of sense to me to think of writing for the dead to read as well as the living and the unborn. The Church of Poetry has a large congregation. If, on the other hand, I am re-creating the image of Hitler to my childish imagination, I will allow the form to be looser, jumpier, more eldritch. I am eclectic, and hope to constantly widen my range of simplicities, complexities and textures; in saying that I acknowledge Auden as a potent master. If I write unrhymed poetry, I feel a pressure to get back to rhyme again, and would agree that, in taking language for a walk, rhyme is a good leash. It is directive, yes, but who knows where one is going anyway, and it produces ideas and images in startling profusion. I have become more responsive to half-rhymes, internal rhymes, but like to mix these in patterns with full chiming rhymes, and recently have developed a debonair habit of using such forms as a five-line stanza, rhyming *abab*, but with a totally unrhymed fifth line riding piggy-bank on the rhyming structure – this seems both uncertain in its certainty and progressive in that it leads the poem on to the next stanza. Rhyme is keeping step with oneself, counting the railings, travelling by mysterious signposts; it is not so much a mechanism for me as the way my psyche works. Only free verse leads me to consternation and confusion.

Here's a recent example from *The Air Show*, an excerpt from 'Blackout':

> Surely the light from the house must stay at the glass
> And pull itself back, into the room again?
> For the light is ribbons, faces; it cannot pass
> Out into the loose garden, and the rain
> Which scrats at the pane with absent, occasional fingers.
>
> And all our drapes, curtains, tackings of cloth
> Closed on these glances, glimmers, openings,
> Where the cold glass sticks tight to the hung moth
> Quivering its white thorax and plumed wings –
> How brief they are, how pale those lookers-in –
>
> Are teaching the light it has nowhere else to go
> But round the angles of things, filling the square
> Where a sofa thickens its back, the bookshelf row
> Scatters in flakes of gold, the arm of a chair
> Wobbles where shine slinks off, and into the corner...

And so, to the famous lexis: Hamlet's 'words, words, words'. I have tried, in an intermittent way, to say something about kinds, and also tried to avoid pinning myself down too closely. To ask a chameleon to describe its colour is a moderately thankless task, and to attempt to comment on my vocabulary and word-choice is really asking me to describe my verbal elective affinities. If the world is a 'buzzing, blooming confusion' translated, in poetry, into its constituent images, related by temperamental blood-ties, and ordered under the control of guiding images, my natural love is for a fairly rich and elaborate vocabulary and sign-language. There are two contrasting modes with which I am out of sympathy. First, the Symbolic Tradition, in capital letters – that club to which all true poets belong in Kathleen Raine's book. I am certainly conscious of in-time and out-of-time experiences and believe in a multi-dimensional universe. I do not believe that the world is everything which is the case, but a Jungian purity of Rivers, Fountains, Moons and Forests is not for me. The Shelley or late Robert Graves bit does not satisfy my sense of the *haecceity* and thinginess of the world, that parade of sensible objects, feast for the senses. Neither am I happy with the stubbornly quotidian worlds of an Amis or a Ewart. Too much spiritual mandarin in the one; too much incorrigible and unwashed linen in the other. My natural lexis is probably an over-literary one, which, as in David Jones's *In Parenthesis*, tries to find the ability to place the Queen of the May against an accurately described rifle or egg-bomb. I like to juxtapose the *realien* of history against tides of light and shadow, redeeming objects from their contexts in the everyday, creating atmospheres and climate for them to exist in. My language is at home amongst metaphorical transformations. Among living poets, I recognise in Anthony Hecht that capacity for mingling a swash, gestural vocabulary with Martini glasses and hotel bedroom, a trick the Americans find easier than we do: that coupling of the high style and the commonplaceness of things has enormous appeal for me. Perhaps working with theatre has heightened my sense of the proximity of glitter to tat. I enjoy the gestural, the rococo, the elaborate and baroque for the sake of the saying – the language of Burton's *Anatomy of Melancholy*, or Browne's *Urne Buriall*, the robust heightened demotic of Ben Jonson, the esprit and sprezzatura of Thomas Love Peacock. There may be dangers in fancy-dress, but I think the age can afford to face them. But, responsive to Theatre, Fireworks, John Piper, Follies, Grottoes, and all ways of calling Spades Agricultural Implements, I draw my vocabulary out of history and the ruins of the high-style, duffing it up a little to teach it not to be too proud of its airs when the themes darken. Elaboration, in this sense, is natural to me. If I thought I was a Puritan, I'd beat myself like a dog, though pure water is also a good drink. The

danger is to be too sonorous, over-adjectival, over-dressed. Peter
Porter once gave me a review in which he said 'Sometimes I thought
I was reading rejected lines from Gray's "Elegy" '. Well, perhaps
Gray's rejected lines have their merits. Or I could paraphrase Roy
Campbell, and say of myself: 'He's got the icing and the fruit all
right, but where's the bloody cake?' And my inter-locking vocabu-
laries are inextricably linked with environments I constantly return
to: gardens, theatre-sets, night, wars and rumours of wars, rooms
and ruins, festivals and celebrations. Pavlova, asked to explain a
dance, replied 'If I could explain it, why should I go to the trouble of
dancing for you?' On this analogy I'll close by giving two poems, an
excerpt from 'Fireworks', where a rich vocabulary is used for its
own display, and the complete text of 'Young Ghost', an elegiac but
rich vocabulary used for the serious purpose of giving my dead
mother her youth back again.

> But there the dark, the dark uncomprehending
> 　　This legerdemain out of close cabinets:
> These filaments and webs at their unwinding
> 　　Of loose-cut brilliants, of dying trinkets,
> 　　These crenellations, crumbly towers and lancets,
> The rose-windows twirling against the night,
> The writing on the wall: crisp, aureate,
> 　　Which must advance its
>
> Case against our backdrop of slow motion:
> 　　Rays, arcs, auroras, pyre on beckoning pyre,
> The galaxies at their long diminution,
> 　　Red giants and white dwarves, the tigerish glare
> 　　Of Sirius, Algol and Denebola.
> There Nero angles in his endless lake
> And mysteries breed about his pleated cloak.
> 　　The near; the far.
>
> 　　　　　　　　　　　　　　　　(from 'Fireworks')

And now the poem, 'Young Ghost':

> Oh, the young ghost, her long hair coursing
> Down to her shoulders: dark hair, the heat of day
> Sunk deep under those tucks and scents, drowsing
> At the neck's nape – she looks so far away,
> Though love twinned in her eyes has slipped its blindfold –

And really she glances across to him for ever,
His shutter chocking the light back into the box,
Snapping the catch on a purse of unchanged silver.
Under those seven seals and the seven locks
She is safe now from growing with what is growing,

And safe, too, from dying with what is dying,
Though her solemn flowers unpick themselves from her hands,
The dress rustles to moth-wings; her sweet flesh fraying
Out into knots and wrinkles and low-tide sands.
The hat is only a basket for thoughtless dust.

And she stands there lost in a smile in a black garden:
A white quotation floating away from its book.
Will it be silver, gold, or the plain-truth leaden?
But the camera chirps like a cricket, dies – and look,
She floats away light as ash in its tiny casket.

I think, to conclude, I'll also give an excerpt from an earlyish
poem, 'The Piece', which is, of course, using the image of a jigsaw
to say something about one's failures as well as one's possible succes-
ses; it does say something about that patient and puzzling process of
trying to make an unuseful sense out of necessary and quite unneces-
sary fragments, and the failure in the last stanza is the spur which
makes one start the next poem.

The Piece

   . . . Between the lines, a tumble and collusion
   Of shades which cancel out to monochrome:
   Fingers coax local colour from confusion,
   Sprawled leopards on the shield, an onion dome,
      A coach's crusty gold, twinned horses' heads,
      Blocked hollyhocks afloat on airy beds.

   They move as islands, distant yet related,
   While patient clouds unscumble, and the wood
   Fills out with leaf-work. Now, the celebrated
   Ride stiffly through a patchwork multitude.
      Untroubled mountains fill with white: the place
      Is seen quite clearly as a crooked space

For that one piece whose blank sin of omission
Has failed the leaning sails, the smiling queen,
And put the heralds out of their commission.
What now can prop the swiftly failing scene,
        Come from some dust world back into its own,
        The ungiven line, the key, the cornerstone?

Notes

1. W.H. Auden, *Making, Knowing and Judging* (1956), reprinted in *The Dyer's Hand and Other Essays* (Faber, 1963), pp.31-60. Auden's views on poetry as a verbal game seem to have made a deep impression (see e.g. Scupham's comments a little later in his paper). See also Auden's contribution to *Agenda* Vol. 10, No. 4 ('Special rhythm issue'), p.9: 'On hedonistic grounds, I am a fanatical formalist. To me, a poem is, among other things, always a verbal game. Everybody knows that one cannot play a game without rules. One may make the rules what one likes, but one's whole fun and freedom comes from obeying them.'
2. All published by OUP. *Prehistories* (1975); *The Hinterland* (1977); *Summer Palaces* (1980); *Winter Quarters* (1983); *Out Late* (1986); *The Air Show* (1989); *Selected Poems* (1990).
3. See also Grevel Lindop's account of his process of composition.
4. In *Out Late*, pp.23-33.
5. 'The poets call on the goddess Echo': pp.55-61.
6. W.B. Yeats, 'Extract from talk on rhythm and his poetry with readings from "The Lake Isle of Innisfree" and "The Fiddler of Dooney" – October 4, 1932'. In *The poems of William Butler Yeats, read by Yeats, Siobhan McKenna and Michael MacLiammoir*; A Spoken Arts Recording for Home Educational Arts Records Ltd.
7. Published by OUP, 1990.
8. In *Summer Palaces* (1980).

Writing Things Down
Douglas Dunn

Accepted wisdom would have us believe that when a poet sets out to explain his methods of working, the risk that is run is nothing less than the possible killing of his gift. I feel inclined to agree. Having accepted the invitation to participate in this series, I now find myself in a state of funk. First of all, just being present means that I'm willing to call myself a poet, and make this claim in public. That makes me feel uneasy. It was Robert Frost or Robert Graves, I can't remember which, who said that poet is a praise word and therefore not a description that a writer of verse should use of himself. Modesty is not what I'm driving at. Instead, I feel a superstitious dread in case I'm tempted to break a code that has always been sacred to me. It's as if I might make unauthorised or preposterous claims for which the Muse will punish me. My other qualm is that while craft and technique are extremely interesting subjects, imagination and instinct are more fascinating by far, if only because less is known about them. Not only do they rise from mysterious, subjective, eccentric, unpredictable and irrational sources, but to consider them is to find yourself led back to mystery, self, strangeness and the unreasonable. To separate craft or technique from imagination and instinct, or from a writer's subjects, strikes me as pointless. On this occasion, though, I admit that the blandishment is a pressing one.

It's always been my belief that a poetic nature, or instinct, has its origins in mysterious and perhaps even spiritual events that happen in childhood, or a little later in what used to be known as 'early youth' in the days when the language was innocent enough to be used without embarrassment. Nowadays it's hard to refer to childhood or youth without sniggering. It's even more difficult to speak of poetry as a gift. But there's a moment at the end of the film of Pasternak's *Dr Zhivago* which never ceases to cheer me up. Zhivago's half-brother, now a KGB general, has been visiting a hydro-electric dam in search of Dr Zhivago's daughter. As the young woman leaves, the general notices that his niece has a balalaika slung over her shoulder. We've seen this balalaika wander from the poet's bereaved childhood through the Revolution and its aftermath until his separation from Lara, pregnant with the young woman whom the general has just found. Not only does it transpire that she plays it extremely well, but she is self-taught. 'Ah,' the general calls to his niece and her boyfriend, 'then it's a gift!' Part of the scene's magic depends on Sir Alec Guinness's voice – the way he says, 'Ah, then it's a gift!' makes me weep tears of delight, the sort which say 'Yes' repeatedly. But it's what the scene expresses that makes it work so well in tying up with the life, loves, profession, and gift of poetry of that miserable historical plaything, and very fortunate man, Dr Zhivago.

Have we lost all belief in poetry as a gift? Perhaps not. But we have lost a great deal of the confidence with which it used to be said that poetry is a gift. There are times even when I wonder if some contemporary poets were drawn into poetry by a gift, by a recurrent epiphany, the moment in childhood which Rosa Luxemburg once evoked by the image of the wind in the birch leaves. At times it can seem as if some poets have *chosen* poetry through a liking for it, or through education, or concern for poetry as a subject, or as a means to appearing in public, or as a way of getting regular, well-paid book reviewing.

Technique would be described neatly as the self-aware dimension of poetry, were it not that instinct and imagination play a part that is virtually impossible to measure and which contribute in a large way to what might look like conscious decisions. Metre, rhyme and stanza can be isolated as the groundwork of a poet's craft, as well as the skill with which vocabulary can be harvested. There exists what I would like to call a secret interplay between the poet and technique, between the instinctive and the deliberated. I'm inclined to think of instinct as deriving from and perhaps responsible for the bias in the language possessed by a poet as it were by the natural circumstance of life. There is a knowledge of poetry that has been acquired from who-knows-where far back in the memory, in forgotten or half-remembered times when poems and songs predisposed a boy or girl to think of what they saw or experienced in terms of rhythms and rhymes. It's a coincidence of poetry with personality, and a heave from and against a climate of self, place and nationality. Why do I write poetry? Why did I devote my life to it? I have no idea. All I can admit to truthfully is that I have no recollection whatsoever of a moment when I said to myself that I would. I find it hard to believe that it was ever a question of choice.

Self-awareness, however, ought not to be neglected. Reading and writing inform that non-choice; they sophisticate it and encourage it to grow. They educate more than the critical mind; they encourage imagination and instinct. The dilemma should be obvious. Technique is self-aware to an extent, but that doesn't mean that the poet knows exactly what he or she is doing. Technique is to a large degree intuitive, but that shouldn't be taken to mean that a poet is working entirely by chance or feel. Choices have to be made and decisions taken; a poet's critical acumen raises the questions, triggered off, perhaps, by intuition; and it is that same instinctive sense of what might be right, or wrong, together with a critical faculty nurtured by reading, which answers them.

When asked how he came up with the image of a toad to represent the ambivalent loathesomeness of work Philip Larkin answered, 'Sheer genius!' Perhaps the interviewer was never likely to receive a serious answer, or perhaps the answer given by Larkin *was* serious as well as correct. Had he been asked why 'The Whitsun Weddings' was written in the stanza he devised for it, his answer might have been similar; and so, too, the iambic tetrameter of 'An Arundel Tomb', or the trochaic Hiawatha metre of 'The Explosion'. Neither that stanza (unique, except for parodies of the poem), nor neo-classical tetrameter, nor the rhythm of 'The Explosion', could have been predicted. Trying to explain to yourself why they materialised comes up with not much more than a shrug in the head. None of them was close to the range of technical options disclosed by Larkin's previous poetry. What I hope these examples suggest is that techniques in poetry might not always, or not often, be a matter of deliberate choice, but of discovery, accident, or luck.

Scottish poetry is so concerned with language that it can seem like a national obsession. You need think only of Hugh MacDiarmid's intentional revival of the Scots language in his poetry of the 1920s, or the geological terms in 'On a Raised Beach', or his erudite procession through languages and linguistics in 'In Memoriam James Joyce'.[1] Fine poets in Scots have followed MacDiarmid, notably Robert Garioch and Sydney Goodsir Smith. Gaelic, which is threatened with extinction, has enjoyed a resurgence of poetry in the work of Sorley Maclean, Derick Thomson and Iain Crichton Smith.[2] Anxiety for the survival of Gaelic has added a nervy touch to the awareness of language in Scotland. Edwin Muir's timeless, balladic poetry also affirms a connection between modern Scotland and its eternal identity, in spite of, or perhaps because of, his European subjects.[3] Elegant, sprightly, intellectual and sentient poetry by Norman MacCaig portrays a temperament that is Gaelic even if his language is English buffed and polished by his voice and accent.[4] Clever, and self-consciously manipulative, Edwin Morgan's poetry calls attention to its language and techniques in a way that English poetry customarily avoids. Tom Leonard's castigatingly political, linguistically shrewd portrayal of Glaswegian speech[5] – the politics of mouth – is paralleled in prose by James Kelman's novels and stories.

It is probably impossible for a writer in Scotland to accept language as one of life's given stabilities. Notional English-English is not a yardstick that a poet in Scotland takes seriously as something against which to measure his or her own use of English. A Scottish accent defines itself in its own country, and, first of all, against traditions of writing to which a Scottish voice relates. There can be a certain kind of snobbishness attached to this awareness of accent and voice, most of it, but not all, of the inverted kind. When it comes to Scottishness in writing, Scottish critics can be as alert as a head waiter with his eyes peeled for the entrance of a gentleman without a tie, or, as I am talking of *demotic* consciousness, of a diner *with* a tie.

From the moment when awareness rises in support of an instinctive poetic urge, young Scots men and and women searching for a poetic idiom true to experience find themselves immersed in a sociolinguistic climate that is quite different from the one explored by their English, Irish or Welsh counterparts. It is a national climate. When you simplify it – and it is vulnerable to vulgar simplification – it looks like a choice between Scots (or Lallans) and English, or Gaelic and English. However, it is not quite as easy as that. Scottish poets who write in English share the same socio-linguistic territory as those who write in Scots (and much the same as those who write in Gaelic). They speak a similarly accented English, read the same newspapers (in English), walk the same streets and catch the finite number of trains on ScotRail's timetable. They are inhabitants of the same country, listening to, and speaking to, a similar range of people and surrounded by the same audible phenomena of language, with their cadences, dialects, humours and social markers, the whole human swirl of speech in a country, its sheer physicality of noise and expressiveness, with many eccentricities, gestures, and individual peculiarities. A poet who is devoted to the Scots language, however, is likely to acquire a quite different imaginative bias from one who writes in English. A poet who writes in Gaelic will inherit a different imaginative power from either. Obviously, a poet writing in Scots is not writing in English but in what, historically speaking, is a form of English which through its separate development cannot, with any accuracy, acknowledge English as 'the mother tongue'. A poet who writes in Gaelic is writing in a language totally unrelated to English. And a Scottish poet who writes in English is not only writing in a form of English peculiar to that poet (as would have to be said of *any* poet writing in English, whether English, North American, Australian, African, Indian, West Indian or Chinese) but specific to a place that is not England, and to a person who is Scots.

Early in my own writing, I suppose I had to negotiate the terms on which I could use the English language in the accent in which I speak it and draw on English and American as well as Scottish poetry to help me. Those who write in Scots might see this as a partial surrender of nationality or an assumption of a wilful Britishness. It so happens that I don't. Writing in English subtracts from a Scottish identity no more and no less than it withers Seamus Heaney's Irishness, or Derek Walcott's West Indian-ness, or questions the authenticity of Les Murray as an Australian, or Wole Soyinka as a Nigerian. A line of Derek Walcott's could be salutary here: 'The classics can console, but not enough'. If 'classics' can be extended to include Chaucer, Henryson, Dunbar, Gavin Douglas, Shakespeare, Donne, Jonson, Milton, Marvell, Dryden, Pope, Wordsworth, Byron, Keats, and so on, as well as European poets from Dante to Ronsard to Goethe and Pushkin, and what you can get to know in translation of Persian, Arab, Indian, Chinese and Japanese poetry, then the dilemmas of a poet whose work falls within the post-Imperial phase of the English language as a result of England's (or 'Great Britain's') invasive, mercantile and colonising history (to which Scotland surrendered rather early) might begin to clarify themselves, if only by a little. Scottish poetic traditions can claim an enviable longevity. They were interrupted by historical decisions for which contemporary Scots can hardly be held responsible. By the 1990s, however, nationalist bitterness is not unlike that felt by Anglophonic African, Indian and West Indian writers, even if the solutions to the political argument are quite different. In politics, and in a private argument with language and history to which it is closely linked, Scottish dismay and soul-searching point to a controversy of a quite different kind. After all, Scottish soldiers, adventurers, emigrants, missionaries and administrators were not exactly bystanders in the British Imperial story. At this late stage it might seem like the height of impertinence – from the point of view of history – to lament the weakening of the Scots language as a consequence of the political Union of 1707 and, in due course, accompanied by the aggrandisement of those Scots inclined to seize opportunities offered by Empire.

Even Robert Burns, the great egalitarian, was poised in the 1780s to set off for a career in Jamaica which would have involved him in the supervision of slavery. Yet the diminishment of the Scots language happened, too, as did the modification of speech which has tended to replace it with accent and the residue of dialect. 'The classics can console, but not enough' – Walcott's line is very fascinating. It leads me to believe that by this last decade of the twentieth century we are all 'rootless cosmopolitans'. We are people for whom civilised standards of literature are not enough. But we have been *forced* into that position, and I think it is time that we began to force ourselves out of it.

'Rootless cosmopolitans' – Gunter Grass has used that suggestive phrase recently. There is something wrong with it, as Grass explains. It was employed by the Right in Germany in the 1930s to stigmatise leftist intellectuals, many of them Jewish. Grass knows that the phrase was once an odious pejorative delivered by the politically aboriginal as an insult calculated to put mischievous or independent artists not only in what was thought to be their place, but in a position of real danger. By the 1990s, 'rootless' can look like a lie as much as the truth. It is a question of perspective, and British critics, Scottish ones especially, are not good at answering it. Whether by Seamus Heaney, Tony Harrison, Derek Mahon, Iain Crichton Smith or Norman MacCaig, a good deal of contemporary poetry shows qualities which are radically indigenous as well as eclectic. 'Rootless cosmopolitan' is a true description of how we have come to be, but only because we have allowed it to happen. It is a bit like another fashionable phrase – 'internal emigré', or what it describes, the condition of being an 'inner exile'. These descriptions originated in post-Revolutionary Russia. 'Rootless cosmopolitan' was coined in Nazi Germany. There is a strong sense in which it is obvious that a good deal of our mental positioning derives from the history that led to the Second World War, and also from the War itself and its Cold War aftermath.

Rootlessness and self-imposed 'inner' exile are clearly undesirable positions in which to find yourself. It is hard to see them as physical or actual; they describe states of mind encouraged by the condition of poetry in Western societies. Increasingly, it's possible to detect a touch of melodrama and self-importance in what these terms represent, taken, as they are, from the oppressive realities of other countries at times when the autonomy of the poetic mind was an intolerable affront to totalitarian regimes. Negative pressure on a poet in the British Isles is a much subtler phenomenon altogether. Rejection slips, being turned down for an Arts Council grant, not being asked to give a poetry reading, or being published and read by a handful of enthusiasts, are all forms of anguish which it would be unworthy to compare with censorship, imprisonment and execution. Parliamentary and media outrage at Tony Harrison's *V* probably offended all of us, but it was difficult, too, to escape from the suspicion that in a country like this nothing could have served the film and the book better from the point of view of publicity and sales. Representatives of the secret police did not turn up on Mr Harrison's doorstep at two in the morning.

In Britain, and perhaps even especially in Scotland, the literary world invents its own secret police force. It would seem that there are right and wrong ways of going about an attempt to make poems, and right and wrong ways of showing a proper indigenousness. A political atmosphere pervades poetry at the present time. It is not just that a poet has to be seen to have his or her heart in the right place when it comes to real political issues, those which determine who runs the country. Your mind has to be seen to be ideologically perfect on matters of race, gender, and sexuality. I sometimes think that these days a stereotyped English male poet is on a hiding to nothing. While there is a certain satisfaction in that state of affairs, it is also full of pratfalls. Not a lot of room is left for imaginative liberties when the priority is to be seen to be in all ways politically acceptable. For instance, English friends conclude from my conversation and some of my writing that I must be a rampant Scottish nationalist with marked republican leanings; and I am a nationalist, or at least, I believe that Scotland should have its own Parliament and run its own affairs. In Scotland, though, I've been described an an English poet.

Sniping of that sort is not limited to Scotland, of course. *Everywhere* is concerned with the establishment of pecking orders, and there's a reluctance to understand individual writers who might not want to peck, or, for that matter, be pecked. In nationalist phases of history, however – and this seems true of Scotland since the 1920s – poetry can be made to take second place to indicators in writing that testify to nationality and political hygiene. Where there are three languages to 'choose' from, and one of them is named for a nationality not yours, then controversy is guaranteed. Wider understanding of what poetry is or might be is likely to be constricted. An eloquent series of remarks by Marina Tsvetaeva might point out what the difficulties are:

No language is the mother tongue. Writing poetry is rewriting it.

A poet may write in French: he cannot be 'a French poet' – that's ludicrous. The reason one becomes a poet is to avoid being French, Russian, etc. in order to be everything... Yet every language has something that belongs to it alone, that *is* it...[6]

To begin to look for that quiddity in a language is the first step towards understanding what might also be its contemporary possibilities for poetic artistry. For a poet who is Scottish, however, writing in English will lead to a quite different apprehension of what 'belongs to it alone, that *is* it...' Literary and actual politics are bothersome distractions that can get in the way of the poet's right to cultivate a workable disinterestedness. Traditions of writing native to a poet's country will be of great fascination, and any poet will want, and need, to become familiar with them. But it doesn't bother me in the slightest that a lot of the poetry I love and that has been useful to me was written in England, France, the United States, and elsewhere.

On the other hand, it's possible to feel uncomfortable with some aspects of a native literature. Hugh MacDiarmid believed that the best line in Burns was 'Ye arena Mary Morison'. Indeed, in its directness and rhotacistic euphony Burns's line sounds decidedly aboriginal. MacDiarmid's remark was instructive, I remember, and I can recall reading Scottish poems in its light. That directness terrified me. A straightforward, forthright momentum can be advantageous, but it tends also to push a gentler, more figurative, or meditative lyric poetry to one side. Edwin Muir wrote that you will look in vain in Scottish poetry for lines like 'And peace proclaims olives of endless age,' 'Bare ruined choirs where late the sweet birds sang,' or 'I saw Eternity the other night'. The feelings and harmonies that we associate with Wordsworth and Keats would not go very easily in the faster tempos of Scottish poetry. Spacious imagery, sensuous pictorialising, and daring figurativeness, too, play very little part in Scottish verse until the twentieth century. Scottish poetry cleaves to a more democratic, libertarian character; it is more open to acknowledging the testimony and significance of the Common Man. Not for one single minute would I want to lose *all* of that; but what I think I've wanted to do is slow down the fast clip that is typical of Scottish verse and give a lyrical preference something like a chance. What I don't want to do is contradict my nationality by fudging my own voice with cadences and diction ill-suited to it.

Now and again, I'm aware of how my accent accepts and pronounces rhymes that most English accents might not hear. In my poem 'Loch Music', for example, I rhymed 'Bach' with 'loch' and 'stars' with 'disperse'.[7] Not full rhymes, perhaps, but I find them assonantal enough, while they bear a direct relationship to a real voice and not a paper one. Occasionally, too, I've used Scots words, but only when they're words I continue to speak – 'dailygone', 'hurcheon' (hedgehog), 'whittrick' (weasel) and so on.

In a fairly recent poem, 'At Falkland Palace',[8] I found myself wanting to echo the formality of late sixteenth and early seventeenth century Scottish verse, particularly that of Alexander Montgomerie, the author of 'The Cherry and the Slae'. The fourteen-line stanza of Montgomerie's masterpiece – 114 stanzas, 1596 lines – is intricate, ornamental, and satisfying to a Scottish voice and ear. Metrical engineering is a conspicuous feature of Scottish poetry from the fifteenth to the end of the eighteenth century. Montgomerie's stanza contains couplets, while line lengths vary from tetrameters to trimeters with a few two-beat lines here and there. This is a stanza from Montgomerie's poem which should convey its sound and movement.

> Our way then lyes about the Lin,
> Whereby a warrand, we shal win,
>   It is so straight and plaine,
> The water also is so shald,
> We shal it passe, even as we wald,
>   With pleasure and but paine.
> For as we see the mischief grow,
>   Oft of a feckles thing,
> So likewise doth this river flow,
>   Foorth of a pretty spring,
>   Whose throat sir, I wot sir,
>   You may stop with your neive;
>   As you sir, I trow sir,
>   *Experience*, can prieve.

Drafts of my own poem considered and discarded several kinds of stanza before I realised that the sound I was looking for was one I identified with Montgomerie's poem. When that dawned on me, I felt more confident of being able to finish a poem which until then had been recalcitrant. The shape of 'At Falkland Palace' turned out to be two stanzas each of thirty lines which vary regularly from iambic tetrameter to dimeter. Falkland was the summer palace of the Stewart dynasty; it is of the time to which the imagined noise of

Montgomerie's verse was beckoning me. Giving myself over to a conviction of how the poem should be written led me to want full rhymes as far as possible. It compelled me to establish a firmer iambic beat, which is less easy in short lines than in pentameters. From the point of view of how lines begin and end, sentences are harder to control in a stanza with short lines. In that sort of form, losing a main verb is not so much a case of mislaying it and covering your tracks with three dots, but a temptation. Saying and thinking in verse have to overcome difficulties posed by metrical phrasing, the position of rhyme words, and syntax. Too many lines beginning with 'The', 'And' and 'Of', for example, occur in my earlier drafts of the poem. For the sake of spontaneity, getting thoughts and feelings down on paper, my habit is to leave these crudities alone for the time being. Instinct and imagination ought to be given their heads in the earlier stages of making a poem, even if the writing is shoddy and wayward as a result and the metrical pulse all over the place. At times, too, it might be necessary to pass on from a passage that refuses to happen to succeeding lines for the sake of keeping up a continuous flow of energy.

If you look down the left-hand margin of Browning's poems you'll notice that relatively few of his lines begin with 'weak' words. Never having seen anything in print on this subject, I suspect that the rules of versification are non-existent. You learn by reading. Perhaps, if you're lucky, you pick up something of what a poet like Browning knew about artistry. You learn from experience that how lines begin is as important as how they end. Metrical poetry, especially when it rhymes, *and* free verse, are obsessed by line-endings. You can often sense that a poet's concentration has been applied vigorously to the right-hand side of a poem, leaving the left-hand side open to a string of weak words and expressions.[9]

Too stern an approach to the line can produce a mannered artistry. Where lines are short the temptation is to accept cramped syntax of a sort that cripples spokenness. You could end up with a poem that looks wonderful on paper but feels like paper between tongue and teeth. I always speak lines aloud when I'm writing. Doing this on trains and buses can be pretty embarrassing. Not long ago, in Tentsmuir Forest, I found myself being overheard by a flock of birdwatchers who very clearly thought I was in need of sympathy. What *they* looked like in pedal-pushers, anoraks, funny hats, and covered in cameras and field glasses, is, of course, their business. Someone giving a line of verse to the wind, however, seems to be a head case. But in revising 'At Falkland Palace' I found saying lines aloud indispensable. Perhaps what the habit does is put me in touch with an inherited Scottish directness. The instinctive principle on which I seem to work might be one in which that directness contests the issue with a temperamental preference for lyrical phrasings and perceptions which, as I said earlier, amounts to an opposite tendency in Scottish poetry.

Part of my nature likes to involve itself with history, politics and society. Another side to it is attracted by personal, intimate and disinterested approaches to whatever I find myself writing. Separating these cleft thematic urges from the technical strategies I employ seems to me impossible. 'At Falkland Palace', then, is several kinds of poem at once. It is a love poem addressed to the woman to whom it is dedicated. It is a poem about being in a particular place at an affirmative moment in a relationship. Because of where and what that place is, it is a poem about the past meditated in the present. As the first poem in my book *Northlight* I intend it to lead naturally from the last poem in a previous book, *Elegies*[10]: the woman addressed in 'At Falkland Palace' is the same woman addressed in the last line of 'Leaving Dundee'. It is a poem of returning to Scotland. Its formality and artifice are asked to create a sound that accords with place. That might be gestural, an echoic delusion on my part; but, at least to me, it *was* the beckoning voice of an old and wonderful poem that enabled my own, doubtless not so wonderful, sixty lines. I could go a little further and confess that in the compositional fantasy found and enjoyed in writing the poem, I was, momentarily, a fake Stewart grandee of the late sixteenth century when Scotland was still itself, and that this Caledonian hidalgo found himself in Falkland Palace with his lady, in 1982, which is when the poem 'happens'; it was begun then and finished in 1987. About thirty years ago I was given very good advice – 'The Muse knows no sense of time'. Here is the poem:

At Falkland Palace

For L.J.B.

Innermost dialect
Describes Fife's lyric hills,
Life, love and intellect
In lucid syllables,
Domestic air.
Natural play of sun and wind
Collaborates with leaf and mind,

The world a sentient
Botanic instrument,
  Visible prayer.
Everything's birth begins
On the moment of the May's
Creaturely origins
– I'll live for these good days
  Love leads me to
In gardened places such as this
Of the flower and apple-promise,
  Lark-sung, finch wonderful;
  Edenic circumstance, not fall,
    Walking with you.
  Balladic moments pass,
  Tongue-tied, parochial,
  A narrative of grass
  And stone's hierarchical
    Scottish Versailles.
These native liberties propose
Our lives, rose by unbudding rose,
  A song-crazed laverock
  Whose melodies unlock
    Audible sky.

  Dynastic stonework flakes,
  Weathers and fails, withdraws
  From shapely time and shakes
  A gargoyle's severed claws
    At visitors.
Here wrinkled time's abolished house
Perpetuates a posthumous
  Nation, monarchy's urn
  In which the Stewarts mourn
    What once was theirs.
  In a country like this
  Our ghosts outnumber us:
  A ruined artifice
  Empty and sonorous,
    Malevolent
In how its past force-feeds with filth
Anachronism's commonwealth
  And history bemoans

> What history postpones,
>   The true event.
> In the hollows of home
> I find life, love and ground
> And intimate welcome:
> With you, and these, I'm bound
>   To history.
> Touching your hair, holding your hand,
> Your beauty blends with time and land,
> And you are loveliness
> In your green, country dress,
>   So fair this day.

Stanza, metre and rhyme lead some critics to identify poets who use these techniques as 'traditionalists' or exponents of an 'archaising mode'. Attitudes to form are supposed to reflect a greater or lesser approval or distaste for an authoritarian, hierarchical view of history and society. However, I don't consider myself to be a traditionalist or self-conscious archaiser; and I know for a certain fact that I am not now and never have been on the Tory side of history, nor of the totalitarian Left. In his book *Poetic Meter and Poetic Form*, Paul Fussell quotes the American poet J. V. Cunningham, who said that

> Prose is written in sentences; poetry in sentences and lines. It is encoded not only in grammar, but also simultaneously in meter, for meter is the principle or set of principles, whatever they may be, that determine the line... We have lost the repetitive harmony of the old tradition, and we have not established a new. We have written to vary or violate the old line, for regularity we feel is meaningless and irregularity meaningful. But a generation of poets, acting on the principles and practice of significant variation, have at last nothing to vary from.[11]

An option that Cunningham might not have been in a position to consider is represented by that very common contemporary poem in which technique suggests a compromise between formal and free verse. It might be a poem in unrhymed, de-metred lines with stanzas of the same size. Without being metrically designed, it might use rhymes with metrical passages cropping up every so often, but organised in such a way as to avoid the more rollicking features of crambo-clink. Ted Hughes's poetry, or Seamus Heaney's, might have encouraged this (perhaps) organicist approach where the concern is less with formal shape than with the possibilities of phrase, line, imagery and a succession of local effects. Incidental narrative will be scarce in such poems. Indeed, a desire for intensity and the audible qualities of the phrase would seem to be what justifies that particular style. Edmund Wilson described these qualities as 'plastic' rather than musical.[12] He suspected that it might have been Matthew Arnold who encouraged this tendency. More convincing, however, is Wilson's suggestion that a narrowing of the function of poetry created the kind of poem which exists to serve a memorable line, image or phrase.

Individual writers have made fine poems from a style that reaches for neither a regular nor an entirely free formality – Michael Longley is a good example. It's a way of making poems that appeals to me from time to time. However, a compromise is a compromise, and I'm nagged by the thought that poetry ought not to be involved in half-hearted treaties. Yet it can be no bad thing for a writer to be open to a range of styles rather than just one. Longley, for example, is a gifted metricist, and the same inspired judiciousness supports his freer poetry.

The remarks by Edmund Wilson to which I referred come from an essay called 'Is Verse a Dying Technique?' Over the past few years, however, verse has staged a comeback on both sides of the Atlantic. At least two anthologies and one periodical have been devoted to this New Formalism in America.[13] It is more worrying than chattering accusations of wasting your time with an archaising mode. Anything that directs poetry to a technical definition is to be discountenanced.

Revision ought to take care of the removal of metrical padding and the poeticisms that can and sometimes do occur. Also, the more slavish habits of formality can be disregarded when other opportunities ask to be taken or when exactness begins to lead a poem away from its experience. When writing 'Love-making by Candlelight',[14] precise line-lengths and a regular rhyme scheme had to go in order to find the poem I wanted. Some rhymes remain, as do an iambic pulse and the overall shape which was more or less the one I'd started with. 'S. Frediano's',[15] however, was written much more quickly although I'd wanted to write it ever since 1982, several years before I found myself doing so. I suppose I believed that the first draft would be followed by many others, and that unmetrical lines would be revised later, that the occasional rhymes would suggest a subsequent scheme. Instinct told me to leave the poem more or less as it is. For weeks, though, I was unhappy with that hunch. Here's the vanity of the poetic process: I fancied that a couple of rhymes in the poem were good, but wasted in a poem that otherwise doesn't rhyme, and whose iambic measure is diverted by passages of freer writing. 'Rake/Gaelic' and 'blur/literature' were the two rhymes that excited me to vainglorious adoration. Holding back from further revision left me with what I felt was a more 'truthful' music (but I don't really know that; it's instinctive). Feeling-in-words seemed to duplicate feeling-itself more satisfactorily were the poem left unrhymed and free. I suppose I'm driving at the annoying gap between what you feel and want to say and what you actually manage to say; and if it's free verse that brings you closer to your desire then you might as well stick with that form of verse rather than impose formality on a poem reluctant to accept it. Yet both poems owe their final form to the regular, metrical verse that was originally intended for them. 'Love-making by Candlelight' was finished in regular verse, found less than satisfying, and then re-written more freely. 'S. Frediano's' in its first draft was meant to be a beginning step towards a metrical, rhyming poem. Neither poem seemed to me to want the formality I'd had in mind. 'Why?' you may well continue to ask, for I doubt if my explanations will have convinced you. Here I have to appeal to instinct, and to these secret transactions which a writer makes between what seems instinctively right and what 'ought' to be technically precise. Much of the reason for my decisions – or so I suspect – stems from the tact and honesty required when writing about intimate subjects. For better or worse, the free verse of this century has left us at least half-convinced of the virtues of spontaneity. Earlier poets must have possessed the ability to compose spontaneously in accurate metre. After more than thirty years of frequent practice, however, I still find myself all-too-often in the position of having to take infinite pains. Oh dear, yes; to be able to compose spontaneously in metre without losing the heat and passion of feeling...Rilke said something that cheers me. It cheers me because it was said by Rilke, possibly the last European genius in poetry (unless – and I'm not sure – that honour is W.H. Auden's):

> Only the very great are artists in that strict sense, which alone is true: that art has become a way of life for them. All the others, all of us who only occupy ourselves with art, meet on the same long road and greet each other in the same silent hope and yearn for the same distant mastery...

Isn't that wonderful?

It is in that district of delicacy and truthfulness where the obligations of form can be of very real assistance. To be any sort of writer at all, then at some point early in your life you have to make a leap from reticence into an artistically and socially acceptable candour that will be hospitable to both mischief and responsibility. Poetry insists of those who would try to write it that they have the courage of their joys and melancholies. You also need to possess the courage of the present tense and the first-person singular. Nor is it permissible to falsify temperament or distort experience. Sentimentality might be the worst sin of all. What that means is an emphasis placed on unearned or undeserved feelings in poems where what is said tends to overstatement or understatement when the subject demands neither but a different level of expression altogether.

You might want to complain that this has too little to do with the art or craft of poetry. What I want to suggest is that because poetry is concerned with the rendering of emotion and intelligence, then, from a moral point of view, the craft of poetry is very deeply implicated in the ethical quality of these renditions. 'Any emotion which cannot be tested and passed by the mind of the man who feels it is sentimental,' Edwin Muir wrote. Another definition can be found in Joyce's *Ulysses*, in the telegram that Buck Mulligan receives from Dedalus: ' – *The sentimentalist is he who would enjoy without incurring the immense debtorship for a thing done*'. A moral tone is distinctly audible in both cases. 'The mind of the man who feels it' drives home fiercely the personal irresponsibility of 'the sentimentalist'. That it is an 'emotion which cannot' – or that has failed to be – 'tested and passed by the mind of the man who feels it' suggests a moral lack or a disgraceful opportunism in neglecting an 'immense debtorship' to an event in which the writer claims to have been involved.

To claim that sentimentality arises from a failure of intelligence or a victory of false emotion over a wavering intellect, or selfishness over responsibility, could be to lay as much blame on a poet's control of his or her technique. Counting stresses and syllables, line- and stanza-making, rhyming, attending to vowels and consonants, harmonies and collisions, assonance and dissonance, diction, syntax, working with the full apparatus of verse, ought to mediate between wrong and mendacious feeling and the chance to head them off. Banal, and certainly practical, as this must sound, the tempo of metrical writing with rhymes and stanzas is slower. If a writer is serious about a poem as an artistic creation then labour itself as well as the recommendations of veracity should expel culpable or mistaken feelings.

To invest a moral significance in technique can sound inhibiting and perhaps even reactionary and priggish. Our suspicions stem not so much from what we might feel about the formality of verse as the informality which contemporary principles go out of their way to court and recommend.

An anecdote: not long ago I gave a poetry reading, having travelled to the engagement immediately after an occasion for which the wearing of a suit was required. As I entered the room where the reading was to be held, I overheard someone say, 'He wears a suit, with a waistcoat. It'll be rhyme and metre, all night long.' How in the name of God could such a conclusion be drawn? Think of those photographs of the French Surrealists buttoned up to the eyes, some of them even wearing *spats*, for Heaven's sake . . . Or T.S. Eliot, who was probably born in a suit, a four-piece suit, as Virginia Woolf once remarked. Tweed = rhyme and metre? I'm no logician, probably not even very adept at consecutive thought, but even I can work that equation out as a statement of nonsense.

One consequence of the contemporary emphasis on informality is that form in its widest sense is perceived as the creature of a powerful but intellectually discredited conservatism. Form in poetry, and form as an abstraction associated with political and social beliefs, seem to me completely unrelated. The connection is forced only by argumentative desperation. They can be linked only if a conservative poet insists on it; and were such a poet to urge this association, then he or she could be criticised as an enemy of poetry. Through that extreme gesture poetry would be placed at the service of only one section of society. The generosity of poetry would be sullied. I believe the same to be true of an anti-conservative poet whose procedures are drawn from a version of the same equation and dedicated to exploiting the same vulgar definition of form.

Poetic form as a reflection of social and political beliefs is a common assumption, and the tenacity with which it is believed creates what I would like to call 'compositional anxiety'. That is, it can fill a writer with unreasonable doubt. But as this is, by its nature, a subjective exercise, let me admit that from time to time I feel unsure of verse, and I'm led to worry if it *is* an archaising mode. Right this minute I can say with complete conviction that the long-lived methods of verse do *not* constitute an 'archaising mode' – so let's have it in inverted commas once again – but I know that in the future I'll find myself in two minds, and far from the first time.

> Other echoes
> Inhabit the garden. Shall we follow?
> Quick, said the bird, find them, find them,
> Round the corner.

Whatever these 'other echoes' in the garden of Eliot's *Burnt Norton*, or in our own real or imaginary gardens, finding them – and a poet is compelled to make the effort – is made harder and harder by the times in which we live and work. So much of the rest of life clamours for attention. Just as

> Words strain,
> Crack and sometimes break, under the burden,
> Under the tension, slip, slide, perish,
> Decay with imprecision, will not stay in place,
> Will not stay still . . .

so, too, can the forms and devices of poetry appear to be 'a worn-out poetical fashion'. *Verse* is not an 'archaising mode'; it is language itself that can be overtaken by time. Art, no matter how specific in its history, aspires to timelessness. Poetry looks for a life as durable as the language in which it is written. As soon as a poet begins the wooing of Yesterday, contemporaneity is unbalanced and a wilful conservatism blemishes the work. Self-conscious attempts to seduce Tomorrow might result in even worse consequences.

What Eliot evoked as 'the intolerable wrestle/With words and meanings' can see a writer pinned to the floor, surmounted by the hefty giant of the language intent on breaking your neck. Searching for clues and the hope of a fresh start in poetry's museum, where so much is probably 'around the corner', can run out of attractions. It is possible to feel dispirited and anxious, unable to write and finish poems to which you can feel reconciled if not completely satisfied. 'It is as if I had completely lost the ability to bring about the conditions that might help me,' Rilke wrote of this state of affairs, 'whenever I reach out for them I find new aggravations and excuses, the days pass, and who knows how much of life? Ought one not to devise some grotesque figure solely to bring in this sentence: "He spent the last six or seven years doing up a button that always came undone again"? . . .'

I would like to finish with just a few words about rhyme. In conjunction with metre it is one of poetry's best ways of keeping alive the hope that poetry can be beautiful. More and more, I feel that there is an inherent *poetry* in verse. Rhyme is a very sociable and considerate device. On many occasions I've asked myself: 'Why do people like to read and hear rhyme? Why, especially, is it enjoyed in silent reading? Why do children in particular take pleasure in rhyme? Why do *I* like rhyme?' And I don't know the answers to these questions. Neither, I suspect, do you. But if nothing else, rhyme, and metre, too, entertain the possibility that poetry can continue to happen between tongue and teeth as well as between the ears and behind the left nipple. Perhaps poetry *is* conservative (with a small and decidedly non-political 'c') in that it is defending eternal pleasures and truths. To participate in an art that is devoted to such verities – even in a minor way – is an immense privilege, and a serious responsibility. In *Elements d'une doctrine radicale* (1925), the French essayist Alain once wrote: 'Many people say that the important thing is to advance; I think rather that the important thing is not to retreat'.

Notes

1. These poems may be found in Michael Grieve and W.R. Aitken (eds), *Hugh MacDiarmid: Complete Poems 1920-1976* (1978; reprinted Carcanet, 1993, 1994). 'In memoriam James Joyce' (from the volume of the same title, 1955) begins Vol. II. 'On a raised beach' may be found in Vol. I, p.422ff. ('All is lithogenesis – or lochia, / Carpolite fruit of the forbidden tree, / Stones blacker than any in the Caaba, / Cream-coloured caen-stone, chatoyant pieces...')

2. See e.g. Sorley Maclean, *O Choille gu Bearradh (From Wood to Ridge): Collected Poems in Gaelic and English* (Carcanet, 1989).

3. Edwin Muir, *Collected Poems* (Faber, 1984).

4. Norman MacCaig, *Collected Poems* (Chatto & Windus, 1990).

5. Tom Leonard, *Intimate Voices: Selected Work 1965-1983* (Galloping Dog Press, 1984).

6. Marina Tsvetaeva, quoted by John Bayley in his Introduction to Rainer Maria Rilke, *Selected Letters 1902-1926*, trans. R.F.C. Hull. (Quartet, 1988).

7. 'Loch music' can be found in Douglas Dunn, *St. Kilda's Parliament* (Faber, 1981), and in his *Selected Poems 1964-1983* (Faber, 1986), p.203.

8. In *Northlight* (Faber, 1988), pp.1-2.

9. See the Introduction, and also the notes to Alison Brackenbury's essay: line-endings are as it were special cases, because they are determinate in metrical structure. If particular relationships – for example, correspondence between word-stress and metrical accent – are exploited in line-final position(s), then it is not too surprising that there is relatively more metrical freedom – and consequent freedom to deploy other, lexical effects – elsewhere in the line.

10. Published by Faber (1985).

11. Revised edition, 1979. First edition (1965) published New York: Random House.

12. Edmund Wilson, 'Is verse a dying technique?' in *The Triple Thinkers* (Penguin, 1962). In this interesting essay, Wilson argued that verse was coming to be used in 'increasingly specialised functions', its other and former functions being usurped by 'prose technique'. One of these specialised functions is the embodying of 'separate lines and fragments... broken mosaics and "pinches of glory" '. As Dunn points out, Wilson traces this etiolation to (among others) Matthew Arnold: 'Arnold, unintentionally and unconsciously, has had the effect of making the poet's "poetry" seem to be concentrated in the phrase or line' (p.27).

13. Timothy Steele's *Missing Measures* (see the notes to Jeffrey Wainwright's essay) is also written from a New Formalist perspective.

14. In *Northlight*, pp.3-4.

15. In *Northlight*, pp.5-6.

Structure in my Poetry

Iain Crichton Smith

I must begin with a prologue which is necessary for the better understanding of what I am about to say.

I was brought up on a religious island – the island of Lewis in the Outer Hebrides – where the religion was fierce and uncompromising, and fundamentalist. This religion converted the world to dogma. To it the sentence of hell is possible and real. There is an attempt at a constant scrubbing away of sin, using the text of the Bible as a detergent. The artist is attempting in his pride to take the place of God as creator. We are familiar with this fundamentalism in Iran. It accepts a religious text as being wholly inspired, even the parts which we might consider as nonsensical. Thus for me my art is an attempt to confront this world which in the end despises what I do and for which spiritual books must be more important than fiction and the psalm superior to the lyric.

That is part of my story. The other part is that I was brought up using a marginal language, Gaelic. I find myself therefore in an ambiguous position both with regard to language and with regard to the preconceptions of what I do in art, and I must say that it has been at times a nightmarish labyrinth. It has resulted in desperate manoeuvres in order to be true to myself.[1]

My early poetry was in fact characterised by what I call the dichotomy of the Law and the Grace,[2] a theological terminology which I adopted. The Law is for all practical purposes the metrical cage which I partly inhabit and partly create, and the Grace the inspiration which beats against the sides of the cage. It is the wind of accident blowing against an adamant justice. If you wish to find a parallel movement you would find it in the work of Robert Lowell, whose parabola from metrical bondage to freedom I also describe.

What is the structure of my early poetry? It is clearly a metrical structure. In that early poetry I was conscious of formal concerns. It would have been psychologically impossible for me to write in free verse. I do not think, however, that metre led me into 'mechanical' harmonies. It was a method of containing the inspiration while the inspiration also fought against the metre, thus creating energy. This duplicated my psychological state. It was poetry, as I have said elsewhere, of fighting tensions.

I deal in my poetry at times with questions of freedom and order. I deal with ultimate questions such as death. There is a poem called 'For the Unknown Seamen of the 1939-45 War Buried in Iona'[3] where the verse has a lapidary feel about it, though there is a continuing argument. The verses lead by questioning towards what might be considered an epitaph. The deaths are seen as random:

> ... Yet these events are not amenable
> to any discipline that we can impose
> and are not in the end even imaginable.
> What happened was simply this, bad luck for those
> who have lain here in a changing pose.

The typical movement of a poem, then, was an interrogation moving by various experiential methods towards a resolution. The poem ended when a resolution was found. The metre helped to control the inspiration, to give it strength, to focus it, to sharpen it. Sides of questions were to have equal weight in the argument.

Sometimes the argument might not be mine but that of a persona, as in the poem 'Statement By a Responsible Spinster',[4] where the question is whether a woman should have sacrificed herself for an aged parent. The idea of sacrifice is probed through a particular consciousness. The duplicity of age and its cunning is mentioned. The idea of self-deception is also mentioned. The poem is more ambitious in its rhymes than the previous one. There are ten rhymes of particular difficulty. These include 'ornament', 'permanent', 'firmament', 'lineament', 'armament', 'element', 'moment', 'merriment', 'emolument', and 'monument'. The rhymes compose a kind of elegant formality which might be suited to a spinster. The idea of freedom versus discipline remains the same. It is much of my thesis and is reflected in the verse.

The elegant formality is also reflected in a curious dandyism which is often found in these early poems and has to do with art itself. It invents phrases like 'musicks us', for instance:

> And lastly I speak of the grace that musicks us
> into our accurate element till we
> go gowned at length in exact propriety...

It delights in form and elegance for their own sake. It sees art as connected with harmony and geometry. (I loved geometry when I was in school.) The poem is seen as a form of geometrical elegance. Typically it is written as a sonnet.

Thus my early work has a metrical formality which I perceived as necessary.

Nevertheless this early work contains soliloquies, usually by women, which though they are fairly formal are also attempting to be conversational. Such a poem is 'The Widow', the persona of which meditates on a scholarly (and now dead) husband. Such poems have run-over lines, that is to say, sentences often end in the middle of lines. This is the ending of the poem.

> To cease growing –
> that is the worst of all. Therefore must I
> hug your cold shoulders all the wintry night
> and summer too? Old woman like a sky
> open to rain and lightning. Am I God
> so to forgive you or to leave the why
> nailed to my cross? Your chair is rocking, rocking,
> as if with grief. I see you with a nod
> whipping your bony body. Stop, I say,
> stop, child, you mustn't, you were all I had.

Similarly in a poem called 'Schoolteacher' I let the character speak in a conversational voice:

> And who stood up? John's father? John? The faint
> graph of her will climbed the wavering wall.
> It climbed for forty years. It made a white
>
> snake on distemper. ('Who was the famous saint
> who crossed from Ireland in a flimsy boat,
> Columba or Columbus? Surely you remember?')

The question, of course, is one method of making the style conversational.

To turn now to the origin of these poems – I would feel first of all an urgency, a sense of lack, a stirring, an inchoate thing moving towards expression. At that stage there were no words, only a restlessness, a dynamic impulse seeking form, needing privacy. The words would come and from then only it was a case of trying to contain the inspiration by metre.

When I was young we had no water in the houses, we had to go to the well with buckets. For balance it was easier to carry two buckets home without spilling a drop. And then again the poem might have two equal arguments which necessitated care.

One poem which I am reasonably proud of and which is quite long is 'Deer on the High Hills'.[5] It has a number of sections and is written in verses of three lines. I think Dante had an influence on this poem. It began with seeing three deer on an icy road on a winter's night. This led to spontaneous images of French aristocrats on a ballroom floor. Parts of the poem I do not understand. Most, however, are a balance between instinct and intellect and are quite clear. (There is another very odd one called 'In a Chinese Restaurant'[6] which seems to be about an old woman and her husband wanting to visit a Chinese restaurant before they die.)

The poem 'Deer on the High Hills' is not simply descriptive. It also has an elegance of language which links it to my early dandyish poems, for example:

> Forget these purple evenings and these poems
> that solved all, or took for myth
> the pointed sail of Ulysses enigmatic.

This kind of elegance I later strove to get rid of. It is found in lines such as 'The witty gun blazed from his knowing hand' (in 'Deer on the High Hills') and in an earlier poem, 'From aloof azures let his ariels go.' Incidentally, one of the things that I think a poet has to get rid of is a lot of literary allusions. I'm not sure that I have done so. One of my books is called *Hamlet in Autumn*. And I often recur to Shakespeare.

I have therefore tried to move away from this elegance to what I hope in later volumes is a weightier plainness.

Now when I examine my own poetry, I find in it elements which I was not conscious of at the time and which derive, I think, from my Gaelic reading, particularly my reading of Gaelic poetry. Let me mention just two of these elements: firstly the use of adjectives and secondly the use of assonance.

In Gaelic poetry, particularly that of the eighteenth century, there was, perhaps derived from Irish, the use of a battery of adjectives to define the noun. There could in this way be as many as eight adjectives. One can see this more clearly in my translation of *Ben Dorain*, the long eighteenth-century masterpiece by Duncan Macintyre (incidentally a poem about deer as well).

The following verse is a description of the slopes of Ben Dorain:

> Precipitous, hilly,
> with hollow and valley,
> ruffled and knolly,
> mountainous, hairy,
> clustered and furry,
> tufted and curly.

and with regard to the deer itself:

> It's the stag, the proud roarer,
> white-rumped and ferocious,
> branch-antlered and noble,
> would walk in the shaded
> retreats of Ben Dorain
> so haughtily headed.

and with regard to the hunting dog: 'His hackles rising, bristling,/ sandy, shag-haired, vicious...' Now when I examine my own poem 'Deer on the High Hills' I sometimes find the same fertile use of adjectives, for instance:

> Deer on the high peaks there have been heads
> as proud as yours, distinctive, ominous,
> of an impetuous language, measureless.
>
> Heads like yours so scrutinous and still
> yet venomed too with the helpless thrust of spring,
> so magisterial, violent, yet composed...[7]

and also,

> And these return in spite of the idea
> the direct reasoning road, the mad Ulysses,
> so unperverted, so implacable...

In actual fact I am not sure that long lists of adjectives don't make us lose sight of the original noun rather than help to define it.

Another derivation, I think, from my Gaelic poetry is my sometimes unconscious use of assonance. Gaelic poetry is heavily assonantal, with echoes between words at the ends of lines and in the middle of lines. I find this too in my English poetry, for example in a poem called 'Luss Village'.

Such walls, like honey, and the old are happy
in morphean air like gold-fish in a bowl.
Ripe roses trail their margins down a sleepy
mediaeval treatise on the slumbering soul.

And even the water, fabulously silent,
has no salt tales to tell us, nor makes jokes
about the yokel mountains, huge and patient,
that will not court her but read shadowy books.[8]

or in a poem called 'At the Sale':

Climbing the dais to such loud applause
as shakes the hall for toiling without fail
at this strange nameless gadget pumping, turning,
each day oiling the wheel
with zeal and eagerness and freshness turning...[9]

I find it also in the poem already quoted, 'For the Unknown Seamen
of the 1939-45 War Buried in Iona Churchyard':

These things happen and there's no explaining,
and to call them 'chosen' might abuse a word.
It is better also not to assume a mourning,
moaning stance...

These therefore are two elements from the Gaelic which enter my
English poetry, I think for the most part unconsciously. And indeed
most of what goes on in the best poetry is unconscious. And I am
sure that in some deep sense the work of mine which partly defeats
the intellect is the best.

In general the language in my early poems is not colloquial. One
of the concerns which appears not only in my poems but in a story
such as 'Mr Trill in Hades' is the collapse of the classical world. I
think that this is taking place in our time. Teachers find that pupils
do not understand simple classical references which to them are self-
evident. University lecturers are finding the same thing. (Of course
it is happening with regard to the Bible too.) Now I know that the
classical world should not be idealised. We know that there were
slaves and much cruelty. But to me the classical world also rep-
resented qualities of gravitas, duty, and so on, which are qualities I
admire.

Also the classical world was filtered to me through a very fine headmaster, whom I admired and for whom I wrote an elegy when he died. I admired in him virtues which arose from his classical training, virtues such as the ones I've mentioned – a high sense of duty, seriousness, magnanimity. I think therefore that much of the vocabulary in my early poetry, certainly, is formal and not colloquial, and that this combines with the formality of the metre. Thus in my poem 'For John Maclean, Headmaster, and Classical and Gaelic Scholar'[10] much is characterised by a vocabulary which is not colloquial:

> I know that it is waning, that clear light
> that shone on all our books, and made them white
> with unanswerable grammar. That the slaves
> sustained our libraries and that the wolves
> and watchful eagles nourished an elite
> and that the elegant and forceful proofs
> of their geometries will not suffice.
>
> I know that Athene is now
> dishevelled in the shrubbery, and the nurse
> beckons at evening to her. Gods rehearse
> their ruined postures and the ruined brow
> reflects from mirrors not of fire but ice
>
> and that our brute Achilles drives his wheels
> across the gesturing shadows: and that kneels
> to cheering legions Aphrodite: packs
> are watching Ajax hacking with his axe
> inanely the pale sheep: and shady deals
> illuminate Odysseus's tracks.

I am not sure whether I have here created effects by a combination of Saxon words and Latin-derived words as in, for instance, the marvellous closing lines in *Hamlet* where Hamlet says: 'Absent thee from felicity awhile/ And in this harsh world draw thy breath in pain/ To tell my story.' How far was Shakespeare conscious of these effects, the contrast between 'harsh' and 'felicity' or 'pain' and 'absent', words which are short, and Saxon, and words which are Latin and more formal? It is in fact hard to know how many effects in poetry are conscious.

I find some of that linguistic contrast in my poem 'Orpheus',[11] where Orpheus is entering the common world after ascending from Hades:

> And Orpheus took his lyre and left that place
> and moved where the shadows moved and the clouds flowed
> and all that had its own changing grace.
> As on an April day there was sun and shade
> but nothing vicious or virtuous
> haunted the various music that he played.

Later of course I had to try to include that quotidian world which Orpheus entered. This attempt is found among others in a series of mainly short poems called 'Transparencies'. Here is one;

BANK CLERKESS

> She builds
> towers of silver,
> unbuilds.
> Riffles
> pound notes
> like a card sharp,
> wears
> a large
> cheap
> white
> ring.
>
> She is unbuyable
> with any currency
> but youth.

and

WAITRESS

> Mouths
> Hands.
> 'The soul of the party.'
>
> After ten hours on your feet
> a smile is a great weight.

and this one, untitled:

One has to be fit
to write poems.

A giant
to lock
small words in place.

And this one, untitled:

I would love
to write
a "great" poem,
big as the Cuillins.
Instead I sniff
a great yellow
bourgeois
garden
rose.
And I stick a
carnation in my
buttonhole.
Deep red inside,
pink outside.
I thrust my cuffs out.
They are like the blur
of autumn
at the edge of a
leaf.

You can see what I was trying to do. I was trying to write about individual things and beings of the day. This attempt was quite conscious. It meant that the language had to change and become less large and Latinate. It meant that lines became shorter, that there was no formal metre. There was perhaps, however, a stiffness.

Nevertheless, the poems appeared quite different. Some of the lines might only have one word. Single words became important, instead of lines and verses, as in the following:

My name
is
Miss Twiss.

I like
biographies.

I speak
in a loud
tremulous
voice.

I admire
fierceness.

I want
to be neat
with a rose
at my throat.

Today
I walked down the road
with my dog on his lead.
Someone was burning
rubbish
in a garden.
There was a nasty tang
from the smoke.

They should stop that.
They should stop that
at once.

It is a difficult process. Sometimes I revert to metre and sometimes I write free verse. Thus my work hovers between the two.

In my latest book, *The Village and Other Poems*, I continue this effort of trying to achieve the registration of the quotidian, especially in the section about the village. Obviously when I am thinking of what I am trying to do I call to mind Lawrence and Williams. It is an attempt to escape the ethical and the judgemental. In my case it is partly an attempt to escape the dogmas in which I grew up.

Naturally there are things one cannot do with such a style. A large music is not possible. Nevertheless certain poignant effects can be attained, as for instance in my poem for my brother who died in Canada after spending most of his life in Africa.[12] The music of this I think is quite different from that of the 'Elegy for John Maclean'.

The style is less Latinate, I think, though curiously enough I was remembering Catullus when I wrote the poem, and his elegy for his own brother. Here is the poem:

> 'Farewell, my brother.'
> The seas separate us,
> a history of salt.
>
> It is as if I had dreamed
> that on an island ringed by waves
> we once walked
>
> when the buttercups blew in the wind
> around the ruins of houses
> in a blank sea-gaze.
>
> The Bible was a hard wall
> which we climbed over
> to touch the consolations of the heart.
>
> Eternal voyaging!
> Among the civil wars of Africa
> you spent the best of your days.
>
> You will lie in a different earth
> far from Lewis
> unlearned in your history,
> with its own legends.
>
> In the early morning
> I heard the raven
> squawking above my ground,
> a rancorous wanderer
> in his bad-tempered province.
>
> Forgive us our misunderstandings.
> Life is not like strolling
> carelessly through a field.
>
> It is not sunset
> over a stubble
> colouring the sharpness,
> a perfection of swords.

The earth shakes
often when we are surest
of the prosperity of our fortune.

Even when the moon
is round as a coin,
our achieved gamble.

Even as I wrote
you were absently sleeping
like an alien on this earth.

My distant brother,
with your own casket
of joys and tribulations.

Barer than the mind
is the soil of Lewis.
It is in the keeping of the wind.
It has the same resonance,

that constant music,
that enchanted cottage,
which enhanced our residence,

our hunger for the unknown.
If we could speak again
would we know better?

I offer this bouquet
from the oceans of salt,
my distant brother.

I send it across the seas
to the spaciousness of Canada,
my flowering poem,

to let its fragrance
be sweet in your nostrils,
though you are now unable
to converse with me.

My distant brother,
in the shelter of my poem
let you be secret

till we are children again
in the one bed
in the changing weather
of an inquisitive childhood.

The roads separate:
see, I wave to you,
you turn away completely
into your own cloud.

See, I wave to you,
you are disappearing forever.
Tears disarm me.

Now you stand like a statue
in the honour of goodness.
My pride and my tears burn me.

Farewell, my brother.

I suppose part of the music of this poem is achieved again by asso-
nance as in 'that enchanted cottage/ which enhanced our residence'
and 'when the buttercups blew in the wind/ around the ruins of
house'. I owe part of that to my Gaelic ancestry.

This brings me to another question which I will have to discuss, I
think, though it goes deeper than structure. But before I do that I
should like to quote one or two other poems from *The Village*. Here
is one:

Each morning
I cross the railway line

towards the kiosk
to collect my newspaper.

Summer,
how lovely you are,
how leafy
just like a newspaper
composed of coloured paper.

And also the rails hum
towards the future
in the midst of such news returning,

those reds and greens.

Very faint echoes of rhymes connect these verses. Thus 'newspaper',
'paper', 'future', and also 'summer' and 'hum'. These echoes are
deliberate. Thus also in the following poem:

I read of *Sevastopol*
   by Tolstoy
   in a train going to my village.

This Russian is my contemporary
   though my sky
   is Gaelic.

I hear the guns
   in the holy silence
   of your prose
   which casts its shadows.

Just as it was,
   bravery and cowardice.
   All the aristocrats
   whom I never knew
   in peasant Lewis,
   dying like lilies
   which are unable to bend.

Again I have used phantom rhymes, for instance 'contemporary' and
'sky'. And 'prose', 'shadows', 'was', 'cowardice', 'Lewis', and
'lilies'.

I hope you will see what I am concerned with, that is, that my
poetry was initially a questioning of dogma, often in a question and
answer form and that this required a metrical structure. As time
passed, my concern became quite a different one, not questioning
this or that dogma, but wondering whether dogma is required at all.
Thus looking out at the world can we exist without dogma? These
village poems are notations of the world as I see it. It took me a long
time to write in free verse, as it took Lowell a long time. And in his

comments on Carlos Williams there is, I feel, an admiration for something that he himself was unable to do. Thus beside the work of Carlos Williams, Lowell's poetry sometimes looks scholastic, and the early work willed as if he were a Roman legionary in armour. His last book *Day by Day* was, I think, an attempt to enter the Carlos Williams world, but the critical reception to it showed that he was unable to do so. *Life Studies*, which was very successful, was a half-way house. It had a strict form of its own.

The last thing I should like to talk about is the question of language as it affects my work.

I have to do this since it is a central question.

I have suggested that, perhaps without my knowing it, the Gaelic tradition of verse has affected my work. This is shown in sometimes unconscious assonance, perhaps even in turns of phrase of which I am unconscious but which an English native speaker might notice. Thus as far as he is concerned my poetry might be exotic.

Another way in which the Gaelic tradition has affected my work has been in choice of subject matter such as exile, such as poems about old people, since the area I come from has an ageing population.

However, much deeper than this is the question of language itself. Thus is it the case that I can get the whole of myself into a language which was not originally my own? My own history is that I spoke Gaelic till the age of five and English after that in school and also in areas where I have lived where Gaelic was not spoken. Is there therefore an emotional and intellectual fracturing? Does the fissure created by the two languages suggest that there is a fissure in the poetry itself? It is a question that has greatly troubled me, of course, since poetry perhaps even more than prose is fundamentally a question of language contracted and intensified. The simple question is, Is English really a language I should be writing in?

In actual fact I haven't tried to use deliberate effects in my English poetry that are derived from the Gaelic, as Austin Clarke has done in Ireland. That is to say, he has used effects and structures derived from Irish. I haven't done this. It is of course an area of my work that an outsider might see more clearly than I do.

Thus it is quite possible that my poems of deepest import are derived from the Gaelic world and that the ones of more superficial import derive from my reading in English poetry.

This whole question goes beyond superficial structure towards a deeper structure which I am unable to examine, partly because of ignorance of linguistic theory and partly because I cannot see it myself.

Deeper perhaps than what we consciously do is what we are unconsciously driven by and dictated to. It is this structure that lies perhaps below the other structures that we can manoeuvre, and it is one that interests me extremely.[13]

I should like to exemplify with two poems, one originally in English and one translated from the Gaelic. I have chosen the same subject matter for the two poems. One is a prose translation and the other in verse. They are both poems that I wrote about my mother. Here is the English one:

> She is tougher than me, harder.
> Elephant body on a miniature stool
> keels when rising till the drilled stick
> plants it upright. Rock
> fills the false room
> who has more air about her.
> Kneaded life till good butter.
> Is at seventy not afraid
> of the perished dead
> who spit and rear
>
> snarling at me, not her,
> though forty years younger.
> Not riches do I wish me
> nor successful power.
> This only I admire
>
> to roll the seventieth sea
> as if her voyage were
> to truthful Lewis rising,
> most loved though most bare
> at the end of a rich season.[14]

And here is the English translation of another poem to my mother:

You were gutting herring in distant Yarmouth, and the salt sun in the morning rising out of the sea, the blood on the edge of your knife, and that salt so coarse that it stopped you from speaking and made your lips bitter.

I was in Aberdeen sucking new courses, my Gaelic in a book and my Latin at the tiller, sitting there on a chair with my coffee beside me, and leaves shaking the sails of my intelligence and my scholarship.

Guilt is tormenting me because of what happened and how things are, and I would not like to be getting up in the darkness of the day gutting and tearing the fish of the morning on the shore, and that savage sea to be pouring down my gloves without cease.

Though I do that in my poetry it is my own blood that is on my hands, and every herring that the high tide gave me palpitating till I make a song, and instead of a cooper my language always hard and strict on me, and the coarse salt on my ring bringing animation to death.[15]

Finally I should like to draw your attention, for the second time, to my twin difficulties, the first arising from growing up in a strongly religious background, which thinks of my work as vanity, and the second to my writing in a language which is not originally my own. These twin difficulties I have found a burden. They have also forced me to write about subject matter which might be considered old-fashioned. To me, however, they are not so, for the first has brought me face to face with the mysteries of language. It might even be argued that even my religious obsessions are not perhaps old-fashioned as they might appear when we think of Iran and the rise of Muslim fundamentalism. I perhaps understand these better than others might, though I may not approve of them any more than others do.

It has also led me in some of my portraits of certain characters into an analysis of the human mind which I find infinitely labyrinthine, infinitely devious, setting up various shields against reality. It is this which drives me to novels and short stories.

Also, I try to imagine what a world without dogma would be like, that is a world in which we imagine the human being as part of the passing seasons and his death so. Would it be possible to exist in such a world?

That is the point I have arrived at now. But then again it is possible that art is itself a form of shield, as I once wrote many years ago:

Girl with Orange Sunshade

An orange sunshade wheels about her head.
The sunshade shading sun is yet a sun
mimicked by colour, halo of the red
and mild attendant of the coloured bone.

Yet it is mimic as if the other sun
should not attack her being saved by this
paper not passion which she learns to spin
as if herself were Fortune, pert faced miss.

And this cool wheel about her ordered hair
is like the art we nourish in our rooms
on little water and a jar of air.

It holds us steady from the searing flames.

We mimic fire to shield us from the fire
and shade our heads with bright and paper poems.

Notes

1. See also the extensive comments by Douglas Dunn here, who similarly notes that 'Scottish poetry is so concerned with language that it can seem like a national obsession ...'.
2. See e.g. the poem of the same title in Iain Crichton Smith, *Selected Poems* (Carcanet, 1985), pp.21-2.
3. *Selected Poems*, p.12:

> One would like to be able to write something for them
> not for the sake of the writing but because
> a man should be named in dying as well as living,
> in drowning as well as on death-bed, and because
> the brain being brain must try to establish laws...

4. *Selected Poems*, pp.10-11. The rhyme-scheme can be gathered from the following excerpt (the last two stanzas of the poem):

> I inspect justice through a queer air.
> Indeed he lacks significant ornament.
> Nevertheless he does not laugh or suffer
> though, like pity's cruelty, he too is permanent.
>
> And since I was trapped by pity and the clever
> duplicities of age, my last emolument
> returns, thus late, its flat incurious stare
> on my ambiguous love, my only monument.

5. *Selected Poems*, pp.23-35.

6. *Selected Poems*, p.80:

> Because we'd never go there, it was good,
> those years together. We'd never need to go
> though we could talk of it and so we were
> happy together in a place we'd made
> so small and airless that we couldn't leave…

7. From Section IX of the poem.

8. *Selected Poems*, p.11.

9. First published in *Penguin Modern Poets* 21 (1972).

10. *Selected Poems*, pp.70-4.

11. *Selected Poems*, pp.88-90.

12. 'Farewell my Brother', in *The Village and Other Poems* (Carcanet, 1989).

13. Some of these questions have been addressed by George Steiner, in his tour de force, *After Babel* (OUP, 1975).

14. *Collected Poems* (Carcanet, 1992), pp.33-4.

15. *Selected Poems*, p.45.

A Chev'ril Glove

Anne Stevenson

CLOWN . . . To see this age! A sentence is but a chev'ril glove to a good wit: how quickly the wrong side may be turned outward.

VIOLA Nay, that's certain; they that dally nicely with words may quickly make them wanton.

CLOWN I would therefore my sister had no name, sir.

VIOLA Why, man?

CLOWN Why, sir, her name's a word, and to dally with that word might make my sister wanton.

VIOLA Thy reason, man?

CLOWN Truth, sir, I can yield you none without words, and words are grown so false I am loath to prove reason with them.

Twelfth Night, Act III, Scene 1.

I have been asked to identify some of the structural questions with which I engage when I write poems. How conscious am I of metrical considerations? Are my poems constructed according to 'bonds' of metre and rhythm, or do I pay more attention to sound-affinities and textures? Do I attempt in verse to reproduce the rhythmical structure of colloquial speech? Do I write by phrase or clause, with nouns and adjectives or chiefly with verbs? On what principle do I choose words, seek rhymes, rewrite, revise and in other ways consciously preside over the process of making poetry?

Let me be frank. I do not believe anyone sitting down with a like set of questions could write a poem. At best he might produce a pastiche or an experiment, a poetic exercise. Nor do I think structural considerations can be ignored. Theorists sometimes delight in mystifying the complicated game of language that poets delight to play. And poets are ready enough to make exaggerated claims for the unconscious. The truth is that critics and poets alike have to acknowledge poetry's long, vigorous, independent existence. Every poem worthy of the name is a personal artifice made of public language, and it is only the foolish who refuse to acknowledge that questions of prosody arise immediately the first cadences of a poem have shouldered themselves into existence.

Let me translate that declaration into personal experience. Like many poets, I began to write verse when I was introduced to Shakespeare and the English Romantics as a child. I have no doubt that it was rhythm, the stressed and unstressed undulations of the iambic line, that first bewitched me. In those pre-television days, my mother and father filled companionable evenings at home by reading aloud to us children and to each other. Mother read history and fiction; Father read poetry, and we all took parts in the more accessible of Shakespeare's comedies. My father, who was an amateur musician, read with intelligence and fervour Scott's 'Marion' and 'The Lady of the Lake', Coleridge's 'Ancient Mariner', Arnold's 'The Forsaken Merman' and 'Sohrab and Rustum'; Browning's 'My Last Duchess', Lord Macaulay's 'Horatius at the Bridge'. Then, when I was ten or eleven, I had an English teacher who out of laziness and fondness for the bottle (or so I was told) insisted that we learn poems by heart. One by one, we had to stand up and recite to the class. I discovered that learning poems came easily to me. Before long I was cultivating my reputation as top reciter of sixth grade. Poetry was something I could do, something that in part made up for my woeful inability to understand what was going on in arithmetic.

I began writing ballads and plays when I was twelve or so, but in my teens I became a thorough-going Romantic, imagining fondly that I was an incarnation of the poet Keats, whose odes and sonnets I imitated, along with those (I fear) of Edna St Vincent Millay. I also fancied myself as a composer – with less reason, for although I practised faithfully on the piano and 'cello, I could never commit to five-lined paper more than a tune or two of music.

My first poems were romantically inspired on two counts. I responded instinctively to the rhythms, language and heroic subjects of romantic English verse; and I created an image of myself-as-artist which suspended me in a myth of creative superiority as I drifted through school in my dream of future greatness. Fortunately, I had three excellent English teachers at the University of Michigan High

School in Ann Arbor. They taught me to write prose and (up to a point) to spell; they gave me C's for carelessness and A's for imagination, and they minded not at all if I imitated Shakespeare, writing and directing my own plays. (Nothing was ever said, either explicitly or by implication, about any handicap I might have incurred through the misfortune of having been born female. Such is the advantage some American women of my generation – mainly those who went to co-educational colleges – have over our English contemporaries.)

I graduated in 1950 and entered the university to study not English (I was wary of the subject even then) but music and the humanities. In the same year an anthology was published which challenged some of my ideas about poetry. I still possess a tattered paperback copy of *New Poets of England and America*, edited by Donald Hall and Robert Pack. In it, Auden-like precepts of order, intelligibility, good manners and responsibility for the world outside oneself set the tone for what looked like a twentieth-century return to classicism.

At Michigan, impressed by John Ciardi, the first 'real' poet I'd met, I began to write lyrical poems in the manner of Richard Wilbur (then very popular) and Adrienne Cecile Rich.[1] The latter was at Harvard, a woman a little older than myself, whose first collection won the Yale Series of Younger Poets prize in 1951. Like Sylvia Plath (of whom I then knew nothing) I was both envious and in awe of her. In some early poems, I tried to emulate her suave, disciplined, informal and accessible style. (Adrienne Rich today, of course, views those early successes with feminist contempt.)

During the same years, in the early 1950s, I was working closely with composers, painters, dancers and actors in a students' organisation called the Inter-Arts Union. Most of my literary productions at Michigan were dramatic and eclectic: a masque for dancing in the manner of Ben Jonson, or Yeats; an Auden-like libretto for a one-act opera, *Adam and Eve and the Devil*; lyrics and conversational monologues in the style of Robert Frost. I learned enough Italian to take a course in Dante. Several of my avant-garde contemporaries worshipped Ezra Pound – whom I privately thought a charlatan. Others were wild about Eliot, whose weary sophisticated tone I chose to imitate in preference to the inflamed rhetoric of Dylan Thomas. But particular 'influences' probably mattered less than the ardent excitement a group of us at Michigan experienced as 'artists'. We felt ourselves, my friends and I, to be in the forefront of the modernist movement. The blood jet was not so much poetry as a fountain of unbounded creative energy. I half believed, in those days, that art could save – if not the world, at least me in the world, or me from the world.

Soon after I left the university, I married and moved to England. My enthusiasm for modernism waned as I became painfully acquainted with the realities of English life and culture, and for seven or eight years I was too confused to write anything. A poem called 'The Women' 'slipped idly from me' in Yorkshire in 1956. I sent it to *Poetry Chicago*, where it was published, but it was not until 1961, when I met Donald Hall after returning to Michigan, that I became aware of a new and nourishing climate in American verse. The poets – apart from Hall – to whom I listened when I began to write again were Wallace Stevens, Robert Lowell, Louis Simpson, Marianne Moore and especially Elizabeth Bishop.[2] Elizabeth Bishop's poems pleased me so much I undertook, in 1962, to write a short book on her work for a publisher in New York. My own first book of poems, *Living in America*,[3] owes a great deal to discoveries I made about diction, tone, pitch and content in the course of studying Bishop.

Now Elizabeth Bishop, although famous for her painterly eye, confessed to me herself that, unlike Marianne Moore, she was really an 'umpty-tumpty' poet. A mentor of hers – who became mine – was the seventeenth-century English metaphysical, George Herbert. Miss Bishop was fond of Baptist hymns; she was a fan of ballad metres and folk tunes – see her 'Songs for a Coloured Singer' and 'The Burglar of Babylon'.[4] Besides, she was contagiously in love with the natural world and with mental adventure of all kinds. Without being particularly learned, she was an admirer of Darwin, an amateur expert on contemporary art, a devout reader of cookbooks, a lover of landscape and language, with a mind always ready to be entertained by the sheer quiddity and oddity of the world. In short, she was, for me, a model of Shakespearian workmanship.

Think what a magpie Shakespeare was, picking up scraps and phrases of valuable language from street and tavern, court and countryside, law-book and chronicle. His little Latin and less Greek were inessential items discarded from a huge working stock of English with which he furnished and embellished a mental studio of inconceivable proportions. I like to think of Shakespeare, of poets in general, inhabiting the world like a warehouse, a factory floor full of molten language and malleable forms, who are always a little impatient with the ways of scholars and libraries, who get bored in museums of sacred phrases and run like crazy at the appearance of high-sounding academic theories.

Elizabeth Bishop, to me, was that kind of working poet, and from her, among others, I learned – not how to write poetry, but how to handle the material laid out on the workshop floor. My first 'professional' book, *Reversals*, fell all but dead from an American university press in 1969. Yet I felt that in writing it, I had set myself a standard of economy and skill. Here's a love poem from that early collection. My love poems, I'm afraid, usually reveal feelings of ambiguity. The trick here was to catch a shift of vision in sound as well as word.

Aubade

Intervention of chairs at midnight
The wall's approach, the quirkish ambivalence
of photographs, today in daylight,
mere pieces of balance. My brown dress,
tossed, messed, upheld by the floor.
Rags of ordinary, washed light
draped as to dry on the brown furniture.
And the big bed reposed, utterly white
that ached our darkness, rocked our weight.

You can see that it was important to rhyme, but not always closely: midnight/daylight/white/weight; ambivalence/brown dress; floor/furniture. There is no line-ending that doesn't chime with some other, although the rhyme scheme is irregular. And having been strict with the rhymes, I let the cadences fall where they would, only restricting the lines to four or five stresses each. The metre is loosely iambic/trochaic, but so is the English language generally. The inner rhymes on an *s* sound – pieces, dress, tossed, messed – were arrived at, as it were, accidentally, in the course of writing. I couldn't, of course, have predicted any of the formal features of the poem before it began to sing of itself.

My first English collection (*Travelling Behind Glass*, 1974) included a number of longish, free-verse meditations which rhythmically imitated Auden or Eliot, though now they sound to me more like MacNeice. In sections of a poem called 'England' for instance, the pulse beats are discursively iambic,[5] with lots of enjambement:

Americans like England to live in her cameo,
A dignified profile attached to a past
Understood to belong to her, like the body of a bust.
The image to the native is battered but complete,
The cracked clay flaking, reluctantly sloughed away,
Inadequately renewed on her beautiful bones.

> The stinginess of England. The proliferating ugliness.
> The pale boys, harmful, dissatisfied, groping for comfort
> In the sodium darkness of December evenings.
> Wet roofs creeping for miles along wet bricks.

(I like, even today, to startle the reader with a short, sharp line, set off from a ruminating description or argument.)

> Lovers urgently propping each other on the endless
> Identical pavements in the vacant light
> Where the cars live, their pupilless eyes
> Turned upward without envy or disapproval.

Unfortunately, the original conclusion of 'England' subsided into vague philosophising (I have since revised it). One of the better bits, however, records a mood of nostalgia and resignation by (as I now see but didn't, consciously, then) breaking off the literary syntax and addressing someone (a friend, a lover) directly.

> September. Already autumnal.
> Lost days drift in shapes under the plane trees.
> Leaves tangle in the gutters.
> In Greenwich, in Kew, in Hampstead
> The paths are dry, the ponds dazed with reflections.
> Come with me. Look. The city
> Nourished by its poisons, is beautiful in them.
> A pearly contamination strokes the river
> As the cranes ride or dissolve in it,
> And the sun dissolves in the hub of its own explosion...

The original poem, unsuccessful as it seems to me now, depended for its effect on lyrical cadences I would be hard put to notate. I still write poems by overhearing the rhythms of what I used to call 'inevitable cadences'. I suspect I simply remember the rhythms of poems I learned in childhood, and any violation of those rhythms sounds wrong.

After 1967, when I wrote 'England', I conscientiously tried to break away from an inherited lyrical tradition (abandoning, incidentally, the convention of beginning each line of a poem with an upper-case letter), swinging towards Carlos Williams's colloquial three-line stanza in some of the dramatic monologues of *Correspondences*; working towards a freer, more cursive discipline of line in

Enough of Green.[6] Questions of style are not, of course, matters of choice. The rhythm of what has to be said determines, in the end, how it *will* be said by any particular poet. The lush, visionary poems of *Minute by Glass Minute* [1982], for instance, were dictated both by a state of mind and the landscape of the Wye valley. In *The Fiction-Makers* [1985] I gave rein to a taste for irony and an increasingly strong belief that a clear distinction must be made between art and life.

Many changes of attitude over the years – debates with myself about the place and importance of poetry, of language itself (the central debate, to be sure, of the age we live in) – have not, I think, affected the way I begin working on a poem once a line or a tune has taken root in me. A given rhythm is usually primary,[7] though an idea may hang around for months before it announces the rhythm in which it must be treated.

I am myself, of course, harder to please these days. Instead of being overwhelmed by tidal waves of creation, as when younger, I often have to dig hard for nourishment. In the course of digging one becomes especially conscious of words, and, like Feste in *Twelfth Night*, alert to the two-way relationship they establish with their presumed masters. If there is a difference between my assumptions now and those of twenty-five years ago, it expresses itself in the first poem of *The Fiction-Makers*, which argues (yes, argues) that writing is the medium of cultural memory, but that – like the Heisenberg principle in physics – the very act of recording human experience inevitably distorts it. Fiction, even the records of 'facts' we call history, should not be confused with the vast complex of feelings we apprehend every moment of our lives through our minds and senses. Any part of that three or four-dimensional continuum we call experience we choose to commit to two-dimensional paper (or for that matter, a two-dimensional screen) is fiction-making, however convincingly mimetic.[8] The effect of organised language is to simplify, clarify, define, celebrate, make beautiful or ugly, greater or smaller recognisable physical or psychological events. There is no writing that is more complex than the language it employs, and that language can never be as complicated as the (multitudinously determined) events it describes. In other words, words can never absolutely tell the truth. I played with this notion in a little poem I take as a serious joke.

> The idea of event is horizontal,
> the idea of personality, vertical.

> Let fiction take root
> in the idea of the cross between them.
>
> The mind of the world
> is a vast field of crosses.
> We pick our way through the cemetery
> calling out names and stories.
>
> In the event
> the story is foretold,
> foremade in the code of its happening.
>
> In the event
> the event is sacrificed
> to a fiction of its having happened.

I am unable to describe the feeling of relief that little poem brought to me. It was like springing the lock on a frame of type and watching the letters spill out freely on the table; like being taken backstage in the theatre of human ideas and shown how many ancient props of language and tradition are still flexibly there for us to use and modify and play with. Never mind the anxiety of influence or the awesome presence of sacred texts, dead geniuses, learned theorists and the rest. They all have their place in the perpetual play of human imagination. The figure of the poet, in such a perspective, presents itself in its old, Shakespearean guise – Lear's fool, or Feste the jester, her ladyship's 'corrupter of words' – who quips and sings his way through illusions of hierarchy and power, delusion and treachery, vanity and virtue, with the liberty of a licenced witness. Superficial changes in culture and language over five hundred years or so (less than a second of geological time) have scarcely altered the myth-making, story-making, fiction-making habits we humans so much need and enjoy.

'All the world's a stage,/And all the men and women merely players' declares the poet Jacques in *As You Like It*, wittily undermining those two recurring fictions of civilisation, courtly pomp and pastoral innocence. Yeats sounded the same note towards the end of his life, viewing the human and political crises of his time with eyes 'that are always gay':

> All perform their tragic play,
> There struts Hamlet, there is Lear,
> That's Ophelia, that Cordelia;

> Yet they, should the last scene be there,
> The great stage curtain about to drop,
> If worthy their prominent part in the play,
> Do not break up their lines to weep.
> They know that Hamlet and Lear are gay . . .[9]

It is unfortunate that the word 'gay' has taken on another, specifically sexual connotation in our time; but perhaps here is just another example of how a word can shift in the harness of meaning and turn itself inside out, altering its effect even within the strait-jacket of a famous poem. Words, in short, are the poet's servants and the poet's masters, most useful when they are most alive, fallible and human, but of very little importance when somebody's theory chloroforms them on the page or turns them into textual beasts of burden:

> Irish poets, learn your trade,
> Sing whatever is well made,
> Scorn the sort now growing up
> All out of shape from toe to top . . .[10]

Enough. Since this paper purports to answer questions relating to my own craft, let me conclude by giving you several passages from a poem I wrote a year ago, after a poetry festival in Toronto. I called the poem 'Ward's Island',[11] and it describes a trip I made by ferry from the city to an offshore island on Lake Ontario. Ward's Island was, I'm told, the site of the first trapper's settlement in the area, but it is now – or was a year ago – a public park surrounded by shabby little run-down houses the municipal council is trying to demolish. It was minus eighteen degrees centigrade when I landed on the island, and I walked for about an hour, first inland, and then along the freezing outer shore, where the lapping waves had coated the rounded rocks with ice. I thought at the time, 'this is the end of the world, this is what it will be like.'

I scratched some lines in my notebook on my return trip: 'waves like fishscales/Brutality of the skyscrapers, blunt-topped metal coffins, all of them banks. The five colours of the city's opulence; silver, jet, gold, burgundy, jade. Ward's little island survives, with its down-at heels shanties of clapboard and synthetic brick, broken toys, rusty iron chairs, lonely cat etc. – what sort of community?'

It must have been March when I sat down, finally, to make something of these fragments. One line especially pleased me: 'silver, jet, gold, porphyry, jade' (I substituted 'porphyry' for 'burgundy' so as to keep the mineral imagery consistent). Using it as a rhythmic base, I soon had a stanza:

> A sunny Sunday, cobalt, with feathery clouds.
> Wind at minus eighteen degrees centigrade
> knifing the lake. I felt on my face
> the grinding of its blade. But water tossed light
> like fish scales in our wake, so I stayed on deck
> in my boots and visible breath
> watching the city recede, a rich brocade,
> silver, jet, gold, porphyry, jade.

The poem was clearly going to be longish and discursive, with sharp points of rhyme here and there, internal rhymes (centigrade/blade/recede/brocade), and also end-rhymes. The casual tone would eventually determine, within a loose syntax, what its exact diction should be. I worked for several days to set pace and tone within a framework of firm or near rhymes.

> On the other side, the open side, colder.
> I saw how ice had hugged and hugged each boulder;
> the beach was studded with layered, glittering skulls.
> I kept on walking, with whatever it was I felt –
> something between jubilation and fear.
> There appeared to be no traffic at all
> on that sea no one could see over;
> only to the airport frail, silver insects
> sailed from the beautiful air.

After the absolute rhyme of *colder* and *bolder*, vowel affinities between skulls/felt/all, and of fear/appeared/frail/air, seemed sufficient to sustain the music during this climactic section of the poem. You'll notice a distortion of normal syntax: 'only to the airport frail, silver insects/sailed from the beautiful air.' Think of the banality of writing instead, 'the only activity I could see were silver airplanes, like angels or insects, sailing down from the air.'

I'm afraid I'm delightfully satisfied with the last lines of 'Ward's Island', in which I found I could pursue an ambiguity already established in an earlier stanza by the word 'banks' – that is, banks of the lake and banks full of money. Here are the final lines of the poem:

> Still, I caught the next ferry back.
> A gaunt youth in a baseball cap and two burly men

> settled themselves and their boredom
> in the too hot cabin,
> there to spread newsprint wings and disappear.
> I paced the warmth, rubbing life into my hands.
> The city advanced to meet us, cruel and dear.

Here, not only was I able to refer obliquely to the ethereal planes – those silver insects sailing from the air – by making these bored men 'spread newsprint wings', but I could use a colloquial expression, 'rub life into my [freezing] hands' to indicate the preciousness of life. And the final line is ambiguous on two counts: 'The city advanced to meet us, cruel and dear': 'advanced' describes the apparent movement of the city towards the ferry as it nears the harbour; at the same time, the word suggests that the city is 'advanced', is in an advanced state of civilisation. The words, 'cruel and dear' of course, play with the advantages and disadvantages of advanced living; 'dear' means expensive as well as loved and precious – which is precisely the kind of ambiguity I longed to express during the actual experience of travelling to the island.

I have to say that I think the poem succeeds. It records an actual experience and the emotion that experience induced. And it does so by playing with language, or by letting a few words have their heads in a play of meaning. In writing 'Ward's Island' I was lucky. I lay no claim to any special gift or 'genius'. On the contrary, I know that in comparison to other more fluent, fertile talents, my slow mind plods and stutters. Nevertheless, as I once wrote in 'Making Poetry', when poets are in the 'habit' of language – when we're alert and rhythmically fit – then with prayers to patience and luck we can sometimes produce good poems.

And why inhabit, make, inherit poetry?

> Oh, it's the shared comedy of the worst
> blessed; the sound leading the hand;
> a wordlife running from mind to mind
> through the washed rooms of the simple senses;
> one of those haunted, undefendable, unpoetic
> crosses we have to find.[12]

Notes

1. E.g. Adrienne Rich, *The Diamond Cutters* (1951). Richard Wilbur, *The Beautiful Changes* (1947); *Ceremony* (1950).

2. Elizabeth Bishop, *Poems, North and South – A Cold Spring* (1955). Anne Stevenson, *Elizabeth Bishop* (Twayne's U.S. Author Series, 1966).

3. Stevenson, *Living in America* (U. Michigan: Generation Press, 1965).

4. In Bishop, *The Complete Poems* (Farrar, Strauss and Giroux, 1983). 'Songs for a Coloured Singer' (p.53) begins

> A washing hangs upon the line,
>   but it's not mine.
> None of the things that I can see
>   belong to me.
> The neighbors got a radio with an aerial;
>   we got a little portable.
> They got a lot of closet space;
>   we got a suitcase...

'The Burglar of Babylon' may be found on pp.132-39 ('On the fair green hills of Rio/ There grows a fearful stain:/ The poor who come to Rio/ And can't go home again').

5. To my ear, at least, there are also triple-time cadences here; see also Fleur Adcock's comments on recognition of 'inner' rhythms.

6. *Correspondences* (OUP, 1974); *Enough of Green* (OUP, 1977). The latter represents an important transitional volume in Anne Stevenson's work.

7. A point made by several of the poets represented here – see e.g. the essays by Adcock, Scupham, and Sisson.

8. On mimesis ('the interpretation of reality through literary representation or "imitation"') see Erich Auerbach (trans. Willard R. Trask) *Mimesis* (Princeton University Press, 1953). On the symbolism (or 'fiction-making') of both verbal and pictorial art and its possible genesis in the physiology of the brain, see also J.Z. Young, *Programs of the Brain* (OUP, 1978), ch.20.

9. W.B. Yeats, 'Lapis Lazuli'; from *Last Poems* (1936-39).

10. W.B. Yeats, 'Under Ben Bulben'; from *Last Poems*.

11. In Anne Stevenson, *The Other House* (OUP, 1990), pp.50-1.

12. In *The Fiction-Makers*, p.29.

Am I doing it right?

Jeffrey Wainwright

Introduction

I suspect that a famous adolescent anxiety is never very far from a poet's mind, and looms very large when called upon to reflect on the details of practice. It is: 'Am I doing it right?' I think that the extremely various expansion of poetry in the English-speaking world in this century may have exacerbated this. From California to the Caribbean to Africa to Orkney there are more and more poetic constituencies and correspondingly more poetics inspired by different cultural reference-points and social circumstances. On the other hand the progressivist imperatives of modernism – 'Make it New!' – have inculcated a notion that there must be a single line forward, one way in which contemporary poetry ought to be written. So, inasmuch as a poet consciously seeks a method, he or she is aware of a complicated plurality, and that one or several parts of it might be helpfully suggestive, or perhaps offer the best way to proceed, or even the only 'modern' way to proceed. The anxiety is that one may have been insufficiently diligent seeking it out, or too obtuse or limited to appreciate what stares one in the face. Whether the omniscient meta-history provided by the increasingly professionalised institution of criticism is helpful I'm not sure. A goodly part of it insists that the bumpkin poet can't know what he or she is doing anyway. That has to be a comfort, for if one is only filling an attic that will in turn fill the Portakrush of History then one is only obeying orders.

But despite these inhibitions, I am asked to give some account of my procedures in writing poems and I have agreed to do so. That implies more transparency towards intention than realistically exists. But we surely all recognise that we are working pragmatically here, and that in matters of human communication it is the only way we can work.

In thinking about these procedures I became aware of one overriding issue which might be said to lie beneath most of what follows. It is the potential conflict between two desires: one being to say what I have to say (though that of course only emerges in the attempt to say it), and the desire to make an impressive poem, to manipulate words to that end, or the willingness to be manipulated by words to that end. This is not an original issue of course. Nor is it an issue confined to poetry. It is at the shifting base of all rhetoric, even of all conversation. Dante saw it very simply as the character of human language: 'based on the senses because it makes use of sound and... based on reason because it communicates meaning'.[1] But because of the deliberation and evident formalities of poetry, it is especially prominent there. The prominence of word-sound, rhythm and metre dramatises the confluence or conflict of the two desires: for solidity of reference and for the sensuous pleasures of language. Perhaps that is why that much despised question about the poet's 'sincerity' comes up so much.

In the following detail I shall pursue, with a disappointing doggedness, the programme suggested to me. It falls into three main sections: sound structure and metrics; syntax; and lexis.

Sound Structure and Metrics

The line has become the defining characteristic of poetry,[2] so where the line turns is obviously of great importance for me. But before that becomes established, the genesis of a poem might lie, as the rubric has it, in 'purely rhythmic suggestions'.

For example, 'Before Battle'[3] began in a fragment I read about an English Civil War battle which used the metaphor of soldiers approaching the field of imminent conflict like reapers, with the crucial phrase being 'descend, like reapers'. The movement downwards, and then the sweep suggested in 'reapers', is the stimulus of the poem. The two lines containing that phrase have a simple pattern of movement: rise... embrace... descend. My sense of the whole poem is at bottom rhythmical. The rhetoric which is the poem's subject is seeking for a resolution, point of rest and accomplishment which it cannot really attain, and the tension of that striving, or the effort of the poem's speaker to convince himself, is meant to be mimed rhythmically.

In scanning that poem for these purposes I noted that the lines have a variable stress metre with some lines going up to twelve syllables, save for the last line which can be scanned as an iambic pentameter, albeit one with a weak third stress ('our'). After the fact, I would rationalise this as trying to represent the composure of a final, reassuring statement in the composure of even, conventional metre. It is meant to read earnestly and ironically.

Another poem which I recall as being fired by 'purely rhythmic suggestions' is the opening of 'Illusory Wars':

> Ambassadors, generals, secretaries for war
> Have done so much to get themselves so far
> And they weep...[4]

An idea for the poem came from a phrase (see its epigraph[5]) from Barbara Tuchman's *August 1914*: 'Tears came even to the most bold and resolute', and I felt a rhythmical impulse to accelerate through to climactic closure, '... And they weep', especially after the brisk rattling along of the second line. I had this rhythm before I had the words.

I'm asked about the dangers of metre producing a 'merely mechanical fluency', but not enough of my verse is strictly metrical to provide an answer. The line emerges from a combination of the demands made by the rhythmical suggestions, and another equally vague sense of overall shape and patterning for the poem.

This may be a way of describing the verse as predominantly 'free'. But often I am drawn also by an attraction towards symmetrical patterns of line length and stanza shape, and the composition of sequential sequences, and these influence where the line recurrently turns.[6] Every line I write is sounded out aloud, yet soon after beginning a poem I am likely to have a determining notion of how the poem will look on the page.

This means that I am likely to work, at least by rule of thumb, with syllables more than with metre – though usually in poems with a longer verse line. I use syllables as a frame, a discipline to work with and against. Recurrence of one sort and another is basic to verse, and besides stanza and sectional formations, I like to work often with equivalence of line length. This might often mean a roughly ten-syllable line because – as I am not the first to note – its ambit has a flexibility which can include gestural effects with a discursive, near conversational naturalism, the qualities which of course proved necessary for dramatic verse.[7]

The verse is free, but not strictly so. Eliot himself noted that free verse worked off an approximation to metred verse. Clive Wilmer, reviewing Timothy Steele's book *Missing Measures*, underlines the point: 'Most of *The Waste Land*, for instance, is written in a loosened blank verse derived from the Jacobean dramatists; and the verse of William Carlos Williams's early lyrics is based on an accentual measure with roots in Anglo-Saxon versification.'[8] It has always seemed to me that metre is most interesting at its moments of irregularity. (There are so many variables at work in word sounds anyway that the supposedly identical, even alternations of, say, iambic metre are close to illusory.) The short lyric 'Love in the Arms of Death'[9] is as regular as anything I have written (it uses rhyme, too). It moves (as it turns out) in and out of trochaic and iambic feet, the first change, in line one, produced by a pause after the initial gain of attention so as to emphasise the next important word, 'arms'. The second stanza trips along in regular iambics until the irregularity at the end of line three, where that extra unstressed syllable enables the change that stresses 'Kinder'. That change, irregular as it is (and even crudely enabling the rhyme), feels important to me for the rhythm of the poem.

At other times I want much more roughness, strain, dissonance even, perhaps in the manner of old accentual metres that bat a few strong stresses through a long line. The opening of 'Illusory Wars, 1984' is an example:

> *Un* and *im* – unimaginable, unwageable,
> Unprofitable, improbable – will
> Keep us calm.

In line one there are only four stresses in thirteen syllables, in line two, two stresses in ten.

Sound effects and textures

Robert Pinsky writes about 'the bodily role of the sounds of language', and of 'what I could feel the consonants and vowels doing inside my mouth and my ear'.[10]

I confess a predilection for pronounced verse, even for a recitation quality which can border on the orotund. I suspect it dates from the early part of my literary education, where public recitation and choral speaking figured largely and included such dubious classics as Vachel Lindsay's 'Congo' and Chesterton's 'The Battle of Lepanto'. That was followed by school acting, mainly Shakespeare, all declamatory, hitting the back wall with as much e-nun-ci-a-tion as possible. Out of the A-level books came the big moments of Wordsworth ('a motion and a spirit that impels') and Milton ('for Lycidas your sorrow is not dead, sunk though he be beneath the watery floor'). And, inevitably, though just as inevitably soon sniffily rejected, Dylan Thomas.

These obvious features have always been important to me and a key problem is therefore how to fulfil that longing without ridiculous inflation. After three or four hours' concentrated work on half a dozen lines or so it's easy to summon enough sonority to convince yourself something's good. You just have to be sure you keep looking at it coldly as well.

Perhaps this liking accounts for my being drawn to personae which give the excuse for an oratorical voice – George III, for instance, or Thomas Müntzer. The third section of 'Thomas Müntzer' shows this close to full volume.[11] Not much of my verse seems to me obviously 'conversational'. Even in a poem like 'The Swimming Body', where the lines are scattered with 'as I say' and 'moving briskly', 'some . . . or other', 'spending some time', it seems I still want to get on to the big number, reached at last with the end of Part IV.[12]

I do however worry about this emotive style. 'Heart's Desire' dramatises this. The sequence mixes a lyric element which is emotional, expressive, pathetic, with an ironic or sceptical element which is knowing, guarded and prosaic. Sandwiched between 'Illumination' and 'Love in the Arms of Death' comes the enumerated prose lesson of 'Some Propositions and Part of a Narrative'. The combination is nervous and uneasy. Not knowing which way to turn for certain, the sequence perpetually watches its back. It is the poetic versus the solid, history and the real versus poetry, 'tall talk' versus plain talk.

Syntax

Do I manipulate syntax to create particular effects?

Yes.

The first of 'Five Winter Songs' would be an obvious example:

> Flower mornings
> Of coldest winter
> Remember my child
> Born in the frost
> Asleep in the frost
>
> Cold December
> Clear iron mornings

> The sky from darkness
> Pours down flowers
> Made there for you
>
> Remember my child
> Born in the frost
> Arm by his face
> Stretched out he sleeps
> Sleeps in the frost[12]

There is no punctuation in those lines other than stanza grouping, and the intention is to emphasise the urgency of vocative exclamation by mixing the phrases almost, but not quite, in defiance of syntax.

But even in 'exclamatory' mode, as opposed to discursive, most of these poems are built in conventionally recognisable sentences. The choice of syntactic arrangement does, I think, reflect particular thought patterns, or rather the genesis of the thought in some rhythmical suggestion (as above) forces a given syntactical arrangement forward. For an 'exclamatory' poem the sentences seem to be slab-like and reiterative. Development is minimal. They almost mark time with appositions. The little group of poems called 'Sea Dreams' work like this.[13]

But I also get intense pleasure from elaborated syntax, from *articulation* (I love the word!) such as that in Shakespeare's Sonnets:

> Thus vainly thinking that she thinks me young,
> Although she knows my days are past the best,
> Simply I credit her false-speaking tongue,
> On bothe sides thus is simple truth supprest...

or Marvell's 'The Coronet'. I will work syntax across the line in an attempt to create an interesting tension between that rhythm that defines the line and that which drives a coherent sentence. There is a various array of devices available in conventional punctuation, end-stops, rhythmic pauses, run-ons, mid-line stops. I've illustrated that last feature in 'Illusory Wars, 1984', and here is another long sentence across several lines that has a movement I like, from 'The Dead Come Back':

> Thus among the tablecloths and cakes,
> The ham and sliced tongue and all the objects

> Of this earth,
> The company known and unknown at this latest funeral,
> Lily, large and powdered in her flowery dress
> Appears to her brothers and all of us
> Like a star, a celebrity back among her own,
> Nearly a sister again, nearly an aunt,
> All of us parting for her, shy of touching
> What we have brought to mind.

The main clause, 'Lily .. appears', comes centrally in that passage surrounded by its subordinate clauses. The build-up of those, and then the movement away again from the main clause provides a trajectory which I hope is rhythmically interesting while it packs in a lot of almost randomly different detail and action – the kind of odd simultaneity that a dream provides.

I have however only rarely run sentences across stanzas or sections – mainly because (as above) their shapes, visually as much as anything, are an important part of the poem's composition and so they need separate integrity.

Short lyrics hardly ever go across stanza divisions, but for particular purpose I do run across the three-line verses which comprise 'Thomas Müntzer':

> I see my brother crawling in the woods
> To gather snails' shells. *This is not*
> *A vision.* Look carefully and you can tell
>
> How he is caught in the roots of a tree
> Whose long branches spread upwards bearing as
> Fruit gardeners and journeymen, merchants
>
> And lawyers, jewellers and bishops,
> Cardinals chamberlains nobles princes
> Branch by branch kings pope and emperor.

This is to enable an acceleration, but more than that, to mime the entanglement and layered continuity of the image as it scales towards its climax. This kind of run-over is more common in 'The Red-Headed Pupil' so far, moving on occasion across its sections.[14] There is an unresolved issue here between sectional sequence and discursive continuity.

A final question I'm asked about syntax is whether my poems are predominantly 'phrasal' or 'clausal'. I must confess I wasn't sure. Tactfully reminded, however, that the question is whether most syntactic/semantic work is done by nouns, adjectives etc., or by finite verbs, I've tentatively discovered the latter – clausal – domination.

An early poem like '1815' relies on heavy, terse, finite sentences:

> Above her face
> Dead roach stare vertically
> Out of the canal.
> Water fills her ears,
> Her nose her open mouth.
> Surfacing, her bloodless fingers
> Nudge the drying gills.

Adjectival and adverbial addition is there but it aims to be solid and unshowy. At this time 'Water fills her ears/ Her nose her open mouth' was a model of hard plainness, impersonality in the modernist sense ('two gross of broken statues . . . a few thousand battered books').

Later the sentences have sometimes become longer and more elaborate, as in this much more discursive passage from the end of 'The Swimming Body':

> What the mind makes of anything comes of how
> The body's made, as through the limb of sight,
> Or what it touches and what touches it,
> Like this water slipping past, happening
> Outside the brain but not simply arriving there
> To be noticed but already having joined us
> At the skin. This is the border of the world,
> The edge of space, the tireless lapping
> Of the thought of truth, the pulse of death,
> The simple outline of the self – here, and
> Here, and here – the edge of inventing the idea
> Of itself
> Of what it is and what it might be
> Of what is is and what it might be
> And so on and so on and so on.
> Everything comes by the body and is streaked by it.

This is the section where all pretence at easy conversationality is cast aside in favour of that big number I referred to above. My sense of what is important in this passage is the movement of the rather complex, slightly hectic, maybe not quite finite sentences. It seems therefore clausal, though it is possible that such effects as there are come more from some phrasal moments; perhaps 'limb of sight', the water slipping and lapping, skin, pulse, edge, streaked. It depends what is meant by 'work done'.

Lexis

Pragmatically we have to assume the 'choice' that my brief refers to. In theory one is operating a conscious process of selection of words appropriate to 'what one wants to say'. The somewhat erratic nature of 'purely rhythmical suggestion' already suggests some 'automatic' quality which might compromise choice, and then of course words prove famously nepotistic – they are always putting their relatives forward: others beginning with the same letter, or with kindred vowel sounds, or those they rub along with in semantic clusters, or discover in extended metaphors, or other long-lost association. They come bearing gifts: the impressive poem.

Ideally, by a mixture of deliberation, intuition, surrender and second-guessing all this pushiness might be turned to account. The most important lexical interest for me concerns the depths or resonances of words, their coagulations of ambiguity and association, their play both in the sportive sense, but even more in the sense of tolerance.

I tend to be more interested in the familiar than the rare. I have been fixated with mining familiar phrases so as to explore how their reference can be extended or carry an ironic or pathetic weight. In this I acknowledge Geoffrey Hill's influence in that part of his work Christopher Ricks described in his early essay 'Cliché and Responsible Speech'.[15] Here is the method, an early example, the second stanza of '1815 I':

> The graves have not
> A foot's width between them.
> Apprentices, jiggers, spinners
> Fill them straight from work,
> Common as smoke.

> Waterloo is all the rage:
> Cool and iron and wool
> Have supplied the English miracle.

Going somewhere 'straight from work' is given a heavier import here, as is the familiar disparagement 'common as [muck]'; the pun on 'rage', and the resonance of an economic vocabulary of supply and demand applied to miracle are all part of the intended effects. The same word-play operates in the second poem of '1815': 'no flies on Wellington', that is, he's not slow and stupid, or dead.

Another, later, instance of this kind of deliberate lexical loading is in 'Illusory Wars 1984'. It begins by a play which isolates the morphemes *un* and *im* to see them as rhetorical in themselves. Then an echo of the cliché 'keep calm', and, developing one of the motifs of the sequence, 'only pretend', as in 'let's pretend', 'play pretend'. Buried in the word 'infantryman' is the word 'infant', and 'clamber' and 'sticky' are also words that collocate with childhood.[16] In the third stanza the garden image from earlier in the sequence recurs with the garden twine – an effort to associate the ordinary and intimate ground-level reality with the geostrategy of the cold war. The hint of nuclear submarines manoeuvring under the polar ice, and the possibility of mutual destruction, gives me the familiar cliché 'all in the same boat' to work with. Also, to increase the resonance, I've adapted a recalled verse from Pound's 'Homage to Sextus Propertius', plagiarising his rhythmic reiteration:

> Moving naked over Acheron,
> Upon the one raft, victor and conquered together,
> Marius and Jugurtha together,
> > one tangle of shadows.

There is more of this kind of play in the poem with the paradox of 'The histories of future fiction . . .'.

'Illusory Wars' is a heavily managed poem even by my standards. Rejection and replacement of words in this instance focused a good deal upon loading but not overloading. So, among others, I rejected: 'hulls scraping by under the ice'; 'unthink war, leave to/in the imagination/With dollypeg periscopes and the broomstick bofurs gun'; the sapper once 'wormed' his way from the roadside drain; the lagoon was once, meltingly, 'lost' before it was simply 'warm'.

One of the attractions of writing poetry for me is its deliberation. Its accepted formal restraints, even if they are invented rather than inherited, require a period of keeping one's counsel, holding one's tongue. It should be the opposite of glibness. But then it should be right.

This exercise obviously gives the impression of high deliberation and self-awareness. But it is a very partial and misleading impression. How much can I know, or honestly confront about composition? For all the demonstrations of rhythmic variation, I would have to have a very unforgiving ear not to deceive myself that in fact I may have a very limited repertoire of beat. Contingency, half or wholly unrecognised pressures in the language at large, and poetic forms and traditions in particular, exert influence that may exceed conscious effort. W.S. Graham's compelling question: 'What is the language using us for?'[17] is never far away. Nevertheless, *quod scripsi scripsi*. I have to take responsibility for what I have written. I might have done better.

Notes

1. Summary of *De vulgaria eloquentia* in William Anderson, *Dante the Maker* (Routledge, 1980 & Hutchinson, 1983), p.176.
2. See also the notes to C.H. Sisson's essay, particularly the note on 'rhythmical' verse as distinct from 'metrical verse'. One could of course always argue that in verse that is 'merely' rhythmical (i.e. non-metrical) then the line has a graphic, rather than a phonological, identity; but one might also wish to argue that the cadences of *vers libre* might be further determined by their isomorphism (or lack of it) with other intonational or syntactic constituents.
3. See Jeffrey Wainwright, *Selected Poems* (Carcanet, 1985), p.53:

> Our precious earth has borne us on her breast all night.
> We rise and leave her, embrace each lovely comrade,
> And descend, like reapers to the battle place.
>
> The cries that come and so break up the air dissolve.
> Tomorrow dances on a field of peace,
> Phlox, carnation, chamomile.
> We wade so deep in our desire for good.

4. *Selected Poems*, pp.34-6.
5. The full epigraph runs as follows:

> Lord Esher delivered lectures on the lesson of *The Great Illusion*...A twentieth century war would be on such a scale, he said, that its inevitable consequences of commercial disaster, financial ruin and individual suffering would be 'so pregnant with restraining influences' as to make war unthinkable.
>   Tears came even to the most bold and resolute.
>
>   Barbara Tuchman, *August 1914*

6. From a quite different perspective, Peter Scupham also notes the attraction of graphic patterns, particularly where these are realisations of rhythmical shapes.

7. While it is certainly true that the ten-syllable line may lend itself to 'conversational naturalism', another reason for the persistence and utility of this form may be that it allows for an escape from dupleness, i.e. from discrete rhythmical or metrical groups of two, four, eight etc. Since stress in English depends on binary contrasts of strong and weak, it follows that the ten-syllable line will often 'naturally' structure itself into a stress-timed five-beat grouping. Since five is indivisible by two, it must then follow that the decasyllable both includes a potential for naturalism, and also resists it.

8. Timothy Steele, *Missing Measures* (Univ. Arkansas Press, 1990); Clive Wilmer's review appeared in the *TLS*, 1 February 1991. See also Chris McCully, 'Missing measures and the matter of metre', *PN Review* Vol. 17, No. 3, pp. 42-5.

9. From *Heart's Desire* (1978). In *Selected Poems*, p.75:

> Look at love in the arms of death,
> So nearly won by his slender hands.
> How he catches her rising breath
> And robes her body where she stands.
>
> He turns his head to weep for her
> – His love is plain for all to see.
> She finds within his touch a lover
> Kinder than any man could be.

10. Robert Pinsky, *Poetry and the World* (The Ecco Press, 1988), pp. 159, 30. See also Grevel Lindop's comments on the kinaesthetic qualities of verse, and verse composition.

11. *Selected Poems*, pp.54-60.

12. *Selected Poems*, pp.20-6.

13. *Selected Poems*, pp.17-19.

14. Published in *PN Review* Vol. 17, No.6 (July/August 1991).

15. Christopher Ricks's essay, 'Cliché and responsible speech', was reprinted as 'Clichés' in *The force of poetry* (Clarendon Press, 1984), pp.356-68.

16. 'Illusory Wars III/ 1984':

> *Un* and *im* – unimaginable, unwageable,
> Unprofitable, improbable – will
> Keep us calm. Perhaps the dead of those wars
> Only pretend: an infantryman clambers
>
> From a sticky field, a sapper rises
> From a roadside drain, like pearl-divers
> Able seamen kick back to the sun
> And bob by their children in the warm lagoon...

17. W.S. Graham, *Collected Poems 1942-1977* (Faber & Faber 1979), p.191.

The Way it Happens

Fleur Adcock

I'm occasionally embarrassed by a poem of mine which has found its way into a number of anthologies and been studied in schools: if I'd known so many people were going to read it I'd have tried to make it better in the first place. I suppose this retrospective wish is comparable with that of the ninety-year-old jazz musician who said that if he'd known he was going to live so long he'd have taken better care of his health: why am I complaining? And anyway, apart from tidying up a few awkward phrases and getting rid of an adjective or two, how could I have made the poem 'better'? I can write only what I can write; it would take a different poet to do it differently.

In talking about how I do it I'll begin with the question of rhythm, because this is the one crucial factor which distinguishes poetry from other forms of writing.[1] It was rhythm which seduced me into liking poetry in the beginning: clearly identifiable rhythms at first, in my early childhood, when I fell for nursery rhymes and Sunday School hymns and the Georgian poets my mother read to me at bedtime; and then, in my teens, the more subtle rhythms of poets I was taught at school or discovered for myself: Milton, Blake, Donne, Eliot. (It's sometimes hard to separate rhythm from tone, in its effects. I remember being transported, at about fourteen, by the poignancy of Blake's line in *The Book of Thel*: 'Art thou a Worm? Image of weakness, art thou but a Worm?' I'd repeat it to myself until it seemed to be nothing *but* rhythm; but perhaps it was the tender, pitying tone which so appealed to me. Whereas in Milton's lines 'Sabrina fair,/ Listen where thou art sitting/Under the glassy, cool, translucent wave' I was aware of the rhythm, but it was the verbal music of vowels and consonants which carried the charge. To talk of one element in isolation is always a little risky.[2])

In my own writing I'm always conscious of the rhythm, without necessarily being always in control of it; quite often my feeling is that a poem is being dictated to me, rather than by me, particularly in the early stages of composition.[3] The metrical form, or the shape on the page, isn't usually determined by a conscious act. It is not in my nature to sit down, like Gavin Ewart, with the deliberate intention of writing, say, a set of stanzas in the form of 'The Wreck of the Deutschland'; nor should I be likely to compose a long verse satire in ottava rima. My endeavours tend to be more spasmodic and unpredictable. Like most of the poets I know, I have to rely on what I can only call inspiration for the genesis of a poem. What seems to happen is this: a phrase arrives in my head, usually when I'm in a relaxed dreamy state – quite commonly when I'm about to fall asleep or have just woken up, times when the barriers between the conscious and the unconscious mind are at their most permeable. This 'given' phrase (which almost always turns out to be the first line of the poem, but can occasionally end up somewhere in the middle of it or at the end) contains, as it were, a genetic fingerprint of what is to follow: the rhythm of the phrase indicates the rhythm and to some extent the tone, shape, texture, and even the length of the finished poem; these qualities are all wrapped up in those initial few words, as the embryo of a plant is wrapped up in a seed, and it is my job to nurture and encourage the seed until it expands into its final form.

It doesn't always work, of course – there are aborted beginnings, as well as completed poems which really ought to have been aborted. Sometimes what has gone wrong is the rhythm, my perception of which (unless I'm using a strictly metrical form) can vary according to my mood and the pace at which I'm thinking; there are times when I get up in the morning, read through the previous night's work, and find that the stresses have mysteriously shifted while I was asleep. Long, packed lines are particularly vulnerable to such transformations, and often need extra work before I can be happy with them. (One of many reasons why I don't enjoy hearing other people reading my poems is that they sometimes stress a line differently from the way I had in mind, distorting what had seemed to me the natural way of speaking it. This would matter less if I hadn't taken care over the rhythm in the first place.)

This may be the place to insert a parenthetical complaint about the dismal fact that fewer and fewer people these days seem able to *hear* rhythms other than the most thumpingly monotonous ones.[4] I'm not thinking merely of the old buffers in audiences at poetry readings who get up at question time and ask me why I don't write like Kipling, but of students and other young people who seem genuinely unable to recognise quite obvious patterns of rhythm in poetry.

Teachers have wondered whether this deficiency is caused by the emphasis on free verse in schools, and the fact that pupils are no longer required to learn poetry by heart; or perhaps it has something to do with the dulling of the senses by pop music. Apparently there is a condition, on a par with colour-blindness and the inability to tell left from right, in which people are constitutionally unable to recognise rhythms of any kind; but unless some mutation has caused an epidemic of 'rhythm-deafness' the problem must be culturally induced. I find it depressing to suspect that the subtle, often slightly off-beat rhythms which so seduce my ear are largely inaudible except to other poets – and not always to them: at the risk of sounding like an old buffer myself, I must say that a few of the younger poets recently promoted by leading publishers seem to me to have given no thought at all to what their poems sound like.

Back to my own work, and the choice between free and metrical forms. I can't state a preference – as I said, each poem brings its own form with it – but in reviewing my practice I can see that my poems nearly always have some skeleton of formal structure, however rudimentary and however unapparent to the casual glance. (I'm thinking here of the misguided 1960s' fashion for syllabics, a pointless form if ever there was one, but a prop to those of us who felt insecure about writing in free verse and found that the chore of counting syllables felt comfortingly like work. My excessively anthologised poem 'Against Coupling',[5] which people take to be a product of recent feminist sympathies but which actually dates from 1969 or 1970, is composed in a strict syllabic form, with each stanza repeating the same sequence of line-lengths.)

Free verse seems to me the purest type of verse, in that its rhythms are entirely innate and inherent in the phrases which make it up.[6] It has no rules by which to adjust them. I find it extremely difficult to write, because you can never be reassured by external considerations that you've got it right. This may be why very few of my poems avoid falling into stanzas of some kind or taking on a pattern of more or less regularly stressed lines. The few which manage to be entirely 'free' are usually short, reflecting my difficulty in sustaining the impulse, and tend to be haunted, middle-of-the-night pieces, arising directly from the subconscious. 'Things' is an example, so are 'The Net' and 'Foreigner', both of which are based on dreams[7]; in the case of 'Foreigner' the first line, 'These winds bully me', describes what my waking self could hear outside my Arvon Centre hut in Devon very early one morning, while the following three lines, 'I am to lie down in a ditch/quiet under the thrashing nettles/and pull the mud up to my chin', represent a slide back into the dream.

My most sustained example of subconsciously dictated free verse, though, is an earlier poem, 'Over the Edge'[8]; I wrote the first eight lines of this in the middle of the night, without putting the light on, and then went back to sleep; I was considerably surprised, next morning, to find the sheet of straggly, wavering handwriting lying on my bedside table. I then had to decide whether it was a poem, and worth keeping. After some reflection I realised that it was a kind of threnody for several of my great-aunts and uncles who had died in New Zealand while I was on the other side of the world. This seemed to justify it; so without further amendment beyond punctuation I added a final line and a title. The results read like this:

> All my dead people
> seeping through the riverbank where they are buried
> colouring the stream pale brown
> are why I swim in the river,
> feeling now rather closer to them
> than when the water was clear,
> when I could walk barefoot on the gravel
> seeing only the flicker of minnows
> possessing nothing but balance.

That was written in the early 1970s, in what perhaps I could call my middle period (it depends on how many there are going to be!). It's important to stress how much I feel my style has changed over the years. People sometimes tell me that I have a distinctive voice – that they recognise my poems as being by me – but if that is so I find it vaguely depressing: I'd prefer to think that I've developed and that I can take readers by surprise. One of the most cheering comments on my work that I can remember was that of an editor who said of some poems he was accepting 'These don't sound like you at all.' I'll come back to this question of stylistic change later – it's more a matter of diction than of rhythm and form, although it involves those too.

At this point I feel a certain pressure to say something about the line-break, and what principles lead me to break lines where I do (I'm quoting the set of questions I was asked to consider). Unfortunately I have nothing to say about the line-break. Some years ago I was asked to contribute to a symposium on 'The Line' conducted by an American magazine; I had nothing to say then either, but I managed to waffle for a page or so, and they politely accepted it. The truth is that I don't operate in terms of principle, or at least not in a prescriptive way. I can analyse practices, mine or those of other writers, and deduce principles retrospectively from this, but when I'm writing it would be false to pretend that my line-breaks are decreed by anything but instinct. I do have certain principles (or prejudices) in the area of euphony, such as not beginning a word with the same consonant as the previous word ended with, and not producing clusters of clotted syllables which are awkward to pronounce. These are prohibitions – 'don'ts' rather than 'dos' – and they may be ignored if the intention of the poem seems to require it. The commands come from within the developing structure of the work itself; it's a question of matching sounds to the mood and tone of what is being said. In some ways I suspect I'm a lazy writer: I'll take trouble over rhyme and metre, but I don't go out of my way to construct other types of sound-effect or to add alliteration and such devices (except when I'm writing texts for music or when I'm translating poems in the originals of which these effects occur; these two activities are not unrelated to my own poetry, but I'll leave further discussion of them until later).

I suppose it's becoming obvious that I believe strongly in the authority of the voice inside my head (which is an aspect of my own physical voice, although it takes on other personae and accents). On the whole the voice speaks colloquial English of the age I live in. This affects the rhythmical structure of what I write, even when I'm using a strict metrical form. More often, though, it dictates a looser, more flexible type of verse, based on stress rhythms, with lines of roughly equal length, usually divided in stanzas of anything from two to eight lines. Sometimes these are self-contained and sometimes not, and there are other possible variations, such as the presence or absence of rhyme.

Some examples may be helpful. First, a strictly metrical rhymed form. In 1983 I heard that a friend of mine, Peter Laver, had died at the age of thirty-six while walking up Scafell. This was a great shock, and I felt rather guilty to discover that the news almost immediately provoked the idea for a poem – which seemed an almost cold-bloodedly selfish reaction to his death. Two things made it irresistible. The last time I'd seen Peter, in a small and hilarious gathering of friends at his cottage in Grasmere, he had amused us all by reading extracts from volumes of *The Keepsake*, the nineteenth-century annual coffee-table anthology, and had given me a copy of the 1835 edition. Now the book had suddenly become an actual keepsake, something to treasure in memory of him: there was my title. As for my first line, the 'given' line to set the whole thing off, that was his inscription in the fly-leaf: I had insisted that he shouldn't give the book away outright – 'Just make it permanent loan', I'd said, speaking as a former librarian to an actual one (he was in charge of the Wordsworth Library). What he wrote was slightly more archaic, a little more elegantly in keeping with the age of the book: 'To Fleur from Pete, on loan perpetual.' 'Perpetual' carried resonances for me – *nox perpetua* in Catullus – and the phrase was a perfect iambic pentameter, which gave me the metre for the poem. I was hooked.

The fact that I soon found myself using a rather complicated rhyme-scheme, six-line stanzas rhyming ABCBAC, served two purposes; one was the therapeutic, consolatory nature of this hard work for me, a substitute for spring cleaning the house or taking on any of the other energetic chores we tend to plunge into when we need distraction from bad news; the other was that a rhymed poem seemed somehow more serious, a more considered and as it were more public monument to Pete's memory than any little free verse effusion might have been. Nevertheless, I didn't want it to sound solemn: there was nothing solemn about Pete. I combed the volume for the quotations that had made us laugh and put them in; and I allowed the atmosphere to be at first light-hearted and then increasingly ominous, until at the end it descended into bleakness with the admission of Pete's death. Looking at the poem now, I can see that in the last two stanzas (of eight) the tempo has become steadier and more contained; there is a stronger tendency for the lines to consist of complete phrases, without over-running. I'll quote these two stanzas:

> 'On loan perpetual.' If that implied
> some dark finality, some hint of 'nox
> perpetua', something desolate and bleak,
> we didn't see it then, among the jokes.
> Yesterday, walking on the fells, you died.
> I'm left with this, a trifling, quaint antique.

> You'll not reclaim it now; it's mine to keep:
> a keepsake, nothing more. You've changed the 'loan
> perpetual' to a bequest by dying.
> Augusta, Lady Blanche, Lord Ravenstone –
> I've read the lot, trying to get to sleep.
> The jokes have all gone flat. I can't stop crying.[9]

I notice that in each of those two stanzas there is a line-break between the two words of a significant phrase: 'nox/perpetua' and 'loan/perpetual'. In both instances the noun comes at the end of the second line, followed by the adjective at the beginning of the third. This lays a particular emphasis on the word for 'perpetual', stressing the finality and eternal nature of death. A neat device, you may think, highlighted by its repetition at the same point in each stanza. I agree. But as far as I can recall no such intention was in my mind at the time of writing; my impression is that I did it simply for the sake of the rhymes. As I often tell students, poets don't always know what they're doing: luck and happy accidents (i.e. instinct and the experience gained by much reading and practice) may take over.

A metre like that of 'The Keepsake' risks becoming monotonous. More typically, in my recent work, I've tended towards shorter lines, not strongly iambic, arranged more often than not in quatrains. Picking an example almost at random, I'll quote from a poem called 'Icon'.[10] This is a little piece of fiction; an unfinished story. It was set off by that useful trigger (in my experience), a cliché. I found myself murmuring 'In the interests of economy', and decided that it referred to economy of narrative; whereupon it summoned up a vignette of an unspecified couple in a hotel somewhere abroad (also unspecified: it could be any town with an Orthodox Cathedral, but in fact the place I had in mind was Novi Sad in Yugoslavia). The tone is neutral or perhaps conversational; the narrator is addressing an anonymous 'you' who may be just the reader or the audience. The first two stanzas are as follows:

> In the interests of economy
> I am not going to tell you
> what happened between the time
> when they checked into the hotel
>
> with its acres of tiled bathrooms
> (but the bidet in theirs was cracked)
> and the morning two days later
> when he awoke to find her gone.

The rhythm there moves fairly briskly. To my ear it has two heavy stresses in each line, together with one or more often two lighter stresses; but it would also be possible to read the lines in such a way that most of them carried three stresses, arranged in an irregular pattern – hence the doubts I expressed earlier about hearing other people read my poems: flexible rhythms are by their nature open to more than one rendering. Toward the end of the poem, when the male character is peering at the icon and trying to work out what the silver shapes on the Virgin's robes signify (and, by implication, what has brought about the absence of his female companion) the rhythm slows down and becomes more clogged and hesitant, with much enjambement:

> . . . they looked
> like flattened-out Monopoly tokens,
>
> he thought: a boot, and something like
> a heart, and a pair of wings, and something
> oblong. They were hard to see
> in the brown light, but he peered at them
>
> for several minutes, leaning over
> the scarved head of an old woman
> on her knees there, blocking his view,
> who prayed and prayed and wouldn't move.

Much of what I've just said is a case of being wise after the event; what I've been doing, in analysing my own poems, is scarcely different from what I do when I analyse Wordsworth or Elizabeth Bishop for BBC Schools Radio: I'm working from external evidence, without claiming knowledge of the writer's intentions. Perhaps it's time now to confess to a few problems I've been faced with. One is to do with point of view: who is speaking in the poem, and how should the speaker's point of view be grammatically expressed?

In most of my earliest poems I knew perfectly well who was speaking: I was; and 'I' wasn't just a device or persona: it was me, no doubt about it. I wrote in the third person too, but that was a quite different kind of exercise: the adolescent poems I published in the school magazine were the safe, impersonal ones about sunsets or seagulls; the ones in my private notebook were about me. A few years later, still adolescent but married (a condition I'd rushed into at eighteen), I embarked on the first of my 'adult' poems – that is, the first to be published in a serious literary magazine. Once again, it was about me – about the way I identified with other people's landscapes, in an attempt to feel at home in the world (or, perhaps, at home in New Zealand, where I'd been living for six or seven years). However, I felt the need for some concealment: the first person would have been too naked. So I transposed it into the third person, and in those pre-feminist days automatically assumed that to be taken seriously the protagonist would have to be male. The poem featured an anonymous 'he'; not surprisingly, everyone thought it was about my husband.

I suppose this taught me some kind of lesson; certainly I had plenty of lessons to learn, and spent most of my twenties learning them; but years later a similar problem arose, in a more subtle form. By now I'd figured out that it was all right to write out of personal experience, if it was experience other people could share or be enlarged by, and that the first person was a useful device for helping readers to identify with the action. I'd been using it in fictional narratives too, as writers of prose fiction do: as early as 1967, when I wrote the purely imaginative poem 'A Surprise in the Peninsula', I'd discovered the value of first-person narration for conveying immediacy.[11] All the same, it eventually began to pall, and in 1977 I went through a minor crisis. I was living in the Lake District, on my first literary fellowship, and for once I had time to think at leisure about what I was doing, and to tinker away at poems that weren't particularly compelling or urgent, just to see what came out. (For years before that, in my crowded London life with a job, a son, a house to run, and a literary career to fit in somehow, I'd had not time for any but the most urgent poems, the ones which positively demanded to be written.) In Ambleside I wrote a lot, by my standards: thirty or forty poems in a year, instead of my usual bare dozen. At least half of them were failures or simply too minor to matter; and in some of the others I found myself increasingly inhibited by a severe distaste for the first person: I simply couldn't bring myself to write 'I' yet again. As a result there are several poems from that period where the syntax is unusually contorted, in order to exclude pronouns as far as possible and to accommodate what was actually a first-person viewpoint without the use of 'I'. The title poem in my pamphlet *Below Loughrigg* [1979] is an exercise in such avoidance techniques; so is 'Three Rainbows in one Morning', in which at one point, finding myself compelled to use a pronoun of some kind, I subsumed the reactions of my two companions into my own and instead of the more natural 'we' wrote 'they'.

All this was rather silly, as I realised even at the time. A few years later I sent the whole thing up in a sort of spoof called 'Personal Poem', which is actually a calculatedly *im*personal piece of writing, involving a large cast of characters, none of them in any personal relation to the speaker, and an almost complete range of pronouns –

we, you, he, she, they – with the deliberate exception of 'I'.[12] It comments obliquely on the confessional aspect of poetry – 'How people give themselves away!/Yet all we have is hearsay' – and ends by relegating the question of viewpoint or 'voice' to the backwaters of abstract theory:

> Too late to take a boat out;
> and anyway, the lake's crowded,
> kids and oars together, and all their voices.
> But really no one in particular,
> unless you say so. Unless we say so.

After this I felt I'd laid the problem to rest, and could proceed to write first-person poems (although not, I hope, 'confessional' ones) side by side with the other kinds.

I've also played games with syntax in the cause of comic effect, and here too pronouns tend to be involved. In 'Smokers for Celibacy' I begin with the line 'Some of us are a little tired of hearing that cigarettes kill', and continue in the first person plural throughout, except in the section where cigarettes become anthropomorphised, as it were, with their passive behaviour being favourably contrasted with that of predatory males:

> Cigarettes just lie there quietly in their packs
> waiting until you call on one of them to help you relax.
> They aren't moody; they don't go in for sexual harassment
>   and threats,
> or worry about their performance as compared with that of
>   other cigarettes.[13]

For some reason the pronoun 'they' strikes me as faintly ridiculous in certain contexts, and I enjoy that; I've used it in several pieces of light verse where the third person singular would look more normal.

Still on pronouns, there's the you-poem. In one kind the second person pronoun is used almost impersonally, as a substitute for 'one'; in effect it's saying 'This is how things are, this is what happens if...' It's a raconteur's pronoun. I've used it, for example, in 'Double-Take', which begins: 'You see your next-door neighbour from above,/from an upstairs window, and he reminds you/of your ex-lover, who is bald on top,/which you had forgotten.'[14]

The other type of you-poem is the traditional one which adopts the really rather peculiar convention of addressing a particular individual and telling them what they did at some time in the past, or, even more artificially and using the historic present, what they are doing or saying in the period during which the poem is supposedly addressing them. One of my early poems, 'For a Five-year-old', falls into this category.[15] I now find it impossible to read aloud without wincing, not so much for this reason as because of its stilted, meant-for-the-page diction; for example, the last two lines are: 'But that is how things are: I am your mother, / And we are kind to snails.' Nowadays I'd say: 'But that's how things are: I'm your mother, / and we're kind to snails' – which of course destroys the metre. The five-year-old in question is now in his thirties, putting a whole generation between me and the solemn early self who wrote the poem: a gap I find hard to bridge.

A sub-species of the you-poem, I need hardly point out, is the one which talks to a dead person. Peter Reading poured understandable scorn on this convention in *Stet* – while employing it himself – when he wrote 'it's pathetic and mad to address yourself to the dead.' Yes, but sometimes difficult to resist.

On the whole I write in normal sentences, with normal grammar and syntax and, as a rule, normal punctuation. I have been known to omit punctuation for occasional effect, or to write a whole poem with none at all; but these were experiments, and half-hearted ones at that: I have no ambition to be 'experimental' in the old-fashioned sense. For me the poem on the page (which I hold to be primary, and not merely a text for a performance) must nevertheless be capable of being read aloud by the human voice. Fancy shapes and patterns don't interest me unless they can be communicated, to however subtle a degree, in speech. I could never see much point in the now rather faded New Zealand (and, before that, American) fashion for lower case and ampersands. But rhythm is another matter, and I like to think (as we all do) that when I run a clause or sentence across a line-break this sets up some kind of audible tension between the rhythmical structure and the syntactical one.[16] I should hate to bore readers or listeners by metrical monotony.

In fact anything that drives readers away is bad news. Poetry is communication, a process which presupposes an audience. This brings me back to the question of tone – and, intimately bound up in that, of language. I try to avoid sounding pretentious or 'poetic': the high style is not for me, except at rare moments or for particular effects. The tone I feel at home in is one in which I can address people without embarrassing or alarming them; I should like them to relax and listen as if to an intimate conversation (or, to be honest, an intimate monologue) rather than to an operatic aria. This doesn't mean that there are no shocks in store for them – by 'conversation' I don't mean banal chat – and when I'm revising I try to eliminate anything too obvious or dull; but my language tends to avoid the deliberately eccentric: no made-up words, no scouring of dictionaries for recherché bits of vocabulary, not too much obscurity. If an unusual word pops up spontaneously now and then I'm rather pleased, but to grub around for one in a thesaurus would strike my puritanical conscience as cheating (and anyway, discoveries are no fun if you've been led to them by a guide).

The point at which it's crucially essential not to drive readers away is right at the beginning. In this connection I once learned something of value, early in my career, from a reviewer. He observed that the first lines of my poems, as listed in the index to some anthology, were not memorable: who, he asked would want to read poems beginning with such unexciting phrases? Since then the selector in my subconscious has been programmed to take note of this point; relatively neutral opening lines are still allowed through, if they're what the poem seems to insist on, but splashy attention-grabbers which plunge right into the action are always favourably considered.

The other end of a poem is equally important; whole books have been written about how poems close.[17] I used to believe that the end of a poem should *sound* like the end, slamming shut with a satisfying and unmistakeable clunk like a car door. This habit proved hard to break, but in recent years I've inclined more to endings which leave a certain amount unsaid; with a more open-ended poem the reader has more to ponder over; the resonances linger more teasingly in the mind. It depends, though, what went before: a poem in a conventional form can stand a relatively conventional ending (look at the difference between 'The Keepsake' and 'Icon').

The fact that I've used the word 'instinct' and 'subconscious' more than once shouldn't be taken as implying that my poems bubble up like water from a spring. Only the initial impulse does that; the rest is hard work. To understand exactly what kind of work, and what processes are involved in any specific case, you'd have to examine my working drafts, and this is not an experience I'd recommend. My drafts are a mess, partly because of my dreadful handwriting and partly because I went to school during the war and have never managed to wean myself from the conviction that wasting paper is a sin. This means that I tend to make most of my corrections and rewritings on a very few sheets of paper – not always a disadvantage, because it keeps the preliminary scribbled notes and the half-rejected alternatives clearly in view. This can be helpful (second thoughts aren't invariably best) or, failing that, consoling: I can never feel sure that I've got a poem right, but at least I can often see that I've improved it.

I've left some time to talk about two activities which are related to writing poetry but not the same as it, although they have to some extent influenced my own verse practices. These are translation and writing for music, and in my case they are historically connected. In 1979 I went to live in Newcastle for two years as Northern Arts Fellow in Literature. During the first of these years the New Zealand composer Gillian Whitehead had a fellowship there attached to the Music Department. She'd been commissioned to compose a piece for a soprano and small instrumental group, and she asked me to write the words. We wanted a local theme, and I decided to write about Hotspur: the historical Hotspur, Henry Percy, rather than Shakespeare's version of him. The result was called *Hotspur: a ballad for music*. It's sung in the persona of Hotspur's wife, Elizabeth (not Kate, as Shakespeare called her), and it expresses anti-war sentiments which are perhaps anachronistically feminist, but the factual details are as accurate as my sources could make them.

I found the combination of a historical theme and the necessity to be simple and dramatic very liberating. Words for music need to be clear and audible, rather than subtle and muted. I used various ballad metres, together with a style which could be allowed to verge on the archaic (without falling into the sins of unnatural inversion and the 'tis'- and 'twas'-ery which I've so excoriated in my advice to aspiring poetry competition entrants).[18] Devices like alliteration came in: one section begins 'I married a man of metal and fire'. Later in the same section I have an echo of a Bessie Smith blues number, and that's in the nature of a private joke; it doesn't interfere with the consistent texture of the verse. What it hints at, perhaps, is that the emotional temperature of the piece is higher than in my usual work. (I have carefully refrained from referring to *Hotspur* as a poem because I don't consider it to be one. The function of a librettist is to subordinate her contribution to that of the composer: the words are a framework for the music which is the point of the whole thing. Hence, perhaps, my feeling of freedom: the entire responsibility didn't rest on me.)

My next venture with Gillian was a shortish piece for soprano and orchestra called *Eleanor of Aquitaine*, another commissioned work. Out of this arose a plan for an entire opera on the same subject, which was simply the fruit of our own obsession; no one offered to pay for it, and Gillian has so far set only part of it to music. But it haunted us for a year, immersed us in research, took us to France, and led me into reading and translating troubadour songs for insertion here and there in the text, while Gillian looked out the original twelfth-century melodies in so far as they have survived.

I had come upon Eleanor of Aquitaine because I was already, during 1980 and 1981, fixated on the twelfth century through my reading in medieval Latin poetry. My degree was in classics, and to translate Latin poetry seemed a reasonable way of keeping my hand in, but I'd never felt tempted to make yet another version of Catullus or Horace. When I happened to pick up the Gaselee edition of the *Oxford Book of Medieval Latin Verse*[19] in a secondhand bookshop I suddenly realised that this was a different matter altogether: this stuff *rhymed*. It was also – or the parts of it which appealed to me were – elegant, sophisticated, lyrical, erotic, and capable of irony; but what most attracted me was the technical challenge of reproducing the formal patterns of rhyme and metre in my English versions without distorting the meaning of the originals. In some cases this meant finding successive rhyme-words for highly elaborate stanzas (sometimes including lines of as few as three syllables), while preserving both the meaning and the metre. It was like doing crossword puzzles.

I'd better give an example. Peter of Blois's poem 'Grates ago Veneri' (to which I gave the English title 'The Conquest of Coronis') appears in two manuscript sources, the *Carmina Burana* and the *Arundel Collection*. It is composed in ten stanzas in five forms, set out in matching pairs: two in one form, the next two in another, and so on. Stanza three reads as follows:

> *Visu, colloquio,*
> *contactu, basio*
> *frui virgo dederat;*
> > *sed aberat*
> *linea posterior*
> > *et melior*
> > > *amori.*
> *Quam nisi transiero*
> > *de cetero*
> *sunt, que dantur alia,*
> > *materia*
> > > *furori.*

Here is my translation:

> To gaze, to talk, to touch,
> to kiss; four things. So much
> my sweet virgin would permit;
>   but she'd omit
> that one item on the list
>   her optimist
>   was craving:
> which unless one can achieve
>   the others leave
> harrowing effects, and can
>   send any man
>   quite raving.

Because English is more compact than Latin, with brusque conso-
nantal word-endings where the Latin has inflected suffixes com-
posed largely of vowels, I have occasionally had to pad out my lines
in order to match the syllable-count of the originals: thus 'virgin' has
acquired the adjective 'sweet', and *materia furori* ('cause for madness')
has been expanded slightly to make two phrases. But otherwise the
English says essentially what the Latin says. (It also, I hope, says it in
a reasonably neutral and unmannered style. Once again, my rule was
to avoid inversions and archaisms. The word 'virgin', which may
sound a little quaint, is more in the nature of a technical term: male
poets of the period were obsessed with virginity.)

The outcome of my reading in the Newcastle and Durham univer-
sity libraries and of pleasantly laborious evenings in front of my coal
fire was a volume of translations called *The Virgin and the Nightin-
gale*,[20] comprising those poems which I both enjoyed and felt able
to do justice to. There were other poems, particularly by Peter of
Blois, which I admired but which no amount of ingenuity on my
part would convert into satisfactorily rhyming English, and these I
had to abandon. Of the versions I did make, a few correspond less
than exactly with the forms of the originals; and several of the pre-
twelfth century poems which I included didn't rhyme in the first
place. But on the whole it was the games with rhyme and metre that
I found so compelling.

One effect of this project, and of writing in regular forms for
music, was that for some time I became addicted to rhyme; it oozed
over into my own poems, and I had to resist it where it wasn't
appropriate. 'Blue Glass', 'Street Song' and 'An Emblem'[21] are pro-
ducts of this period, and there were other rhyming poems which
didn't survive. The actual content of the medieval poetry had less

effect on my own work, but 'Mary Magdalene and the Birds' had its origin (indirectly) in a hymn for that saint, intermingled with memories of the early monks' poems about birds (as well as the skylarks I heard on the Town Moor); and another poem, 'Drowning', was triggered by a chapter in a linguistic treatise on medieval Latin.[22]

The other language from which I've begun translating is Romanian, and here my motivating impulse was an entirely different one. Apart from anything else, I had to learn the language before I could begin. I visited Romania in 1984, on a writers' exchange trip sponsored by the British Council, and arrived there with very little prior knowledge of the country except what I'd picked up in the few preceding weeks. In Bucharest I met a number of writers and became friendly with several poets (mostly women). They were so expert in my own language that it seemed impolite to remain ignorant of theirs and cut off from their literature. So I decided to learn Romanian: after all, it's a Romance language (although its long isolation from the other Romance languages and the turbulent history of the people who speak it have given it a substantial proportion of Slavonic words and other elements).

For the next couple of years I never went on a train without one of my collection of grammars and teach-yourself books. When I found myself becoming involved in projects to do with Romanian poetry, such as writing introductions for two of the Forest Books series of translations, I made a point of reading all the Romanian texts first; and inevitably I became tempted to try translation myself. It was exciting to have access to a language which wasn't the common property of half the writers in Britain, and to be able to pick up a book with no idea of what I'd find in it. Romanian books aren't easy to come by, but I was fortunate in having friends who gave me copies of their own works, and I managed to collect more on my second visit to Bucharest in 1987.

Not surprisingly there are limits to what I can tackle: anything too idiomatic is either risky or impossible, and I have to beware of unfamiliar references and allusions. My practice is to read through collections of poems and pick out the ones which make sense to me and which I feel have something to offer to English readers. I'm not interested in the activity (often described as 'translation', but for which I feel there ought to be a different word) in which a native speaker makes a literal version of a text and the so-called translator then polishes it up. For me the pleasure is in the discovery, in the process of finding out what's there in the text itself. Once I've made my version, though, I'll take it to a Romanian for advice if I'm in the slightest doubt.

The first priority, of course, is getting the meaning across. I begin with a basic and fairly rough transcription of what the poem says. Where several possible English equivalents for a word or phrase occur to me, I bracket them together, leaving the choice until later. Then I go through this draft again, trying to make it read more smoothly; I double-check the meaning of any tricky phrases, and battle with the synonyms in both languages. Romanian, for example, has several quite distinct words for snow: *ninsoare* is what falls through the air, but when it's lying on the ground it's called *zăpada*; then there's a poetic word, *nea*, and a popular, slangy one, *omăt*. English, for all its richness of vocabulary, seems slightly impoverished here. But in other areas it offers more options than Romanian.

During these processes I've been mentally repeating my translation to myself, testing it for euphony and for naturalness of utterance, as I'd do when composing a poem of my own. After all, this is contemporary poetry, and it ought to sound natural to the ear. Then comes the question of line-endings, more exacting when I'm dealing with something that's already set out in lines than when I'm starting from scratch with freedom to do as I like. Not many of the Romanian poets I've translated use rhyme or conventional metres, although Marin Sorescu has recently shocked his contemporaries by a return to rhymed forms in his latest collection. When I take on one of these, the problems are similar to those of translating from medieval Latin, and involve much walking around and rehearsing alternatives in my head.

But on the whole the poets I've tackled (Grete Tartler, Daniela Crăsnaru, Ioana Crăciunescu and a few others) use free verse. Here my duty is to match the layout of the originals as closely as possible. This can be fairly straightforward, but not always. Sometimes a line which is very short in the original comes out longer in English: for example, there is a compact Romanian word *cearcan*, with two syllables, which in English has to be paraphrased as 'dark circles under the eyes' – seven syllables – because we have no equivalent. At other times the mismatch is in the other direction: there are grammatical features, such as the long word-endings for the genitive and dative cases, which can extend Romanian phrases considerably. Then there are times when the Romanian word-order doesn't correspond to English usage and needs to be inverted. The juggling all this necessitates is the routine stuff of translation; there have to be compromises, but as long as they don't involve placing a crucial word or phrase in a position where it loses its impact, they needn't be too damaging. The rhythm also needs to be taken into account, and here too compromises may prove to be the only solution.

However, there is a degree of interference which goes beyond mere compromise, and I must confess to having been tempted by this and to having occasionally succumbed. The point at issue is poetic fashion: now and then the practices found in Romanian verse can appear clumsy, old-fashioned or amateurish to a British eye. I'm thinking, for example, of the use of one-word or two-word lines at the end of a poem, or of short lines set out in little descending steps for dramatic effect. If I find these in a poem which I otherwise admire, I've been known to make a slight silent adjustment; I tell myself it's for the sake of the poet's reputation, but this may be misguided charity. Likewise with exclamation marks in unfashionable abundance: should one take them out or leave them in? On the whole I've forced myself to leave them in – whereupon my publishers, as likely as not, will edit them out!

The temptation, of course, is that of trying to make these poets more like myself. I'm aware that this is unethical as well as aesthetically misleading, and for the most part I've succeeded in resisting it. But what about the other kind of influence, theirs on me? It's not always easy to tell when you're being influenced – these things often don't show up until enough time has elapsed for a detached view. But just as my work with medieval Latin poetry revived my interest in strictly metrical rhymed forms, it's possible that contact with the cryptic delicacy and surrealistic imagery of Romanian poetry may now and then lighten the tendency of my own poems towards matter-of-factness and what Empson called 'argufying'. If so, it's probably a good thing.

Notes

1. See also the comments by Sisson and Scupham here. Sisson claims, for example, that what he is 'most conscious of recognising' during composition is 'the continuation of the rhythm'; Scupham also writes of how 'the heady garlic of swingeing rhythms' attracted him as a boy. The priority claimed for rhythm, by these and other poets, can usefully be compared with the centrality afforded to rhythmic concepts in contemporary linguistic work on sound-structure (phonology), where those rhythmic concepts are seen as shared, rule-governed entities comprising a structural hierarchy of syllable, foot, word, and phrase – ever-larger constituents within and across which rhythmic rules generate well-formed patterns. The output patterns generated by linguistic rules are very strikingly reminiscent of the patterns of poetic metres, which suggests that the claim by Adcock and others – that poetry necessarily includes stylised rhythmical and/or metrical patterns – is strong, and strong for linguistic reasons. See also the essays by Donald Davie and Charles Tomlinson.

2. This observation is telling. As noted above, stress and rhythm are products of a hierarchy of linguistic constituents: the smallest functional sound-units of English, phonemes, are gathered into syllables; syllables are gathered into words; words are gathered into phrases. One or more syllables of a lexical word (i.e. noun, adjective, verb) may be stressed (but only one will carry strongest stress); and one or more words in a phrase may be stressed (but only one word will carry the intonational peak and nuclear stress of that phrase). Significantly, for a particular syllable to be perceived as rhythmically prominent under normal circumstances, that syllable must have a minimum structure – it must contain either a long vowel, or a short vowel followed by a consonant. This fact helps to explain why (again under normal circumstances) there are no stressed monosyllables containing only short vowels in English (e.g. *ba). Stress in syllables depends on phonemic configurations of vowel and consonant. These interrelationships are summarised in Richard Hogg and C.B. McCully, *Metrical Phonology* (Cambridge: C.U.P., 1987).

3. The given-ness of 'inspiration' – whether this is culturally determined, or whether it is the product of some other form of intelligence – is discussed thoroughly, if anecdotally and inconclusively, in Brian Inglis, *The Unknown Guest* (Chatto and Windus, 1987), ch.3.

4. That there are rhythms within rhythms is well attested. Again this is a matter of hierarchy and periodicity, where, for example, widely-spaced, phrasal rhythmic pulses contain relatively less-prominent, but more frequent, word-stress pulses. Periodicity is valuably discussed in Derek Attridge, *The Rhythms of English Poetry* (London: Longmans, 1982).

5. Fleur Adcock, *Selected Poems* (OUP, 1983), pp.33-4; see also Blake Morrison and Andrew Motion, *The Penguin Book of Contemporary British Poetry* (1982), pp.92-3.

6. This view – reminiscent of Sisson's – can perhaps be traced to (and certainly finds a very clear expression in) the work of Herbert Read. In Read's *Form in Modern Poetry* (1932), for example, he drew a distinction between 'organic form' and 'abstract form'. The former he desribed as follows: 'When a work of art has its own inherent laws, originating with its very invention and fusing in one vital unity both structure and content, then the resulting form may be described as *organic*' (pb. edn, Plymouth: Vision Press, 1989). As Read stated, however, this view ultimately corresponds to Coleridge's formulations of 'organic form' and 'mechanical regularity' (Read, 1989, p.9 fn.).

7. ''Foreigner' was first published in *The Inner Harbour* (OUP, 1979); see also *Selected Poems*, p.87.

8. First published in *The Scenic Route* (OUP, 1974); *Selected Poems*, p.59.

9. In *The Incident Book* (OUP, 1986), pp.10-11.

10. *The Incident Book*, p.36.

11. First published in *High Tide in the Garden* (OUP, 1971); *Selected Poems*, p.23.

12. *The Incident Book*, pp.29-30.

13. In *Time Zones* (1991), pp.36-7.

14. *The Incident Book*, p.44.

15. *Selected Poems*, p.8.

16. Since the end of the line is usually determinate in the rhythmical structure (at least in metrical poems), then clauses spanning line-breaks will certainly produce this effect of 'tension'. This seems to be particularly evident at the end of lines which contain an odd number of realised beats (= rhythmical and/or metrical pulses). It has been argued that such lines – the trimeter, the pentameter, for example – may end with a 'silent stress' (a better term is a 'rhythmically salient pause'). Where the end of the line is co-extensive with a clause boundary, then the salient pause is realised and the effect is one of end-stopping. Where the clause is run over the line, then the syntactic movement of the lines demands that the salient pause is suppressed, and we perceive enjambement, a kind of metrical dislocation dependent on the interplay of line, metre and syntax. See also Davie's comments here, particularly with regard to the vexed issue of whether enjambement is possible in free verse.

17. E.g. Barbara Herrnstein Smith, *Poetic Closure* (Chicago, 1968).

18. 'The Prize-Winning Poem', *Selected Poems*, pp.115-6.

19. *The Oxford Book of Medieval Latin Verse*, chosen by Stephen Gaselee (Clarendon Press, 1928).

20. Published by Bloodaxe Books, 1983.

21. *Selected Poems*, pp.122, 120, 115.

22. *The Incident Book*, pp.27-8.

Distinctive Anonymity
Robert Wells

When I put to myself the questions which have been proposed and try to give an account of my poems, I find myself hesitant, and for several reasons. And it strikes me that the best way to begin an answer might be to describe the reasons for my hesitation. The questions are admirably clear and direct, and if I take issue with them or seem to mistake their meaning, I'm using them not with hostile intent but to help me give as clear an account as I can.

My first doubt is this: how far is a personal answer possible and what does it amount to? It's the poem that counts; the process by which one reaches it is an irrelevance by comparison. The solutions to the difficulties which one meets in writing a poem remain a part of the finished design, it's true. But I sense in the questioning an emphasis on the process – on the poet, that is, and the poet's own way – which can work to the exclusion of the poem. It's rather as if I were being asked to reinvent the art of rhetoric, but to reinvent it in my own image according to a new dispensation in which the nature of language is determined by the needs of the individual voice. I sense the hope that perhaps I, or perhaps my fellow-essayists, may be in possession of a private key. But I have no such key and I don't believe that anyone does. The nature of the language remains the same for everyone, and I'm afraid that when I reduce my view of these matters to the bare bones, what I'm left with will be no better than a collection of commonplaces. On the other hand, I reflect that commonplaces always need to be rediscovered, and the fact that we all live under the same laws shouldn't stop me from talking about them or from having something of my own to say about how these laws work in my own case.

My second doubt is this: the reasons behind the choices made in writing a poem are largely unconscious; they have become second nature. It's a practical matter of seeing what will work, of knowing what is right or wrong in a particular set of circumstances which never exactly repeats itself. It may be possible to look at the result and detect a set of principles at work, but in the actual writing I'm simply out to please myself. Within the form I've chosen I work entirely by ear, and choosing the form too is largely a matter for the ear, of hearing the potential for shape within a body of material which may itself be only vaguely apprehended, so that I have the form of a poem sometimes before I discover the content.[1] The terminology of metre provides a useful way of describing poems once they are written, but I seldom feel the need for it when writing. I will count syllables and listen for pauses, but I've never asked myself in so many words whether an iamb or trochee is required in such-and-such a place, or where the caesura should occur in a particular line. The work of getting the poem right is done by the ear, or rather by the ear and voice together, as one hears oneself when one is speaking. Of course, the ear's instinct isn't an innocent one. Reading, observation and practice all play their part in it.

This, then, is my sense of the limits to the account which I'll now try to give, and with these caveats, I'll begin by saying something about how my poems take shape. There are times when a poem comes all at once, fully formed or almost so, and I afterwards need to change or cut no more than a word or two. These poems are usually of a particular kind. They describe physical experience – moments of intense contact between the body and the world – and the heightened sense of the world that comes with it, the trance-like state when the objects of one's perception take on an equivalent mental existence within oneself. They are written very soon after the experience which they describe. It's as if the experience creates a mould and all that needs to be done is to provide the words which fill the mould and take its form. The work that goes into such a poem has all been done before it's written and bears only an oblique relation to it. The language has already been quarried out and is lying about in the mind ready for use. Or – another way of thinking about it – the words have already been enfranchised, taken into my head and made my own. But for me these are the rare and lucky poems. Usually my first draft is a prolix and shapeless affair; most of the work remains to be done and my progress is slow and painstaking.

The process of revision has become a problematic one in contemporary poetry.[2] What is the aim or ideal toward which one revises? Without such an ideal, without the sense of some determining principle, there is no way of judging whether a change is an improvement. It becomes simply another version, no better, no worse; and the poet is helpless in the face of a first draft. Lack of finish becomes the guarantee of authenticity, as if the poem were justified and given form by the moment of its own genesis, which it records. The poem as a photograph, perhaps, rather than the poem as painting. This formal impasse is an aspect of a larger impasse, the relation between the specifics of a poem and the belief, or sense of meaning, which governs and justifies their selection. Past poetic conventions are easy enough to identify, while those of the present tend to be nearly unnoticeable – they are the water in which we swim. One of our chief conventions, I think, consists in the heaping up of specifics, details, parts instead of a whole, the accumulation increasing as the need to conceal the lack of a governing principle grows more pressing (contemporary French poetry has tried the opposite way out of the same impasse and has tended to eliminate specifics). I would guess that to future readers this convention will seem as obtrusive as the generalising convention of much eighteenth-century poetry seems to us with its references to 'the finny tribe' for fish, 'the fleecy kind' for sheep, etc.

At best, a first draft has a freshness, a sense of the moment and of the voice falling just so, which are easily lost or flattened out in revision. But I want a poem which depends on something more than a turn of voice and a moment. It seems to me that these only have value if their uniqueness is preserved incidentally in the achievement of a form which does not exist simply to register them. Writing a poem consists of getting something clear, and what lures me on in revision is the promise of form which allows that to happen. What I look for in my draft are the beginnings of form, a line here and there, those moments where the language is sharpest, the phrasing most realised. As the elements of the poem begin to appear, they begin to modify one another and the conditions are created in which the poem starts to generate itself. The demands which it makes begin to be precise enough for precise answers to be looked for. Once this happens, I feel that I'm merely assisting at the process. The poem starts to take on an independent existence, like a child learning the use of its own limbs. Poems are meant to be spoken, and the criterion which my ear uses in composition is that the poem must 'say itself'. It must fit itself to the voice without impediment, so far as is possible. I know that something is wrong with a poem of mine when in saying it to myself I keep on stumbling at some point and forget or garble what comes next. The current on which the voice rides is broken. It's through a process of continual repetition that I test out a poem, choose between alternatives and reach a final version. I don't count a poem as finished unless I know it by heart. And there would be little point in the undertaking otherwise, since my chief pleasure comes from having something new to say over to myself. I tend only to write new poems when the old ones have been worn out by repetition and cease to satisfy me.

I find composition a deeply enjoyable, deeply frustrating process. I'm working at the limits of what I'm able to do and, except at rare moments of ease, it's the limits and the area of incapacity beyond that I'm mostly conscious of. I feel hindered and encumbered, as if I were walking through thorns or had been set to clear a field of brambles. (This is my version of Keats's 'leaves to a tree'.) I long to free myself of this feeling, to achieve the clarity of the finished poem. There are three rules – if they can be called that – which I've found to be of help. The first is that between two alternatives, one is always the better. The second is that the line or phrase which I think essential to the poem – it may be the bit that came first – can turn out to be what is holding it up and may have to be jettisoned. The third rule, hard to accept with a good grace, is to be grateful to the obstacles in this respect at least, that they show where the way through to the finished poem lies. The door may be jammed, but at least I know where to push. This means that it's important for me to identify what is wrong with a draft, fault by fault, as exactly as possible.

A hazard of poetry which I become more and more conscious of is that if it's any good it tells the truth, and that means, incidentally, that it tells the truth about oneself. It is painfully self-betraying, in a way which makes the moralising of some critics often seem far too glibly censorious. I find it uncanny how, the more a poem seems to reduce itself to the mere resolution of a technical problem, the more unerringly it homes in on the truth I didn't know was there to tell. I'll give an instance of this as it once happened to me. Some years ago I was caught in a terrorist attack at an airport. Grenades were thrown, there was some shooting, and a general panic. I had several nightmares about the incident, but I didn't write about it or think of doing so. Soon afterwards I set out to write a poem which would gather up some impressions of Iran, the country in which I'd been living. In particular, I had been reading about the Mongol invasions of what are now Iraq and Iran in the thirteenth century. The poem, which touched on these historical events, was to be in four parts; I had the first three, though not a word of the fourth, which was to be about the sack of a city. The form was tightly determined; I set about mechanically fulfilling its conditions in this fourth part and was pleased with the result. But it was only much later that I realised what I had put into these reflections on a sacked city: my recollection of the airport massacre. I tell this anecdote to show how the demands of form can take one further into one's subject. But it can also serve as a caution against judging a poem by the apparent contemporaneity of its material. On the face of it my poem might seem a piece of aesthetic or antiquarian indulgence. But as my story shows, the present is there, painfully so, beside the past, and when I think of what has happened in Iran since I wrote the poem, I begin to believe that something of the future was there too. The habit of measuring poetry by the apparent up-to-dateness of its subject matter easily turns it into a kind of debased journalism, and one of the vices of much recent English poetry is that it sets out to answer this expectation. We should not expect poetry to flatter us or enter into conspiracy with us by overvaluing our own habits and surroundings or mistaking them for the entire world. One thing I require from poetry is an awareness that there are other places, times, and lives, and that these are also part of our own time.

These generalities about form are taking me very far from the specifics of metre and language which the rubric invites me to consider, and it is to these that I'll turn now. I repeat what I suggested at the start, that there is a kind of know-how involved in writing a poem, as in doing any job, which is essential and which can be demonstrated instance by instance, but which doesn't usually lend itself to prescription. There's no mystery about it, but one might as well try to describe how to ride a bicycle, with no bicycle to hand. But I do have some observations which survive this inhibition, and here they are.

The effects which I aim for in a poem are quiet ones. I want a poem to be characterised by evenness and sobriety, the energy expressed in – perhaps I should say, derived from – balance rather than movement. There's a passage in Anthony Blunt's book on Poussin which catches something of what I'm after. He is writing about Poussin's painting *The Adoration of the Golden Calf* (the painting is in the National Gallery), and he makes this observation about the group of dancing figures in the foreground:

> In Poussin's dance each figure is at the extreme point of his [or her] action. In fact their legs [and arms] are at the one stage where they are not moving at all; they are at the end of a movement forward, just about to begin the back swing and thus at a moment of instantaneous rest. That is to say, Poussin has chosen the action which gives the clearest definition of movement and marks its full

extent, but one which does not give the impression of movement nearly so effectively as [a] moderate halfway pose.[3]

I don't want it to be possible to point to a particular place in a poem of mine and say 'This is the centre of it' or 'This is the high point'. I would like someone reading it to think, 'It is here' and then in a moment, 'No, it is here', and then to realise that it is everywhere in the poem. I want to give the sense of a meaning brimming in the poem, a meaning which doesn't declare itself but is embodied as enigma, presence, our own desire for the world as we lean toward it. The technical problem which confronts me is how to achieve such an effect. I'll talk about the problem first in relation to metre and rhyme, and then in relation to choice of language.

I use rhyme often, but with a latent distrust which is easily awakened. I think of Milton's dislike of what he called 'the jingling sound of like endings'.[4] Rhyme can seem noisily intrusive, drawing too much attention to itself and getting in the way of what the poem is meant to show. The form which I come back to and tend to prefer is the unrhymed stanza. I need the stanza because the impulse behind a poem of mine isn't usually of the sustained kind which needs an extended verse paragraph; and for a series of short flights the stanza is the natural formalising device, balancing the poem, giving it steadiness and coherence. I like to remember the Italian meaning of the word *stanza*, a room, and to think of a poem in stanzas as a series of connecting rooms – a house in which the sense dwells, where a prevailing order and decorum allow it to articulate and realise itself. If so, many of my poems can count as no more than a single room, since they consist of just one stanza. I was pleased when a reviewer once said of these very short poems of mine, 'they give the impression that the matter can be taken thus far for the moment, and no further'; and in this case it may be the other Italian meaning of *stanza*, a stopping place, a resting place, which is the primary one. If a poem consists of a succession of stanzas, not just a single one, what we have then is a series of such stopping places. The matter of the poem rests with the close of each stanza, to be taken further by the one that succeeds.

A couple of instances now, where I've found rhyme may come usefully into play. First, rhyme is often used to reinforce an epigrammatic point; I prefer to use it precisely where there is no such point. The inconclusiveness or openness of the poem softens the rhyme, and the rhyme provides just that degree of fixity which the poem needs to cohere. This is the case, too, where rhymed and unrhymed lines are combined within a stanza. Second, when in writing a poem I find myself trapped in language which I can neither use nor throw away, the search for rhymes helps me to free myself (I think of the chick pecking its way out of the shell). Thirdly, I've discovered for myself in translation how rhyming couplets help in leading a reader through a narrative; they blend with the story, holding the attention, drawing the reader forward. Of course, if couplets are well turned they can bring alive any body of material no matter how unpromising. I found this when I was translating the *Idylls* of Theocritus, and came to the Idyll I had left till last, the one nobody reads, not even scholars of Theocritus – his panegyric of his patron Ptolemy Philadelphus, the Greek king of Egypt.[5] Since I had contracted to translate Theocritus complete I couldn't leave the poem out. I set about the labour of transferring the poem into couplets rather unwillingly. But as I worked I found myself drawn into the poem. Its flat splendours began to evoke for me the landscape of the Nile valley, as well as the atmosphere, at once oppressive and exciting, of an opulent semi-colonial court.

If I'm writing a poem which requires rhyme, then the rhymes will be found. They come with the poem – part of the work of the poem – and if they don't come, then they shouldn't be there. The best prescription for finding rhymes that I know – the best because of its guileless truthfulness – is the one given by George Gascoigne in his *Certain Notes of Instruction Concerning the Making of Verse or Rhyme in English*, published in 1575:

> When you have set down your first verse, take the last word thereof and count over all the words of the self-same sound by order of the alphabet: as, for example, the last word of your first line is *care*, to rhyme therewith you have *bare, clare* [an obsolete form of clear], *dare, fare, gare* ['a sudden and transient fit of passion' OED], *hare,* and *share, mare, snare, rare, stare,* and *ware*, etc. Of all these take that which may best serve your purpose, carrying reason with rhyme: and if none of them will serve so, then alter the last word of your former verse, but yet do not willingly alter the meaning of your invention.[6]

One way of overcoming the obtrusiveness of rhyme is of course to use half-rhyme and assonance. But often in contemporary poetry the merely casual or random substitutes for the unobtrusive; half-rhyme and assonance tend to be thrown in to provide a superficial appearance of form, an illusory form. In this case they only distract, and it would be better if they weren't there at all. To my ear, half-rhyme and assonance should fall with the same inevitability in the verse as full rhyme, and as much discretion should be brought to bear in their use.

Some comments now about metre. I want a poem to exist in lines, each one a separable unit, making sense to the ear and marked off by a slight pause even when there is no grammatical break (though I would modify this requirement at least in the case of some free verse and syllabic verse). A metrical effect which I value, but which I think must arise of itself and cannot be calculated, is ambiguity of stress, a play with the fact that stressed syllables are not stressed equally, the voice falling more faintly or uncertainly on some than on others. It's as if one were crossing a stream on irregularly spaced stones, treading firmly on those that look secure, and lightly and quickly on those that look slippery or likely to tip up. What I'm touching on here is the relation between metre and rhythm, the poet's distinctive voice making itself heard within the scheme of the poem. Of this I would say that one may bend the metrical scheme to serve the content of the poem, its thought and feeling, but not to serve oneself and above all, not to imitate oneself. We tend to think of an individual voice as if it were an end in itself. We speak of a poet 'discovering' his or her own 'voice'; and 'the poet's voice' forms part of the title of this series. But this is a discovery which can only be made incidentally in the course of a different search.[7] Once poets begin to cultivate their own voices, that is, to imitate themselves, the poetry turns into a Parnassian exercise; it becomes tediously solipsistic. I think of some lines from a late poem by George Seferis:

> The white paper speaks with your own voice
> your very own
> not the one that you like...

My own voice, if it really is my own, won't be the one I want to seek out or imitate. I'll find it if at all by trying to escape it, or best of all, by forgetting about it; and I'll only find it in finding something else. The aim of poetry is not to develop a voice. It's to reach out and articulate something beyond oneself, other than oneself. We want more than the poet's own features, the poet's own personality, staring back at us out of the poem; we want company in a poem, certainly; we want to find another human being, we want to share, but what we share, the contents of our sharing, lies outside both of us. The fine line needs to be drawn in a poem between self-acceptance and self-imitation; to counterbalance my own comments I'll quote George Seferis again (he is addressing himself, first of all, in these lines):

> Accept the man you are.
> The poem –
> do not drown it among the deep plane trees
> feed it on the rock and the soil that you have.
> If you want more
> dig in the same place.[8]

Now choice of language. I think it's easy to make too much of sticking to the language of one's time. What strikes me about English – and other languages so far as I know them – is constancy rather than change. The language adds to itself, varies and shifts within itself, even contradicts itself, but it has a central nature which, if it changes, changes extremely slowly. The great poets may have moved very far out on different limbs of the language, but the central trunk remains the same. Of course I'm not going to send my poem out dressed up like a Nicholas Hilliard miniature or a Gainsborough portrait; but it's the nature of the language – my closeness to it or distance from it, so far as I can judge that – which provides my standard. This nature can be felt at least as directly, in its everyday form, in writers like Bunyan and Defoe, who have the ability to talk on to the page, as in contemporary speech; and five minutes spent looking through *Moll Flanders* or *Pilgrim's Progress*, or the *Canterbury Tales*, come to that, will produce a string of phrases which are still involuntarily on our lips. It's not rare words or nonce words that we need to look for in writing – they are easy to find – but everyday words, English at its most expressive and useful, and this is not quite the same as the speech of our time. The language that is current is archaic too; a vast anonymity that we reach back into as soon as we speak. If we are aware of its ancientness we'll have a better sense of its precision as well.

My mention of Bunyan and Defoe may suggest that I identify the nature of the language with a plainspoken quality. So I should add that I take an extravagance and a capacity for adornment and elaboration to be inherent qualities also; and rather than mark off the plainspoken from the adorned I want to insist on their interconnection. There's a line of Seferis – to quote him a third time – which I think must stand as a fundamental poetic maxim: 'it is time to say our few words because tomorrow the soul sets sail'.[9] But in English poetry it happens time and again that elaboration is needed in order to come at plainness. The elaboration frames and sets off the plainness, and the one wouldn't be possible without the other. In some of my poems I've tried to make use of this effect, though not consistently, and much less so since I've worked as a translator of Latin poetry. I'm always conscious of the division between the Anglo-Saxon and Latinate elements in English, how they balance in what I write, and how those metaphors contained within words of Latin derivation fit the surrounding sense. Translating Latin has made me avoid an over-Latinate diction. I prefer to climb hills rather than ascend eminences. Yet when, years ago, I spent some time working as a woodman, James Thomson's *Seasons* was one of the poems which meant most to me. I felt the accuracy of his Latinisms and understood something of the need which they answered, a need to abstract the physical world, to make it transparent, to keep the idea of it, when its substantial reality bears down too directly.

Writing according to the nature of the language means keeping to its usages as revelatory, as having a beauty, good sense and usefulness of their own. In this view our language is what we have in common, an inheritance, the creation of all the dead who ever spoke it, the embodiment of what they knew. Language carries the individual voice, but it only does so because of this larger anonymity. What I value in poetry – in all art – most, I think, is this quality of distinctiveness and anonymity together, a distinctive anonymity; and so far as they are separable I value the anonymity above the distinctiveness. The voice must fit the language before the language fits the voice. It's language that I want, not poetry; I turn to poetry because it is the best way of getting at language. In one of my poems I describe an axehandle, the shapeliness and balance of its design, a design which has become standard because 'generations of hands' have found it to be best. I don't think I intended the axehandle to serve as a metaphor for shapeliness of language, but that is the way I read it now.

I come back to the question of form. What do I mean by it, and what is the need for it? The discovery which a new poem brings with it is always also a discovery about language and the possibilities of form inherent in it. The mere repetition of a stanza shape or metrical pattern on the page is not enough to give form, nor can it be found in the distortion of an established pattern with no other end than to serve a personal quirk or whim. Form means finding the right way of saying something. It's a quality of absolute expression in which words and meanings have become inseparable. But since the attempt to define form is bound to end in tautology, I'll try to suggest what

I mean by some personal history instead. When I was a boy I used to collect fossils, and would range about disused quarries or new road cuttings with a hammer to see what I could find. What fascinated me was the power of intense design in a small space, the pattern gathering itself and emerging or half-emerging from the stone, sometimes crushed and broken, sometimes near-perfect. And it was possible to put a name to the shapes too – ammonite, belemnite, trigonia, echinoderm, crinoid – and to know the derivation of the name. I see now – I know I'm laying myself open in saying this – that my hunting for fossils was little different in impulse from my writing of poems. I can think of a critic or two who might laugh and say that this bears out what they had always thought of my poems. But think of fossils as evidence of a life and a world, think of their ancientness and permanence, their frequent beauty and intricacy, and my admission doesn't seem so damaging. Later my passion for fossils gave way to a passion for Greek and Roman coins. Again, what fascinated me was intensity of design in a small space, increased in the case of coins because the image and inscription work together and have been chosen for their symbolic power, their concentration of meaning. I also loved the irregularity of the minting. Again, there are the associated words, the names of places and people, cultures and historical events. And again, there is evidence of a life and a world; what is ancient and remote has been brought close.

I'll add one more analogy and one more fragment of personal history. In a poem of mine about an archaeological dig, 'Median Palace',[10] I mention an elaborately painted clay model of a foot, sandalled and the ankle encircled by snakes, which I discovered. Whatever its purpose, it seemed to be complete in itself, and not a part of a larger image. I remember the moment of discovery. I had been set to excavate one room and had worked down through various levels of occupation to the original floor. In a corner of the room I came on an odd configuration of mud bricks, like a small altar, and in a cranny beside the bricks this strange object. It had been an excavation without many finds – the aim of that year's digging being chiefly to establish the original layout of the building – and the marvelling moment of discovery was so intense that it was as if I had lost consciousness. I must have shouted out, because the next thing I knew was that all around the walls of my deep trench were the faces of the workmen on the dig looking down. My acutest moments in writing poetry, as in reading it, have been of the same kind.

What can I deduce from these analogies? First, my old enthusiasm for fossils and coins suggests that the need for poetry, in my case at least, has something in it of a collecting impulse. (We speak of a collection of poems, and of a collected poems.) I think the notion of a poem as a self-sufficiently beautiful object, something in which we find rest and mental security, rather as a collector or connoisseur might, is undervalued at present. Second, my analogies show a desire for the archaic, a need to get back to beginnings, to stand on the original floor. What is ancient is experienced as something new, something that has been lost and found. It freshens the present and is freshened by it. Like travel, it answers a need to break out from too well-known limits; and as with travel, an erotic sense of promise draws one on. Make it new, then, also means make it old; and failure to make it new means failure in contact with the past, failure to acknowledge that, in this sense too, the world is wide. We tend to undervalue and underuse the models which English poetry provides. Many of the models are obvious; but the more I read beyond them, the more I discover that received opinion bears no relation to what I find. We all have to check everything up for ourselves, and the hidden possibilities crowd around, if only we can make something of them.

It has been a part of modernist practice to advertise its sense of the past by decorating poems with historical references, tags of quotations, and not-so-explanatory notes. But a wilful obscurity, based simply on the poet's having read a few books or visited a few places which the reader may not have strikes me as absurd – it makes a mystery where none exists – and I fight shy of the convention which loads the body of a poem down with historical baggage. If notes are necessary let them honestly explain; and let the learning in a poem be, so far as is possible, implicit – a tradition absorbed rather than advertised. True, every poem has a history. It stands in a relation to the language and tradition. Its words are surrounded by and depend on other words. But this shouldn't be allowed to obscure the poem's relation with its subject, the reality which it evokes. And in this relation, which takes precedence, the poem is surrounded by silence. The words arise out of the silence and return to it, and it should be as if they had been spoken for the first time.

In one of my poems, 'Hellenistic Torso',[11] I describe a fragment of a marble statue, recovered from the rubble of an ancient crypt, and the moment in watching it when the marble seemed to take on the movement of my own breathing – as if I were the marble and felt myself coming to life. A preoccupation with the archaic is bound to come back to the body, since that must be the ground of our understanding, our way of reaching back behind difference to a common experience of the physical world and our own mortal limits. By paradox, the poetry which is most of the present – a poetry founded on the senses, on the body's contact with the world – is also the most ancient in its reference, because the experience it describes is constant and the belief which sustains it – a trust in the existence of things – is constant too. What I have in mind here is an ideal of poetry, a poetry which remains to be written, as well as the existing poetry in which it seems to me that the ideal comes closest; and behind the questions proposed in this series, the question I've really been considering is, What does this ideal mean in terms of language and technique? I would sum up my answer with a quotation and another analogy. The quotation, from the book of Jeremiah, runs like this: 'Stand ye in the ways, and see, and ask for the old paths, where is the good way, and walk therein...'. I take the imagery here – the way, the path – absolutely literally because I'm reminded of a landscape of my own (one which often appears in my poems), a stretch of hill-country in central Italy, and of the system of paths, used mainly for driving cattle to pasture, which runs through it. Walking in these hills I've learnt how one must trust to the logic of the paths, to their good sense, to a relation with the land that has been worked out long ago and offers the best way through. I may not be sure where I am, but the path is never lost. It offers a clear direction and an assurance. The path has an ancient, anonymous existence, and as I follow it I belong with the others who have used it and made it. The passage from Jeremiah is a prescription that I might offer for poetry, but with the proviso – an essential one – that the old paths always have to be rediscovered (they are hidden or semi-derelict) and that the discovery can be recognised by its newness and freshness. '...and ye shall find rest for your souls', the passage from Jeremiah concludes – the rest, in my reading, that poetry should give.

The direction of this essay has been toward a subject which I've left myself no time to talk about, translation – an activity to which I've given a lot of time. What draws me to translation will be clear if I list some of the themes I've touched on: getting back to beginnings, the old rediscovered and made new, the need for other times and places, appetite for language and desire to live with it, love of the anonymous, fear of self-revelation, dislike not of the personal – since translation is nothing if not that – but of claiming the personal as my own. But translation requires a separate piece of work, and I'll turn back instead to the ideal of poetry which I've just mentioned and close with three quotations which go some way toward describing it.

There has been so much talk, so much description, so much alarm about our life, our world and our culture, that seeing the sun and the clouds, going out into the street and finding grass, stones, dogs, moves us like grace itself, like a gift from God, like a dream, yet a real dream, which lasts, which is there.

(Pavese, *Diary* 7 December 1947)

I try to delight in the sunshine that will be when I shall never see it any more. And I think it is possible for this sort of impersonal life to attain great intensity – possible for us to gain much more independence, than is usually believed, of the small bundle of facts that make our own personality.

(George Eliot, *Letters*)

He did not want to cry, – had never felt less like crying in his life, – but of a sudden easy, stupid tears trickled down his nose, and with an almost audible click he felt the wheels of his being lock up anew on the world without. Things that rode meaningless on the eyeball an instant before slid into proper proportion. Roads were meant to be walked upon, houses to be lived in, cattle to be driven, fields to be tilled, and men and women to be talked to. They were all real and true – solidly planted upon the feet – perfectly comprehensible – clay of his clay, neither more nor less. He shook himself like a dog with a flea in his ear, and rambled out of the gate.

(Kipling, *Kim*, Chap. 15)

Notes

1. Alison Brackenbury notes that Hardy sometimes used this procedure: Hardy 'would sketch out the metrical pattern of his poem as blanks, and then fit words to his scheme'.

2. C.H. Sisson comments that 'first thoughts ... are so often better than second thoughts'.

3. Anthony Blunt, *Nicolas Poussin* (London, 1967), p.129.

4. From the Preface to *Paradise Lost* (added to one of the later issues of the poem in 1668): 'true musical delight,' Milton wrote, '... consists only in apt numbers, fit quantity of syllables, and the sense variously drawn out from one verse into another, not in the jingling sound of like endings, a fault avoided by the learned ancients both in poetry and all good oratory' (*Milton: Poetical Works* (OUP, 1969) p.211).

5. Robert Wells, *Theocritus: The Idylls* (Penguin, 1988). Idyll 17, 'Encomium to Ptolemy', may be found on p.110.

6. Gascoigne's essay is reprinted in G. Gregory Smith, *Elizabethan Critical Essays* (OUP, 1904), p.52.

7. Grevel Lindop adopts a similar point of view.

8. The quotation – like the quotation from Seferis given earlier – is adapted from the translation of *Three Private Poems* by Peter Thompson, *Agenda* Vol. 7, No. 1.

9. 'An old man on the river bank', in *Four Greek Poets*, trans. Edmund Keeley and Philip Sherrard (Penguin, 1966).

10. In Robert Wells, *Selected Poems* (Carcanet, 1986), p.65.

11. *Selected Poems*, p.62.

The Rough Basement
Alison Brackenbury

Rilke, I believe, once refused psychoanalysis because he thought that after it he would never write again. I do not know if Rilke was ever asked to analyse his own work, or how he replied. The techniques of poetry seem to me safer ground than psychoanalysis; to be asked why you do peculiar things with line-endings isn't an invasion of the soul. I suspect that anyone who has written poetry for a time is conscious of their own technical repertoire and can illuminate their own work by discussing it. Thom Gunn said recently that he deliberately filtered experience into a poem of contrasting form. As well as making me appreciate Gunn's work better, this remark left me thinking for a long time about the degree to which all poetry does this. Life does not happen in iambic pentameters. It is odd that the artificiality of art comes home more strongly as you grow older; perhaps the techniques are too new and close when you begin. The doves get stuck in the sleeve. Only the experienced magician is cool enough to stand rifling through the box of tricks, or is as clear-headed about the whole show as Thom Gunn. I was once asked to tutor on a creative writing course and refused, not least because the course notes told me I was not there to advise on technique, which was the one area in which I would have offered any advice: the safe ground. But the doves do squeak, and I find that my only reservation here is a refusal to hunt through old work looking for illustrations to a point if none springs to mind. So I hope you will forgive a few generalisations.

Here are some to begin with. The people whom I find most confused and worried by the variety of form in modern poetry – which I applaud – are people who read poetry but don't write it. They are rightly suspicious that incompetents or charlatans may be serving them filleted prose. They are looking, I think, for intensity; that sense of much in a little, a pleasure that is not the frivolity of light verse, which haunts and distorts English writing, but a passionate and moving understanding. A poem should not leave you where you started. It should get under your skin, or more exactly, into your ear, for it is possible to remember the rhythm of a poem without its words. I have come out of sleep with a rhythm going through my mind like running footsteps. These readers are right to ask us for the dream of rhyme or the lift of rhythm just as they would ask a composer for tunes. It is this hunger which makes minimalist composers like Glass so immediately appealing. They are the new baroque. And the baroque composer is my own model, prolific, repetitive, yet pulling off the oddest coup as freedom and form fly together.

But what is our raw material? Blake knew:

I call them by their English names – English, the rough basement,
Los built the stubborn structure of the language, acting against
Albion's melancholy, who must else have been a dumb despair.[1]

English is intractable. It is not Latin. It can be made smooth, elegant, brief, but these are not its chief virtues. Awkwardness and discursiveness are part of its strength. They are there in the buckled-together syntax of Anglo-Saxon poems, from which you can often remove whole sections without the house collapsing. No lapidary surfaces there! They are there also in the long line of *Piers Plowman*, gathering and going forward like a wave:

'I am Ymaginatif,' quod he, 'ydel was I nevere,
Though I sitte by myself, in siknesse nor in helthe.
I have folwed thee, in feith, thise fyve and fourty wynter,
And manye tymes have meved thee to [m]yn[n]e on thyn ende,
And how fele fernyeres are faren, and so fewe to come...'[2]

They are there also in Blake. But as I list my supporters and invent my tradition – as each writer does – you may think you hear a defensive tone and you are right. I wonder if other writers of my age also have the sense that writers of their parents' generation, whose education included practice in Greek and Latin metres, belong to a different class. I am not simply speaking of the English class system, though that is involved here. There are practical results for the writer. Am I also alone in hearing, in these older writers, a grace and assurance in the handling of metre which I suspect I shall never attain? There are always instant consolations to be found. It is possible to write too easily. Look at Tennyson, and those acres of competent versifying, those calculated metric effects imitating bows or sword-arms on which he commented with such pride. If you find writing more difficult, perhaps you look harder at what you write, and the life of the thing disturbs your poem's surface more. The younger Tennyson knew that the mirror cracks.

Many of us have grown up too, not only under the shadow of the classical elders, but under the teaching of academics on formal courses in English literature. I do not regret this formal study. Would I now, with six cats and a child, find time to learn Anglo-Saxon, to cross the ring of ash into that green winter world of Sir Gawayne? I doubt it, and I am glad to have read them soon enough. They have had time to become part of the darkness out of which I write. But I wonder if I am alone, too, in feeling that I should be able to take on the critics at their own game, and to use their terms with assurance? I do not think I even know the names of many of the metrical features I am using or abusing. No doubt those luminous classical elders did, and used them. No doubt practising academics do. And I am quite sure that I am not the only writer who, in my early twenties, after years of reading English poets, realised that I had really no idea at all how to articulate a single line, let alone a stanza or a poem, and that if I were not to be a cunning purveyor of filleted prose I had better sit down and learn.

Perhaps it was in reaction to the 1960s' misplaced trust in inspiration that poets of about my age seem to have learned techniques so carefully, and tried so hard to practise them. I notice a masochistic desire to produce villanelles. As far as I am concerned, riding horses in semi-hurricanes on the Cotswolds in December is quite self-punishing enough, without coming home and trying to write villanelles about it. But one of the few pieces of technical help I have ever been given concerned verse form. It came from Avril Bruten, one of my tutors at Oxford. She said, 'You ought to write sonnets.' I thought she was mad. I have never, to this day, written a decent sonnet. But trying to do so brought me immediately to wrestle with what must be the ground metre of English poetry: the iambic pentameter.[3]

The iambic pentameter is to my ear, the metre of authority. Authority should not, I believe, be our best friend all our life and the iambic pentameter is not mine. It tries to dictate your choices as a writer, especially in diction, which I will talk about last. It is, quite frankly, a little too long for me. Space often appears in it which I don't really want to fill if my subject is racing past me. It slows me down. But there it is, demanding its fill of syllables, and in my early days I padded it cynically, usually with adjectives, as a critic of my first book noticed. I have noticed that it is usually critics in the most obscure magazines who make the most penetrating technical observations.

So why and when, early struggles apart, should I should use this metre? If you play by its rules, it has stamina; it will tick on for you for line after line. It has space for description and for argument, which I am not averse to in poetry. It has room for other voices to quote back at you and dramatise the argument. (A poem is speaking to someone who may not be there; it can help to let their imagined voice into the poem.) It leaves a poem well-defended. Why do children learn standard English, as I insist my daughter does, in addition to speaking Gloucestershire or Neighbours-speak to her friends? By standard English I mean usage, not Received Pronunciation; her accent remains Gloucestershire throughout. Most of my Lincolnshire accent was drilled out of me as a child, and I am not grateful for that; it leaves me with anonymity, and a passing resemblance to Margaret Thatcher, who went through a far worse version of the process. It may have weakened me as a writer. But I am glad to have learned standard English, and its abstract vocabulary. Without it, as English society runs, I could not have had jobs which allowed me to influence institutions, however temporarily; my letters to my MP about housing or the aid budget would not be taken seriously. The poem, flying off into a less than friendly world, also has to earn the right to be read, to enter the minds of people who decide to be sympathetic to it and to be registered as a worthy antagonist by those who do not. In all this, the iambic pentameter is a valuable ally.

These are diplomatic words: yet we are not really at peace. I still find this respectable, potentially elegant metre nearly as intractable as the stubborn structure of English itself. For the two are at war with each other. Of course you can let the iambics tick on for page after page as I described. But this is monotonous; part of my poem 'Breaking Ground'[4] was criticised on these grounds, perhaps justly. It is vital to disrupt that metronome beat. My first long poem, 'Dreams of Power'[5] was criticised for ignoring the authority of the metronome and being too free with the iambic line. I have read manuals of poetics with interest and profit (if you know any good ones, please recommend them). Their strictures on iambic pentameters have confirmed to me that you can delay stresses towards the end of the line, but that it is difficult to get away with altering the stress at the beginning, and that you have to be careful in piling up stresses together.[6] I am still frustrated by all these constraints.

At moments of stress – and I don't mean the metrical kind – I abandon the iambic pentameter, or it abandons me. At the end of every long poem I find I have broken back to a shorter metre, with greater freedom to place stress. In fact, looking back, I find the lines are even shorter than I thought, effectively four syllables at the end of 'Dreams of Power', six at the end of 'Breaking Ground' and, at the end of the poem '1829',[7] which I wrote two years ago, the lines end as eight syllables. I am delighted to find some sort of progression over ten years. Perhaps on my death-bed I shall master the iambic pentameter! But I think not. We must keep the right enemies. In the poem '1829', because Mozart was the final speaker, I was unusually worried about elegance, and if I could have let the iambic pentameter in, I think I would have done so. But it was kept out, stubbornly; partly, I know, by one of my few threadbare principles of syntax, to which I will return.

There are advantages in ignorance, and one of them is a kind of innocence. This too is stubborn; having seen possibilities, it will not lose sight of them. This is true of scansion. I am on dangerous ground here; I shall not give examples or they will be shredded by the academics. But in at least one academic book on scansion I have seen agreement with my sense that many lines in English poetry can be scanned two ways; that there is a tension between syllabics and stress, between, I suppose, Latin and Anglo-Saxon. Giving poetry readings brings this problem into the open. You have to choose. Or do you? Is there a tune and an undertune which a reader more skilled than I am could bring out? I read very monotonously, but I hope I show the listener that there is a pattern there which I am trying to bring out, although I lose many parts of it. I am always interested to hear poets read their own work, especially if I have not found their work metrically sympathetic or even comprehensible on the page. I think I have always gone away with a better understanding of the rhythmic drive of their work and read their later work far more eagerly.

Most poets now give readings. I was surprised how soon I was asked to do so and I think this has had an insistent, though intermittent effect on technique. It shows the writer very clearly which poems work best off the page. In theory it could incline them to the throwaway, the poem's answer to the good one-liner, which only works once. In my case, I think it has confirmed a belief in a certain kind of formality, in the poem as a confident pattern, as a musical speech.

Can ordinary speech be set into poetry? Yes, I am sure it can. I am on high ground here, as critics have told me I am able to do this myself. I suspect there are different ways to do this. I do not attempt to write long monologues that sound like natural speech. Someone once pointed out to me, shrewdly, that the speakers of radio drama are not speaking 'realistically'. They are voices. My poem 'Christmas Roses'[8] has a voice; it has caused some confusion because the voice is clearly not mine. It was a poem more like a dream than a construction and I did not detach myself from it in time to make clear, as I wrote it, that the speaker was a man.

Perhaps I should say in passing that I am generally against using poets' biographies to understand their work (novelists, I believe, are a different animal). I think poetry is a far more dramatic art than is generally realised and poetry audiences really are being naïve if they believe that the person standing in front of them is always reading, however movingly, about their own experience. I find that altering factual details in a poem can be technically useful. Technique must be shameless. I would change my best friend's name if it gave me a rhyme. This truthlessness also enables me to judge if the whole poem is truly working, by setting a distance between me and my subject.

Setting speech into a poem is also an artful process. We don't talk in poetry, but we sometimes talk in fragments of it, and I am always eager to lift these and use them. But I find it is hard to use speech much longer than a line, and a part-line is easier because you can bend the poem round it more easily. I do not believe, by the way, that the rhythm of English speech is basically iambic, although the length of the ten syllable line is useful to fit in one of these plagiarisms.

Before I try to talk about free verse, which is definitely not a form of chopped-up speech, I should mention the eleven-syllable line as one of my favourite escapes from the pentameter. I think I acquired this from modern German poetry, which at its best has a drama, an urgent respect for its subject and its listener which I admire and think is lacking in much of our work. I remember using it at the end of a poem called 'Last Week': 'The sky/ stays further than I thought, further and higher.'[9] It is the line I like for new sight, for possibilities. Here I am, trotting out my darlings like Tennyson with his line about the bow! Well, he came from Lincolnshire too.

As far as longer lines go, I can do little with twelve syllables. There is a famous example about a wounded snake, and as far as I am concerned the reptile should be put out of its misery. Later I shall be quoting an Emily Brontë line which has twelve syllables and is magnificent. But I hear a break in it almost as abrupt as Langland's. I am convinced, though I don't think the professionals agree, that these breaks have the weight of a beat, an extra breath.[10]

If you are going to use a long line, why not have a really long line, and then you can pile up effects and spread out stresses – I think of American poets as the masters of this art. But Anglo-Saxon poetry, Langland and the Bible have also impressed their patterns.

When does the strength of these lines ebb to prose? I do not believe in the validity of the prose poem. Even its writers, I think, are conscious of its monotony, which explains why the content of prose poems is so often strained and lurid. Poetic prose is another matter, and excellent in small quantities, but it cannot hold out for the length of a novel. What can still make a poem is that unrhymed language held together by a net of rhythm, tighter than that of prose, which we call free verse. Perhaps we should call it, after Thomas, 'fixed and free'.

Someone said to me recently, after a reading, that they noticed I habitually set up a pattern in a poem, and then disrupted it. I pulled a face; not least because this was in Zurich and I keep scenting psychoanalysis during conversations in Switzerland. 'Ah, this worries you!' he said triumphantly. Superficially, yes. I like to feel that I am in charge, that I am technically competent. Consciously, I have not always meant to make that disruption. But it is the most important thing for me to do. We learn the patterns to break them, we take the tradition to do something new. The most radical mistake I can make with a poem is to put it into the wrong form. The choice is often too quick for me to examine, but there are times when I decide that I am not starting with a stanza, that I may not have rhyme, that the poem's pattern will be its own. I know that when I write like this I am in most danger of losing the poem completely; if I am interrupted I will not be able to pick it up again and if it comes out rhythmically wrong, tinkering will not mend it. Let me call this free verse. As everyone has always said of it, correctly, you cannot start to write it until you have mastered other forms and it is free, I think wryly, in that it fails, when it fails, most completely.

What has influenced me in the way I write these poems? My prose punctuation has always been eccentric. I was very struck by Virginia Woolf's attempts, as she said, to change the 'masculine sentence'. Although in many ways I count myself a feminist, I don't myself count the enemy as the masculine sentence. Language is intractable for us all and Joyce too made the sentence dance differently for ever. I know that I am trying to re-work punctuation in my work, at a very deep level. I think I will come back to this later, to try to excuse the horrors of my syntax. Indeed, syntax largely determines the form of a short fragile 'free' poem in my work. About ten years ago I was reading American poetry intently, especially Paul Blackburn, whose work I found in Foyles by chance. It is often luck if you stumble over a writer when you need them. I remember the term 'free field' from this period and it does express the sense I had that you could move words around more than English poetry often does and leave visual gaps to show spaces in rhythm. Anglo Saxon poetry had such breaks too.[11]

In this phase I was more unconventional with layout than I am now. I have been persuaded by irritated editors that if a rhythmic device works it is juvenile to plaster it all over the typesetting. But I have kept some of my favourite tricks. I use lower case at the beginning of lines when I want to indicate particularly quick movement between lines, even if I have used capitals elsewhere in the poem. I still insisted on this in some of the early work being edited in my *Selected Poems*, which made me re-consider the point. It disappears in reading; the voice must do the work. But it is a useful colour on the page. I admire the kind of iconoclasm that wakes the reader to something new, as in Cummings's deft punctuation. And I still make and leave spaces in poems.

Whether any of these devices works in my freer poems, especially the shorter ones, depends on that poem's own rhythmic spring. If it doesn't have this, it is broken-backed and dies. I discard at least a third of what I write. The kind of drive I mean, in an unrhyming poem, can be seen again in the most forceful modern German poems, as in the last lines of one by Enzensberger: *sie allein bleibt, ruhig/ die Furie des Verschwindens.* There is a kind of fury driving poems like this, and they aren't tractable to rules. I think I write them best when I have been reading other poets who write them better – for poetry is theft. And I am conscious of being a thief with a patchy record as I go on to discuss syntax.

I hold the perhaps old-fashioned belief that a poem is about something: that language is not simply self-referring. How could we be moved by such a paper-chase? But if a poem refers to an event, that event is, as Wordsworth said, recollected. The writer's mind plays upon the past. It seems only fair to warn the reader of what is going on and to implicate them by the way the poem moves. Syntax, I think, can help here. I am addicted to parenthesis to set up an initial distance, the glint of warning, 'These are not, you understand, the figures/ Which send cold judgement into the backbone –'.

Should a poem's syntax be smooth and Latinate? Are our lives classically calm? Sitting in front of a newly acquired computer, which periodically terrifies me, I consider the clutter of events which have disturbed me between the paragraphs of this didactic piece: lost keys, blocked motorways, wet washing. Why should poems be immune to our mess and hurry? Any calm they achieve, should, I think, emerge from an imitation of it, and not simply be announced by a writer who is ignoring it. Lists, much punctuation, and the long rocking horse of the Anglo-Saxon sentence are useful here. The result may not be the most elegant of literary forms. But this is one of the points at which I think of, and agree with Brecht's proposition that literature comes from life, not from literature. In writing, as in politics, there are times when you must choose.

In this choice, I am again indebted to Virginia Woolf for showing how syntax can be disrupted from the conventional to the expressive. Her insights seem to me of particular use to a poet, for stream of consciousness in a novel always risks monotony. A poem can stop before the reader is jaded. I have tried in my own poems to use colons and semi-colons to link nouns or phrases without conventional syntax, sometimes to suggest the quick flight of objects into the mind, sometimes to present objects, or the solid and the abstract, in what I hope is new company. Poems can make us look again, re-value. At the close of the poem I often begin to use these devices differently, to mark a conclusion.

I suspect that this, too, is unfashionable. But this is where all the accumulated clutter stops: at the moment of reminder. Why else do we bother? There would be no point in planting and cherishing the garden if we never came back to it in stillness. Herbert is a poet who does this startlingly, time after time, and with the same devices I have clumsily described. James Fenton recently chose 'Prayer' from Herbert's work. There must be a kind of guiding ghost that takes writers to the same places at the same time. The end of 'Prayer' though beyond reach would be my own favoured ground: the thief in Paradise: '... the land of spices; something understood.'

I sometimes wonder if breath determines syntax in poetry more than is realised, just as a phase in music must be within the player's endurance. 'Why have you put that comma there?' asked a puzzled radio producer. 'So I can breathe,' I said. The syntax of breath shapes that quiet line which is the heart of Blake's *Jerusalem*, when amongst the wheels and the confusing heavens, Albion wakes. 'Ah! shall the dead live again?' Blake asks questions. I have become addicted to questions, especially at the end of poems. They give a good rhythmic lift – if you have the rhyme on the right word. Philosophically, I think they can represent the worst in modern poetry; a feeble echo of what was once the revelation of ambiguity. (I am not attacking Empson. Anyone who wrote a poem where the Sphinx is waiting for the sun to take her for a walk is a force to be reckoned with.) I would like to think that I use the question differently. It can arraign the reader.

> There is no past here. The only future's
> The hidden gallop's heat. It is a place
> I did not mean to love. Do you live so:
> Walking your own space?

It can try to involve the reader. The end of '1829', the Mozart poem, which I re-wrote obsessively, asks the reader:

> What planets now wear my old coat
> Washed by the rain, as fine as grass?
> What lost suns from the shadows' height
> Throb radiance through my cheap glass?

It is an invitation to sympathy; a kind of chorus.

I think it is time to admit a major problem with syntax. I have always been criticised by editors, quite justly, for using awkward and artificial inversion of word-order, especially at the beginning of lines. Why is this? At first, I think, it was the price of cramping what I wished to say into unforgiving iambics, which are particularly inflexible at the opening of each line. But editors, and I, still wonder why I am so blind to these monsters. Perhaps it is a lingering prejudice that poetry is different, a last whiff of the Tennyson, and very much worse, in school textbooks. Perhaps I am sometimes so concerned with sound that I still don't notice the violence I am doing to conventional English, and so underestimate the amount of distraction I am putting before the reader.

I must admit that there are times when I envy other languages. I studied Latin for a long time (though without any metrical training). Perhaps I have not entirely forgotten its freedom in word order, and the rhetorical advantages of choosing the vital word to be first or last. I also like the German pattern of sending the verb to the end of many constructions, so we are finally very clear what is going on. Look how that sentence faded out! I like adjectives far too much; I admired Keats and Tennyson for too long before I found Wordsworth. I like nouns too, inhabitants of the solid world poetry must bump into, or a quicker world of thought it must work to freeze. But it is in the verbs where I would like energy to rest. I manage it occasionally at the end of poems, as in 'Bookkeeping': 'he, the tireless angel:/ Unaccountably, he sleeps.'[12] This attempt to end with the energy of verbs is an underlying reason why the ends of my long poems break back from the pentameter. It is difficult, in English syntax, to end in a verb, except in the rather theoretical infinitive; it is often difficult, in the pentameter, to begin a line with a verb, especially with a monosyllable. 'Dreams of Power', by breaking back to a four-syllable line, managed two verbs in tension: 'touch light: wake you.'

A stanza in particular determines syntax. In a long stanza, especially with the pentameter, there is room, and a need for, adjectives and nouns, for a diffuser writing. The ballad is taut. You need to know what to say, and usually to get through it in a short unit. There is no chance of covering the bones of the syntax by an embroidery of adjectives. The ballad is the uncoverer: 'over his bones, when they are bare/ the wind shall blow for evermair.'

Recently, and without conscious intention, I have begun to use shorter stanzas. I have made periodic forays into ballads before, but the poem 'Tewkesbury' came out in a tight three-line stanza which I would not have expected that I could have used. It depended on two circumstances: that I wanted to write about old, but shocking facts, with adornment, with a concentration on verbs, and that I knew where the poem was going to end. It was to be the name itself, 'Tewkesbury', the echo of the world in the head.

As you will have gathered from what I said about the Mozart poem, I am obsessed by endings. They are, to put it bluntly, the point of my poems. If there are passing virtues I doubt if I am qualified to appreciate them, and I am very bad at revising the openings of poems, which do not interest me as much as they should. I know a few tricks for beginnings: imperatives and assertions wake up the audience, at the risk of irritation. Questions lure them further on – but it's further on that my interest lies. I tend to think that life becomes more interesting and more things seem possible as you build up experience; are poems the same? My unsuccessful sonnet writing did bring home to me a clear sense of the poem as a three-part movement, with a strong conclusion. If I cannot write a sonnet, what form can I handle?

One form I do use happily is an unrhyming or partially rhyming poem which concludes with a rhyme, like 'Constellations'.[13] This is not, in fact, always a happy process. The two different parts of the poem have to link in rhythm. Sometimes I come to the end – and my beloved conclusion – and find that the rhythm is demanding a couplet, but the length of what I want to add needs three lines. This happened to me recently with a poem about Africa, and the unwanted middle line had to be compressed into two words and rehoused in line one. I am still reading through this poem to decide if the ending works. Often, in my finally rhymed poems, it does not. Sense remains at war with rhythm. I can't resolve this. A poem is not music, or simply sound: what is more tedious than sound poetry? Its undertune is sense. Its syntax frames the bars of its music.[14] The poems where this war breaks out are doomed.

I shall mention one more stubborn preference, before I leave my syntax to rot, or grow. It is a tolerance of provincial usage. My editor once found the phrase 'Out the sky' in one of my poems. 'Nobody has said that,' he said, 'since the fourteenth century.' Well, throughout my life I have been surrounded by people who do say that, and a great deal more; I am sure that Anglo-Saxon survives intact in some of the darker valleys of Gloucestershire. I doubt if I could identify all the non-standard usages in my poetry, if I wanted to. I expect that this piece is littered with them. To be truthful, I am less than happy with the standard English of job applications and management reports. It is bloodless. Thanks to the eighteenth-century grammarians, it is frozen. But like a child who has had too many antibiotics, it is prone to being swamped by any jargon from time to time. We need a language which is more vigorous, more alive, which has some roots. Poems do not ask for a job or the approval of the managing director. They go out in the world to make their own way. You do not achieve universality by a nervous suppression of the inflections of your own voice, although you may, as I have mentioned before, become Prime Minister. I still like Ezra Pound's advice to the non-conforming poem: 'say that you do no work/ and that you will live for ever.'

One of the most conscious parts of poets' work must be their choice of words. Here, at times, English is bewilderingly rich. It is less like the rough basement than an attic in a convent school, which someone recently described to me, filled with huge baskets of clothes, Roman soldiers' helmets, Victorian ballgowns, slinky little numbers from goodness knows where. The children scarcely knew what to choose for their play. I am told that for a translator whose native language is not English, a major problem in translating is to find the right tone. There are too many levels, too many different clothes spilling out of wicker baskets. 'Today, heaven knows/ Anything goes –' But anything does not go. Are we to take refuge in decorum, in the Augustan gilding which almost stifled Clare, in the Georgian prettinesses which Edward Thomas had to leave behind him, in the grand carapace in which Wordsworth trapped his revisions of his own early work?

Wordsworth in old age is an awful warning. What if those clear early versions had not survived? At the other extreme, there is Hardy. If I have the story right, he would at times sketch out the metrical pattern of a poem as blanks, and then fit words to his scheme. It is clear that Hardy had an acute sense of a poem as music. It is one of his haunting women who 'Draws rein and sings to the swing of the tide.' But he over-estimates his reader's admiration of sound. Sense is the undersong. You can find lists in the manuals of different ways to use words, inventing them, hyphenating them, reviving them. Hardy tried them all, and more. It does not work; so often a word jars, distractingly. The poem becomes a surface, hollow at heart; yet Hardy is a poet of wilfully fierce feeling. Of course I am not condemning the whole of Hardy; I think most of us are powerfully influenced by him, as by Edward Thomas.

Why are these garish surfaces of his so wrong? I believe it is because they come between the reader and Hardy's subject, like a piece of particularly lurid stained glass set between the eye and the sun. They insist on the poet's individuality, too often and too loudly; when at some point the lyric should cast free of self, should be dramatised. Hardy, I believe, re-wrote parts of his novels to make them grander. It is easy to sympathise with this; it is a statagem of self-defence. He did not wish to be despised. But he put the value of his own work in danger, by caring more about the good opinion of his critics than the inner value of his subject. Writers can enjoy themselves – they are fools if they are not conscious of the glint of their own feathers – but writing is not about showing off. It is silly and wearing to try to shock the reader all the time, most obviously by writing about sex. It is equally futile to use language as a constant titillation. The end is monotony. There are more interesting choices to be made.

One of the deepest choices in the use of English is that between Latin and Anglo-Saxon words. There is a gulf here which our class and education system ensure remains deep and dark. What is the enduring role in English of Latinate words? It is no accident (Latin word) that the iambic pentameter, the metre of authority (Latin word) requires the writer to use longer Latinate words to articulate it. And do we all need to know and use Latinate words to be articulate?

Yes, I say regretfully. I would like to say no. I have caught myself using Latinate words simply to be impressive; I have poured scorn on management reports – especially in the world of education – where they feature like a nervous tic, to ensure respectability in the eyes of academics or the mandarins of a ministry.

But most abstract nouns in English are not of Anglo-Saxon origin. Many people I know, as I have said jokingly, are still speaking a remarkably pure version of Anglo-Saxon. I am not being in the least original when I say that this dialect of English does not allow the speaker to enter very far into any theoretical or political discussion. It may not even allow them to explain a practical task without demonstration. This is a wholly unoriginal point, but I have seen, you have seen, people stop short at the edge of this chasm, run out of words, wave a hand, in what Blake called 'a dumb despair'. Or, perhaps worse, they produce a chunk of someone else's speech, the newspaper's verdict, the television's voice. I hear this also in the doggerel poems in the Tewkesbury Admag, which accepts my own work with alarming regularity.

So there is a space in English poetry, I think, for Latinate words; and I use them. There is one area of abstract vocabulary which I would not use in poems, unless satirically, which is beyond my powers. It is to me, in the voice of a poet, the equivalent of the comment lifted lazily from the television's cosy glow. I am speaking of the vocabulary of literary criticism, with which, to be truthful, I am now barely acquainted, but which, from closer quarters, I made Clare attack in 'Breaking Ground'. 'Consciousness,' she says, cold and straight.

> I cry,
> Never use those words to me again:
> paradox, paradigm, unconsciousness,
> what light can such raise, flicker warm between us?
> The world is dead enough before my eyes.

But why do people cling to Anglo-Saxon? Someone of formidable quickness once said to me 'Most people are wrong most of the time.' They are not. Education can blind good instincts. I believe that the Anglo-Saxon words are still the heart of English. They are strong, both because they are brief and because they often keep a strength of sound, a thickness of consonant, a breadth of vowel, which lends them power. When I hear reconstructions of the spoken English of the past, the long vowels of Chaucer, the still-broad vowels weighting a Shakespearean sonnet, I do not think we have progressed. If the grammarians have frozen our syntax, the mandarins have chilled our songs. In this instinct, hopefully, and beyond my control, my poems break back to their short final words. They risk becoming, as Latin would have it, inarticulate. But let me be hopeful. One of the most terrible lines in Shakespeare repeats the word 'Never' – and I daresay, breaks the pentameter with its strength. One of the bravest lines in Beckett is the word 'No'. In an anthology recently, I came again upon an opening line of Emily Brontë's, which has frozen and haunted me for twenty years: 'Cold in the earth, and the deep snow piled above thee!' They survive on their own, out of context, these Anglo-Saxon lines, quite as powerfully as any Latin tag. And since I chose to attack Hardy for his garishness, I should pay tribute to the poems of 1912, where his own flourishes are muted and the music penetrates our dull skin: 'So coldly, so straightly, such arrows of rain.'

I have never tried to count the words that cluster in this powerful core of language: the bees at the centre of the swarm, the living heart of the star. There is always the danger that a poet's own vocabulary will be too narrow. I think mine is, or that obsession rules too often. Proof-reading hammers this point home. I have been warned off the words 'cold' and 'eyes'; probably in vain. I may use them more sparingly, but they will still come. As the Vivaldi poem in my first book warned: 'There is only one tune.' I remember, before I had written anything publishable, reading an article about the bankruptcy of romantic vocabulary which cited every word I had planned to rely upon: 'Bright, dark, wild –' and so on. Still, they were mostly adjectives; I had yet to discover verbs. The poet being blamed for bringing about the final collapse, was, I need hardly tell you, Tennyson.

A sense of limits haunts me when I think of choosing words for rhyme. You will have gathered by now that I am addicted to rhyme; not to its constant use, but to its regular return. It is needed to set up an echo of sound in the reader's mind which sets off another echo of sense. Why can rhyme be so powerful? It is not just to make poetry pleasant; that is as evil as light verse. It rests deep in what poetry is.

It is very hard to explain the poem's relation with the outside world, if, of course, you believe it has any at all. 'Shadows of the world' said Tennyson and the cracked mirror remains haunting; but since Tennyson's time we have heard too much of 'images', as though poems were paintings. I wonder if the critical stress on imagery has completely distorted some writers' approach. I do not think there are images in Shakespeare; there are themes. Poetry is far more like music than painting. It needs a clearer sense of shape than film and it derives that from sound. It is an echo of the world; it can play around a fragment of speech or a place name, expanding without betraying its source. Rhyme admits this echoing, just as parenthesis admits the play of the writer's mind.

But back in the basement, or the attic, as vexed translators know, there are very few rhymes in English. Shake out the wicker baskets and you are left with a few rather battered feathers. How many rhymes are there for 'world'? I am sure I should be able to tell you; I must have used most of them, not without some forcing of sense. But rhyming dictionaries are, I think, abominations, like thesauri. We must search our own attics.

It is easier to rhyme if you don't hanker after monosyllables. They can be too bare, but there are many times when I think a poem needs their clarity, their hammerblows. If I am using them at the end of a poem then I must try to rhyme them. Gradually, of course, I have learnt to evade this problem by other devices, by echoes within lines, by the various shades of rhyme. One device I have come to rather late is that of using place names, which only seem to need a smudge of rhyme to set up their own echoes. Here I am indebted to Jenny Joseph, and to her reading of her fine ballad about Rodborough Common, which has 'Rodborough' as its conclusion.

Despite my attack on Hardy, I think that some critics are too Augustan about diction. It is not a term I like. There are pens in the country where reared pheasants are kept before they are shot. Outside the mesh, puzzled and intrigued, the wild pheasants stalk. They are more tattered, but since they have escaped winter, the fox and the gun, I think they are the stronger birds.

Any word could be used in a poem. Poems have their own decorum. A word belongs to the poem it is in. It may not fit in any other poem the poet has written, or will write, but that does not matter. The poem, especially a long poem, can lend strength to words weakened by time and use. The awful can occasionally awe. This is an uncertain process, but I think it is more dangerous to grasp at the slang of an era, in the hope of seeming contemporary or authentic. Larkin is one of my favourite poets, but I think he weakened some of his best poems by this practice. In a curious way, it is Augustan: a surface convention threatening to smother his own voice.

What is the range of such a voice? Are we trapped too soon in that clear identity that blurb writers love? One danger I see in the present marketing of poets as personalities, of their work as a consistent product, is that people involved with literature may dislike or discourage variety and experiment. It makes it so much harder to sell the book. Editors write to me sometimes, clearly wanting more of a type of poem I have already published. They are reproachful when I offer them another, because that is what I am now writing, or confused if I send a ragbag of kinds.

And what of differing styles within a poem? There is a poem in my first book called 'Two Gardeners'.[15] My best friend, who is a critic, said the conversational, unrhymed beginning was fine but that I should scrap the rhetorical, rhyming end. My husband, also trained as a critic, said the end was fine but I should scrap the beginning. The reviewer in *British Book News* said it was the only poem in the book which worked as a whole.

We earn nothing if we do not take risks. I am sure that our conclusions, our break back into simplicity, need to be earned. Words that are rejected, poems that are abandoned, deserve to be if they are not doing enough. I always worry if people tell me my poems are well-crafted. I don't care for the term 'craft'. Women in particular, it seems to me, have messed around with craft for long enough. It is time we moved on to art. Would you rather have Mozart or a raffia mat? If people have had time to notice craft, then they have not been dazzled or moved enough. It is time to write another poem.

As I do so, will I think about technique? Well, not in the eager and anxious way I did fifteen years ago. At times, when I have just read someone whose work excites me, or I am conscious of needing to try something new, I will think of it, with interest. It would be unbearable to know where you were going in life. I have no idea how many technical phases I might push my work through. It will be very interesting to see. If I find myself re-writing my own poems, I hope I will have the sense to take up serious gardening. But at the moment, the hardy perennials look after themselves and I worry about technique only when I have a line that won't work or a poem's end that won't echo; just as a healthy person only worries about their health when they fall sick.

I must admit that I do not understand how someone could write very few poems a year and preserve technique. I am very cynical about fellow-writers. I always wonder if people are lying when they claim to write little, and whether there are drawers or bins full of drafts to prove me right. Burn everything while you can! But this is a reflection on myself, as I know that I need to write regularly to maintain a semblance of technique, and while I never set out to write a poem as a technical exercise, that must be the only function of many of those I don't publish and condemn to envelopes and suitcases for their lack of that mysterious and unacademic thing, life. As long as I know I have practised, and continue to practise, the stubborn basement will hold. This paper is wheeling and skirting; it is dodging the mystery. We each have our source of life, the angel. Listen to the Unfinished Symphony and hear Schubert's. In music, the angels sound louder.

That is the dream. But what is the nightmare? Let me end by telling you. You get up, as usual, to the clutter of radio, hungry cats, a child's lost shoe. You switch off the radio; it is your morning for writing. The cats go out in the sun, to their own mysteries. The child goes out to play. You climb the stairs with a growing sense of something being wrong. But nothing is wrong! You breathe more slowly. You sit down.

There is the old table, with the sliding piles of books, magazines, a manual of poetics. You have hours before you. The winter sunlight shines on your page, perfect and empty. There is nothing more to say.

Notes

1. William Blake, *Jerusalem*, ch. 2, lines 58-60.

2. *The Vision of Piers Plowman*, B Text, ed. A.V.C. Schmidt (J.M. Dent, 1978). The excerpt is from Passus XII, lines 1-5.

3. Whether the iambic pentameter is 'the ground metre' of English poetry is arguable, as is the often-repeated assertion that the iamb is somehow 'natural to English' (a view Brackenbury does not share, as she makes clear later in the text). While the pentameter is certainly one of the great lines of the English verse tradition, this centrality seems largely to depend on what Brackenbury later calls 'authority', rather than on some innate syntactic or phonological characteristic of the line which makes its centrality inevitable. Antony Easthope (*Poetry as Discourse*, Methuen, 1983) has argued that the pentameter is a 'hegemonic form' with ideological meanings, a metrical sign 'which includes and excludes, sanctions and denigrates, for it discriminates the "properly" poetic from the "improperly" poetic' (p.65). Easthope's is a useful reminder that any separation of form and content is arbitrary, and that linear (or stanzaic) forms are themselves meaningful.

4. In *Breaking Ground* (1984); sections of the poems are also represented in Alison Brackenbury, *Selected Poems* (Carcanet, 1991), pp.91-102).

5. Carcanet (1981); see also *Selected Poems*, pp.32-64.

6. Although it is quite noticeable that, at least in the pentameter line, metrical freedom can be greatest towards the beginning of the line (where there are most effects of metrical tension and/or complexity), and most tightly-constrained towards the line-end. The last two feet of the pentameter seem particularly resistant to metrical variation.

7. In *PN Review* Vol. 16/ 5, pp.22-3.

8. See *Selected Poems*, p.141.

9. From *Breaking Ground* (1984); *Selected Poems*, p.72:

> ... The martins have returned, from unimagined seas'
> wind-blinded miles, as sudden as they left
> their bow of wings, stubbed tails, boldly black
> wheel and turn above the crumbling flats;
> how tall they make the houses look. The sky
> stays further than I thought, further and higher.

10. In McCully (*The phonology of English rhythm and metre* [Manchester doctoral thesis, 1988]) I argued just this: the twelve-syllable line does tend to fall relatively naturally into two groups of three accents each. When this occurs, there is a tendency (also found in the three-beat lines of the ballad) to end each three-accent group with a silent beat. The twelve-syllable line may therefore be realised accentually as 3 + 1 (silent), 3 + 1 (silent). English metres in general seem to be based on a duple system of contrast, i.e. two-beat, four-beat and six-beat lines will, on this view, be the prime underlying structures. The possibility of silent beats is also discussed in Abercrombie (1965) and Attridge (1982) – full references to these works may be found in the notes to the Introduction.

11. Although in Anglo-Saxon poetry these visual gaps serving to graphically demarcate half-line constituents were additions of later (nineteenth and twentieth century) editors; they were not employed by Anglo-Saxon scribes.

12. In *Breaking Ground*; *Selected Poems*, p.84.

13. In *Christmas Roses*; *Selected Poems*, p.106. These are the concluding three stanzas:

> Lolled back, she sleeps
> In the icy sun, the moss-green pram,
> Still with her arms held stiffly out
> The wings of a swan. So Cygnus flies –
> They tell me – through the winter heaven;
> I cannot find him from my book.
>
> That we must, still, be told, then look,
> Forcing old lines round fleeing light,
> Is that your way? I tremble, see
> Bright Castor, Pollux, held and free;
> Lovers, beasts, who once they were
> Does not disturb them, constant pair.
>
> Look back, past me. White streams of sky
> Wheel over; I stand, trying
> To track lost stars this night. She was not
> Swimming. She was flying.

14. See also the comments by Davie and Crichton Smith here.

15. In *Dreams of Power*; *Selected Poems*, pp. 22-3.